See Dick and Jen Run

See Dick
and
Jen Run

by Tim Skubick

The University of Michigan Press
Ann Arbor
&
The Petoskey Publishing Company
Traverse City

Cover photograph by John Addis
Copyright Elbinger Studios 2006

2009   2008   2007   2006   4   3   2   1

ISBN-13: 978-0-472-11607-2 (cloth : alk. paper)
ISBN-10: 0-472-11607-X (cloth : alk. paper)

Library of Congress Cataloging-in-Publication
Data on file

*To Gayle, my wife, to Carly, my daughter,
and to Eleanor, my mom.*

Thank you for all your love.

Contents

Preface

Covering a race for governor is a lot like going into one of those carnival fun houses with all the mirrors. Once you get inside, it's tough to get out. I know. I was in one for 10 months. Everywhere you look, you see distorted images, and trying to decipher the real from the unreal can be a disconcerting if not a confusing challenge. While you are in there, you run into dead ends and bump into all sorts of interesting-looking characters, and when you finally get out of the maze, there's a tremendous sense of relief as you return to the real world. Such was the 2006 race for governor in Michigan. It goes into the history books as the most expensive campaign ever. One of the contenders spent an unreal amount of money—over $35 million of his own cash to win—yet Dick DeVos lost. The other contender ran against the backdrop of a Michigan economy that was ravaged by the unprecedented upheaval at GM, Ford, and Chrysler. Jennifer Granholm miraculously dodged the bullet, as voters did not take it out on her. You'll see all the craziness including how the Detroit Tigers figured into the outcome. You'll feel all the triumphs and failures, meet all the characters, learn what strategies worked, and you'll return to reality with a clearer picture of how the political game was played in this historic election. Take my hand; the fun house is just beyond that next page.

1
Showdown in Motown

For three long minutes, there is dead silence in the car as they head to Detroit City airport. Candidate for Michigan governor Dick DeVos has just completed his first toe-to-toe quasi-debate with the incumbent democrat Jennifer Granholm.

The event was in Detroit—not exactly a home-turf advantage for the West Michigan, conservative GOP hopeful trying to make history by sending the charismatic Granholm to the showers.

It's left to media secretary John Truscott (J.T.) to break the silence with the question everyone in the SUV wanted answered, "So, how did you do Dick?" Campaign manager Greg McNeilly and the candidate's wife are along for the ride and anxious to hear the response, too. "It wasn't my best performance," he quietly reflects. Weeks after the event, he put it another way, "At the end of the day, I must say that I wasn't totally pleased with my performance."

But back in the SUV that night after his initial comments, a harsh critic begs to disagree. "Are you kidding?" wife Betsy blurts out. "You did a great job. That was a tough environment." McNeilly joins in on the positive analysis and J.T. adds, "There was so much potential for a downside. You gained a lot of respect by just showing up. That took a lot of guts." After the chorus of "way to go," the candidate thinks again. Truscott says, "After that, he felt better."

Weeks after the historic event, Truscott describes DeVos's first reaction this way: "It was like taking an exam in college and believing you blew it, only to find out you got an A." DeVos adds his personal postscript, "Apparently, just my being there scored big points—even before I said a word. Maybe I was the beneficiary of low expectations."

The media reviews of the DeVos performance seemed to echo the analysis of his inner circle, but it was a performance that almost didn't happen.

Everyone knew in late April 2006 that this Granholm vs. DeVos match up was going to come down to the wire. What happened in Detroit in the first face-to-face meeting had all sorts of political permutations. And for the majority of the DeVos team, all of them were rotten. The six out-of-state DeVos handlers, who were being paid big bucks to share their wisdom, advised him to go to the beach or find something else to do that night. DeVos recalls they were focused "mostly on the downside risks involved if I hit a sour note."

"Don't do it. What's the upside of doing this event in Detroit?" was the wisdom that poured in via a flurry of e-mails over two or three days from the hired guns. These were not second-string rookies telling DeVos to duck the event. Among them were Kurt and Wes Anderson, who did polling and consulting work, along with Brad Todd, who was crafting the DeVos ad campaign. Then there was Alex Castellanos, who also dabbled in media and ad consulting, and finally George W. Bush confidant Matthew Dowd. He helped candidate Bush become Texas governor by engineering a stunning upset over incumbent and very popular female Governor Ann Richards. The DeVos team was hoping he could work his magic one more time against another popular female governor in Michigan. If a vote had been taken in the DeVos camp on avoiding the Detroit meeting, it would have been the six outside consultants voting "no" and the two local guys voting "yes."

McNeilly was practically a member of the DeVos family, as he had endured years of service with both Dick and Betsy. He suffered with them on the political setbacks and stepped back to allow them to savor their victories. Through it all, his devotion never wavered an inch.

Truscott cut his teeth in 1990 as he and political unknown John Engler rode around Michigan in the latter's rundown Oldsmobile. Penniless at the outset, the duo hoped somehow to unseat the sitting Governor Jim Blanchard. Twelve years later when Governor John Engler left office, Truscott got out of government to open his own consulting firm. Having first sworn off anymore statewide campaigns, here he was back on the campaign trail. However, this time there were lots of pennies from the millionaire DeVos, and Truscott was more upbeat about winning than he was 16 years ago.

McNeilly and Truscott, having grown up in Michigan, knew the lay of the land in Detroit. Sure, the mostly black audience at the NAACP Freedom Weekend event would be stacked against their guy. Sure, this was Granholm country. And sure, the stakes were off the charts if DeVos bombed. But they also knew that they had spent months quietly working the black ministers in Detroit and other African-American civic leaders.

"We told these people," Truscott explains, "that we were going to fight hard and play hard in Detroit." They were not going to concede the city to Granholm, even thought they knew she would win the pro-democrat enclave on Election Day. However, they also knew what the out-of-state consultants might not have known. Granholm was not the most popular person in the city. She finished dead last in the three-person democratic primary for governor in 2002. Her relationship with the democratic mayor, Kwame Kilpatrick, was not exactly a match made in heaven. And they knew if they fought and played hard, they could make some inroads into her margin of victory in the city. It would be one thing if she got 85% of the Detroit vote. It would be quite another if her "bounce" was 70% or less. That would mean DeVos had a better chance of beating her, assuming he did well in the rest of Michigan. That's why, despite the recommendation from the outsiders to take a powder, "Mc" and Truscott never budged.

The back-and-forth e-mails finally ended when DeVos wrote to everyone in bold letters, "I AM DOING THIS." "I was determined to go ahead. I wanted to be sure there was no doubt about

my willingness to go to the city and speak my piece in person."
DeVos acknowledges that he had heard from some circles that he
was "afraid of Detroit." After the event, he confidently reports,
"Well no one is saying that anymore!"

Once he made it clear this was a go, the next challenge was
to prevent a political pratfall at the April 28th Showdown in Motown.
The first admission the campaign made was that the white candidate
and his all-white team needed more guidance from persons they
trusted in the black community. DeVos was not exactly a novice
at race relations. In 2002, he made extensive contacts with black
ministers as he and they fought for a school voucher program. The
black ministers knew that many black families wanted an alternative
to the failing urban schools. They could ride the vouchers, underwritten with state tax dollars, to a better education for their children.
So they opened their doors to the West Michigan republican who
was on a mission to legalize state support for private and religious
schools.

How ironic. While DeVos lost that fight, he could now dust
off his e-mail list and renew those old friendships, which might provide the margin of victory in his bid for governor.

Weeks before the event with Granholm, two sessions were
scheduled, lasting a combined total of almost three hours. There
were six African-American leaders gathered around a conference
table. DeVos, McNeilly, and Truscott listened intently.

"Be yourself." "We know when you are lying," were two
observations.

They also kicked around the issues that would likely come
up including insurance red-lining (the practice of charging more
for car and home insurance in the inner city), receivership for the
financially troubled city, control of the local water board that involved a nasty battle with the suburbs, and the proposed ban on
affirmative action that would appear on the November statewide
ballot. Interestingly, one of the participants in the room was William
Phillips, a noted black attorney. One of his clients was none other
than the mayor of Detroit who was anything but a republican. Put
another way, Kwame Kilpatrick had a possible mole inside the
DeVos camp.

The debate prep continued over the ensuing days with the exchange of position papers on this issue or that, and then it was show time. DeVos rented a room at the posh downtown Detroit Athletic Club and holed up with his inner circle for an 11 a.m. meeting on the day of the event. It lasted about two hours as they went over final details and then everyone left. The candidate headed for the workout room, where he followed his usual routine of treadmill, swimming, and the stationary bike. Ninety minutes later, he got ready for the trip to Cobo Hall to meet Ms. Granholm head to head.

Truscott observed as the afternoon went on, DeVos got "a little quieter and withdrawn." But that changed when they entered the cavernous Cobo Hall at 5:45 p.m. for the 7 p.m. event. DeVos flicked the "Mr. Personality" button and did some glad-handing on his way to the holding room. First, there was a side trip to the room where the actual program would take place. As they finished their scouting mission, they walked past another room filled with about 15 persons scurrying about. It was the Granholm "war room" as Truscott described it, filled with fax machines, telephones and every other instant communication device you could imagine. That stuff would be used later in the evening to spin their version of the debate. The message was going to be, Granholm won even if she did not.

"We thought it was overkill and just laughed," Truscott recalls as they headed for the Green Room. The war room, by the way, was vintage Granholm and no laughing matter to her. It underscored her competitive nature, as she left nothing to chance.

DeVos and company had another good laugh as they read the program. It identified DeVos as the chairman of Amway. Wrong on both counts. DeVos left Amway years ago, and the company is now a subsidiary of Alticor. DeVos has nothing to do with it other than to use the company as the backdrop for his barrage of TV ads that would blanket the airwaves soon.

As the minutes ticked off, the candidate, his spouse, McNeilly, and Truscott remained in the bubble, shielded from the crowd that was gathering across the way. One democrat who peaked in through the window reports DeVos was walking around looking nervous. Fifteen minutes before it was time to go on, DeVos walked over to the corner by himself. He is observed going over his notes and rehearsing by talking to himself. In the hall, some 500 NAACP boosters are waiting, along with about 15 TV cameras and a host of reporters. Since this is the first face-to-face encounter, it has lots of box office appeal.

But if the advisors in the Granholm camp had anything to say about it, there would have been no cameras, no reporters, and no debate. Ironically, as in the DeVos camp, those surrounding the governor were also telling her to avoid the event but for completely different reasons.

The last time Jennifer Granholm did an NAACP event, it was also against the advice of her inner circle. It was during her first bid for governor, and then-candidate Granholm had been asked to attend the civil rights group's Detroit convention. After everyone recommends against it, she takes matters into her own hands. While driving along, as one source puts it, "She told the driver, take me over there," where she proceeded to produce a bombshell that caused some real consternation.

While taking questions from the audience, Granholm announced that she favored reparations, which was the notion that African Americans should receive compensation from the federal government for all their years in slavery. Her announcement drew raves from the black audience, but her handlers were aghast. They knew her pronouncement would be devastating in the white suburbs in what was known as the "donut" around Detroit.

Politically, it was bad enough that she had said it, but it was discovered that somebody had videotaped the remarks, which ended up in a GOP attack ad later on. The campaign went into a crisis management mode, and out of that came a feeble attempt to undo what she had done.

Everyone knew reparations meant money. But like former President Clinton trying to parse the meaning of the word "is" when the GOP wanted to impeach him, the governor lamely explained that when she said she favored reparations, she did not mean money. It was as transparent as could be, but that's the way they spun it, and while it was used against her and cost her some votes, she won anyway.

So here was another campaign and another invite to appear

in Detroit before the same group, but this time there was no fear she would screw up again. "There was not a lot of nervous energy put into the discussion on whether to do it," confides one source, but nonetheless all the pros and cons were weighted. Doing the weighing were long-time Granholm confidants Rick Wiener, who first met her on the Mike Dukakis presidential campaign in 1988; Mark Fox, a Lansing attorney who did the debate negotiations for her; Chris DeWitt, who handled the media in the first run for governor; Howard Eldelson, who was campaign manager; Jill Alper, an outside consultant; David Katz, who was married to Alper and ran the 2002 Granholm effort; and last but not least, the gov's hubby, Dan Mulhern.

Note the contrast in camps. DeVos had all those high-powered outside consultants with their meters whirling and only two Michigan guys in the inner circle. Granholm, on the other hand, was surrounded by friends she had worked with for years, and that's the way she likes it. Her group tackled the task at hand. "With both of them on the same stage, there are some risks," one of them opined, stating the obvious. While it was unlikely that the now-seasoned Granholm would pull another reparations gaff, anytime you debate, you cannot control everything, and who knows what could go wrong? But even if that happened, this was so early in the race that whatever happened would likely fade away as the campaign droned on, her folks figured.

Some felt there was a good chance DeVos would be a no-show. Little did the Granholm team know they were almost right. While on the DeVos side, they were pretty sure she was trying to duck the event, too. As both sides debated whether to debate, DeVos had told the sponsoring group there was one date he could not honor. He explained that he made a promise to his daughter Andrea to chaperone her prom dance and then host an overnighter at the DeVos home for about 18 teenagers.

"I will not break that commitment," he said as he displayed his family values for everyone to see. Well as it turned out, that is the exact date the governor picked. The DeVos folks smelled a rat. They were sure she had picked that date on purpose to force him to choose between his daughter and the debate. DeVos personally felt at the time, "I think they were stunned that I had accepted." But my source says the governor was not trying to put her opponent on the spot. If that was going on, "somebody was freelancing" because "there was no attempt to spin the date" by the gov's gang, this source suggests. Besides, the somewhat cocky Granholm crew knew in a face-to-face format, she would out-perform him. They used such terms as "empty suit" to describe DeVos and recalled his appearance four months earlier on the statewide public TV series, "Off the Record" (OTR). He looked uncomfortable, shaky and not much like a governor who was in charge.

Granholm and company most surely did not underestimate the opponent. They knew they were in for a battle but were confident "he was not ready for prime time." "He's not very good. He has no history [about state government]. This guy doesn't know very much," was the sentiment around the Granholm table as they debated the debate. So if she was going to mop up the floor with him, why did the group tell her, "There is no reason to do this"?

The reason was simple: why give him a chance to clean up his act? "Every time you do a debate, you get better. Why not let him be nervous all summer long?" was one observation from a Granholm insider. That way, when there were debates in the fall, DeVos would be starting from scratch, which, of course, gave her the edge. Awarding him this practice debate did not make sense, they told her. But just as it was in the DeVos camp, when it came down to it, the candidate made the final call.

"I'll do it," Granholm told everyone.

Here's part of the reason why. She wanted to please the Rev. Wendell Anthony, who was emerging as one of the black leaders with significant influence over the governor. One black democrat went so far as to say, "She's afraid of Wendell." Remember that Granholm had a problem with Detroit voters, even though she would never fess up to that in public. But in private, as her team considered their decision on this joint appearance, it was noted that doing it would buy her some badly needed good will. "We need to do better in Detroit, and this will help," was one observation.

To understand the gravity of her "problem" in Detroit, go back to the November 2005 election for mayor. Even though the governor never said so in public, it was clear to most in this town that she favored Freeman Hendrix over the incumbent Kilpatrick. On top of that, Kilpatrick, who is not blind, knew many of her supporters were working for Hendrix. Everything would have been great for the gov if her guy had won, but he did not.

The very next day after the election, someone in the governor's office made a phone call to one of Kilpatrick's insiders, and, in effect, suggested that whatever the mayor needed, the governor would consider it. The peace offering was the first time in her three years that such an overture had been made to Kilpatrick, according to this source. Now with her own political neck on the line, the governor was trying real hard to cooperate with the sometimes-mercurial mayor. Doing the NAACP event in the mayor's backyard was certainly a signal that she was serious about making their relationship work.

So once she made the decision to take on DeVos, the group moved into their debate prep mode. They did a couple of rehearsals with Wiener playing DeVos. As in the DeVos camp, the governor went over questions that would likely come up, and everyone knew there would be something on affirmative action. They also revisited a strategy Granholm had used on Jim Blanchard and David Bonior when she debated the two democrats running for governor in 2001. If she got the chance, she would ambush DeVos with a zinger he did not anticipate designed to pull him off his game. They also devised another trap based on what DeVos had said on OTR about the City of Detroit. Asked if he would bail out the city if it was on the financial rocks, DeVos declined, while saying he would work with the mayor to iron things out. If she got the chance, she would spring that on him, too, in an overt attempt to make him look bad in front of a Detroit audience.

"The thing with this strategy is that the issue has to come up naturally," explains one source. You can't take a question on the environment and then ask your opponent about stiffing the city. The attack would look phony and opportunistic. The trick is to make it look spontaneous so as to fool the viewers. Trained as an attorney, "She knows how to turn things on people. She is good at that," boasted one handler.

In the midst of all this prep work, Wiener offered a suggestion that caught everyone off guard. Being careful not to embrace it himself, he suggested the event should be televised live and in prime time on one of the Detroit TV stations. That way, he went on to explain, DeVos would be "exposed" for what he was: that empty suit. As they sat in the governor's campaign office in downtown Lansing, the idea was just quirky enough to deserve extensive discussion. But another participant rejected it. If the governor agreed to a live TV debate this early on, it would lay the groundwork for DeVos to come back in the fall and demand even more. "Then we are committed to doing it," was the reasoning, and based on the group's unwillingness to open that debate door, the group turned to other business. They finally adjourned and waited for the big day...the first face-to-face confrontation of this infant campaign.

2
Let the Games Begin

On the day of the event, the Granholm squad was in full campaign mode. As noted earlier, they had all the electronic gear to "move some paper" after the meeting to make sure their spin got in all the stories the next day. DeVos had nothing like that. The governor clearly had the crowd on her side as she triumphantly entered the arena. DeVos got polite applause. She got a standing O.

But one of DeVos's folks swears the Granholm appointees in the first two rows jumped up first as if on cue and the rest of the audience had no choice but to follow suit. Even DeVos stood up with everyone else. Afterwards, he explained it was out of his "continued respect for the office." He says he did it "without hesitation." Note that he didn't say it was out of respect for her.

After they were both on stage, she and he met to shake hands before they came out fighting, but DeVos feels she is already in a fighting mood. He describes what happens next as "the pre-fight attempt at intimidation."

Intima-what? The nice, unassuming and mild-mannered Jennifer Granholm into intimation? You bet. She is a gamer. DeVos remembers, "She came in close to me, gave me the signature extra firm handshake and asked, 'Have we ever met?'" He responds in his most gentlemanly way, "Yes, Ma'am, we have, and it's nice to see you again." The picture of this handshake in the papers was a hoot. She was standing as tall as can be with her game face firmly in place — no flashy toothy grin from her this time. He bends slightly toward her, and he is smiling. The contrast was striking.

For the moment plunk yourself in the challenger's shoes as he concedes, "We really didn't know what to expect. There were very few 'ground rules' established prior to the event, so we were clearly walking into a fluid situation."

That's a remarkable statement. In this day and age of mapping out every detail and wanting to reduce the chance for errors, why the heck did they send him out there without knowing all of the ground rules? In fact, while on stage waiting to do his thing, DeVos hears for the first time that there will be questions from the floor. There's a wild card that can drive you nuts. Whatever he was paying his team, somebody blew it. You don't send your candidate into the lion's den without knowing the rules under which he might be devoured. Amazing.

Onto the program, but before we get into the content of the debate, two confessions: first, I have a strong bias against the format that was used. The candidates were restricted from interacting with each other, although there was some interaction. The two reporters who read questions from the audience did very little follow up even though it was clear from time to time that the two candidates were skirting the issue. And the second confession, I missed the debate. To be honest, my wife and I were just back from a glorious spring break, and I was not ready to suit up just yet. Hence, the observations here are based on what I saw on the videotape supplied to me.

As the game is about to begin, here's what DeVos was thinking. "I must admit that I was a bit concerned as we waited to be introduced." Understandably so, since he knew, as he puts it, "The governor is an experienced debater and a very skilled communicator, and I'm just a business guy who is new to this type of format."

The governor went first and immediately seized the moment to paint a not-so-subtle contrast between herself and DeVos. Her objective was to promote herself as someone who knew Detroit compared to her opponent, who grew up in Grand Rapids. She cleverly began by chucking her title. She was now talking to the audience as "Jennifer" not "Granholm the governor." "I want to talk about the person. My decisions rely on who I am," she goes on in her opening remarks. The sincerity juice is all over the stage and we're not five minutes into the thing.

She recalls how she "worked like a dog" to get into Harvard, noting that she did not have rich parents. Here she could have added, "unlike my opponent who was born with two silver spoons in his mouth." "I'm for the underdog," she went on, hoping to connect with any underdogs in the audience. And to make the audience bond even stronger, she says she and her husband moved to Detroit after law school where they were married, had children and bought their first three homes in the city. It was all very touching, but nobody bothered to ask her why she and the family moved out of Detroit to the suburbs, and she, of course, left that out of her monologue.

She draws the audience in even more by using the affirmative action issue. When GOP Attorney General Mike Cox refused to file a brief on the landmark case that was pending before the U.S. Supreme Court, she says she filed it instead. And to close the deal, she tells everyone that "We are a family of faith," and to prove it, she recites a passage from St. Matthew about doing good deeds "for the least of these."

Finally, since she knew everyone in the audience detested former GOP Governor John Engler for taking over the local school board, Granholm teed-up a theme she would repeat and repeat until November. She noted that she walked in as governor to a $4-billion deficit she "inherited" from Big John, and with that, she sat down to thunderous applause. It was a great opening.

DeVos, the outsider, gave it his best shot, too, as he tried to prove that he had something in common with the audience as well. First, he reveals that he was advised to skip the debate, but he quickly adds, "I knew it was important to be here and have this conversation." Next, he admits the obvious, "We come from different places." Watching the tape I chuckled. What he should have added was, "That's because I'm a millionaire." And following in

Granholm's footsteps, he makes his attempt to identify with the audience with: "We have the same hopes and dreams." Then he launches into a description of his family, complete with wife and four kids, and says he has "never been about division." He asserts that he can bring people together, and, "I'm here to talk about how we can work together." Then, perhaps without knowing it, he swipes a line from Granholm's first campaign for governor by saying, "This is the longest job interview of my career." It got a polite laugh. He finished and sat down.

And now, we finally get to the questions, and when the first one is popped, Truscott feels his heart drop. It's one question they did not anticipate. Egads. If you thought J.T. was having a panic attack, here's what the candidate was thinking: "Despite all the preparation we had done for the event, which was thorough but not excessive, I was immediately surprised by the first question...so I was initially a little bit on my heels."

"I felt like I had let him down," Truscott discloses as he waited anxiously for the response to the first toss up. It was on the use of photo IDs to vote. That has huge racial overtones, because many minorities don't drive and don't have a license with a picture. Others don't have a job and therefore no company ID either. The State Supreme Court had been asked to rule on the legality of the GOP idea of, no picture, no vote.

On a question such as this, clearly the incumbent has an edge. She has been living and breathing state government since she arrived in town over three years ago. The last time DeVos spent anytime around these parts was during his brief stint on the State Board of Education way back in the early 1980s. Consequently, she could talk circles around him with her more intimate knowledge of the subject. She noted that former Attorney General Frank Kelley had ruled years ago that demanding a photo ID in order to vote was discriminatory.

This audience certainly knew something about discrimination, and Granholm played to them. "What's really going on here [which is one of her favorite lines when she wants to hit a home run] is an effort by the far right to depress the vote." Blacks had fought the old Jim Crow laws that prevented them from voting in the South, and now the governor was telling them it was wrong for legislative conservatives to pull the same stuff all over again. You know the audience loved the response.

DeVos is next.   He begins his unrehearsed response by saying the high court should look at the issue as he expresses his concerns about the integrity of the voting process. (It's generally felt by the media that republicans get very uptight about voter fraud and mandating the use of a photo to vote was their way to eliminate that.) To the governor's argument that the disadvantaged could not afford a photo ID, DeVos countered that the legislature would provide the funds, which several weeks afterwards, it did. And the governor vetoed it. Nobody in the room, except DeVos and his guys, was aware that he was winging his first answer, and frankly, while watching the replay, it was not obvious to me either.

Fast forward to question four, which was aimed right at the governor, and she gave her best response of the night.

Given her well-documented "problem" with some Detroit voters, the writer of this question talked about the elephant, or should we say, the donkey in the room. The woman in the audience wanted to know, why should democrats, who have doubts about her leadership, vote for her now? My, my, the governor was ready, as she launched into her analysis of Lansing and Washington. She noted that everything in the state and in Washington was under GOP domination, and in the Michigan House and Senate that control was from the "far-right." And then she masterfully outlined for the audience what that meant to them. She reported that the GOP wanted to increase state aid to the cities by 2%, but they left Detroit out. (She declines to tell them that she never introduced a revenue sharing increase, either.) She recalled that they wanted to allow Grand Rapids to create a new mass transit authority, but left Detroit out. And for a dab of frosting on the cake, she said the GOP was increasing funding for every university—except Wayne State, which was in Detroit. "They have engaged in divisive tactics" that divided the state by region, race, and democrat vs. republican. She basically said, I'm it. She was the only democrat in town; the only firewall between those right-wingers and the persons sitting in the audience. "It's important to have balance," she adds. That means one party should not run the whole show. Her audience loved that, too. She is clearly on a roll.

However question 7 gave DeVos a chance for his shining moment. Since June of 2005, democrats had been hammering him on "sending Michigan jobs to China" when he ran the old Amway company. This was the corporation that sent legions of sales folks into your home to sell soap and other products. He had rehearsed this answer for months, but that night he seemed to show the same kind of passion and personal conviction she possessed. Did he send 1,400 Michigan jobs to China, the questioner wanted to know? There were over 1,000 layoffs in Michigan, but he tells the audience the China charge is false. "Not one job was transferred from Michigan to China...we have to be there" because the Chinese won't allow any industry to sell products unless they build in that country. DeVos closes the deal by saying the jobs in China actually helped create 300 jobs in Michigan. After his unsure start early on in the program, DeVos reflects weeks later, "As the debate progressed, I think I was able to better hit my stride."

The questions continued as both candidates demonstrated their ability to bob and weave to avoid direct answers to very direct questions, and nobody on the panel called them on it. But at last, the moment Granholm had been waiting for, popped up from the audience. Here was that "natural" moment where she might catch the challenger flat-footed.

DeVos went first on denouncing the ballot proposal called the Michigan Civil Rights Initiative to ban affirmative action. On this, he and the governor agreed. He noted that he was "not popular" with some members of his own party for opposing the plan. He even repeated the mantra from the coalition fighting the amendment saying the language of the amendment "doesn't advance civil rights." It's a good answer and the crowd liked it, but little did he know what would hit him next.

The trap is now set as he sits down and she stands up. She advises everyone that the plan "damages Michigan on the moral and economic fronts" and then seemingly out of nowhere, she turns to DeVos. First she softens him up with, "I applaud you for opposing that. I think it is great that you are doing that..." (Aw, isn't that sweet.) But then, she looks him in the eyes, puts both her hands together with fingers extended and points at him and asks, "I assume that you are also in favor of affirmative action?"

The audience erupts into wild and thunderous applause. If this had been the old Batman TV show, there would have been cartoon bubbles over DeVos's head with the words, "zap, bam, boom, and splat." The governor stares at DeVos as the camera shows him just sitting there. We call it the "deer in the headlights" look. All he can do is smile, but it is definitely not a happy one. With her game face again in place, she looks like the cat that swallowed the Amway soap peddler. He, on the other hand, is obviously pondering his next move as the 25-second audience reaction reaches a crescendo and echoes in his brain.

He reveals his thoughts at that very moment. "While I thought the format was for us to have an open conversation with the audience and not each other, her turning to me [with some real fire in her eyes] and pressing me on affirmative action was the biggest surprise of the night. She clearly came armed and looking for a fight...an interesting insight into the attitude [or frustration] on their side."

The applause begins to subside as the audience and media await his retort to this torpedo fired by the governor. He slowly rises and buttons his sport coat. It reminded me of a knight making sure his armor was in place. With arms outstretched, he's seemingly trying to say O.K., listen to this. He begins with, "My friends." Oh yeah. He only wishes he had some friends in the audience.

"May I make just one observation? We came here, we came here for a conversation, and that's what I intended to have." My translation: That stinker. She just broke the rules. But he doesn't say that because his consultants have drummed into this head: don't attack her or show disrespect because if you do, you will lose votes. He carefully continues with his response. "I'll be happy, however, to comment to the question that's been raised," he diplomatically wades in deeper.

Looking at the audience and not his opponent, he says, "If you'll please define for me exactly what affirmative action means to you, then we can have the conversation." There is some audible murmuring in the room, as this attempt to skirt her attack falls flat.

In retrospect, what he should have done was turn the tables on her and ask for her definition first. But he didn't. He tries to wiggle out of this mess by tossing in the name of Sam Logan, who writes for the *Chronicle*, a widely respected Detroit newspaper. He quotes Logan as saying the definition of affirmative action is "quite confused." It's a crafty move to validate his own statement that no two people can agree on what it really means. Then he offers a response that came off very sincere and from the heart. It was his home run of the night.

"Do I believe that everyone deserves an equal opportunity to get to the table of opportunity of success and the American Dream? Absolutely," he answers his own inquiry. "Do I believe that we need to assist individuals who aren't able to get to that table themselves? Absolutely," he repeats. He concludes with a statement that flips the audience murmurs into approval, "We are a nation built on hope and opportunity for everyone…no matter where you come from, your background, skin color or otherwise."

Note that he does not get into racial quotas or other buzzwords associated with the inflammatory issue. He hits chords that resonate with this audience, thus giving them an answer they cannot reject.

The Granholm camp afterwards felt that he was damaged by his attempt to avoid a direct answer to her question. That may be true, but the rest of what he said, came off quite well, thus blunting the impact of her left hook.

This little exchange dominated the media coverage. The governor looked in command. DeVos looked anything but. Image is everything in politics. The rest of the debate was pretty bland. DeVos did get her goat, however, when he brought up a recent screw up by the Granholm state corrections department. A convict who should have been in the slammer was mistakenly let out on parole. He proceeded to plug and murder three innocent victims. Suffice it to say, it is not the kind of story a governor running for her own life wants to read.

"We've seen mismanagement," he explains. "We can't afford mistakes." Truscott thinks Granholm's stare showed she was not pleased with the comment. As they moved toward the finale, DeVos says his former Amway Company, where persons are recruited to go door-to-door to hawk soapsuds and would not leave until they had the check, was actually "the ultimate civil rights initiative." Given the widespread public dissatisfaction with how those products were sold, I was surprised he brought it up himself.

Finally, we get to the closing remarks, which were typical and uneventful until the governor stepped into it, right at the end. She leaves the stage "for one second" and goes into the audience where she says, "When you're governor you've got a great team." She introduces her husband of "20 years this May" and then goes to nine of her appointees, who just happen to be black. She hugs, she kisses, she smiles, and she milks it for all it was worth. The subtext, of course, is for all the minorities in the audience to see what the governor has done. She is smart enough to tell everyone, "It's not just that they are African American. It's they are excellent. They happen to be African American." Make no mistake, this governor has worked hard to make her cabinet reflect all races, and she gets high marks, but that night, she got low marks for pandering to the audience.

DeVos felt the same way. "Her willingness to pander so aggressively to the audience—where she personally introduced almost everyone who was a person of color in her administration—was pretty superficial stuff."

One of those Granholm appointees who was asked to stand that night confided to me that he or she did not feel used, but "it would have been better had the governor invited all of her cabinet to be there." One Detroit lawmaker who was there also confirmed the pandering thing and agreed that every cabinet member should have attended. "The audience was smart enough to figure out that she had done a lot to include minorities in her administration." Even one of the governor's team members confessed they had heard the "pandering" slap.

But there again was the competitive side of the governor vividly at work. She wanted that audience to love her, and she wanted to leave no doubt that she had persons of color working with her, but by trying too hard, in some circles it actually backfired.

DeVos ended his performance by suggesting that Detroiters

were not better off after four years of Granholm, but he was not that direct. "You can't confuse motion with progress." He notes the jobless and crime rates are the same as four years ago. "That's not progress," and he tells them it will be different with him sitting in her seat.

The event ended, and both combatants proceeded to the reception. The governor did not stay long. DeVos hung around for more than an hour. On the whole, the event will probably be a blip," suggests one Granholm handler a month after the Showdown in Motown. But this next tidbit may stick in the craw of those handlers who urged her not to go there in the first place.

DeVos got out of the test run debate exactly what the Granholm folks were afraid he would get: experience. "I think I learned a lot and can do better next time...whatever it was, this event provided a chance to learn a lot about myself and a lot about the governor, and actually gave a very positive lift to my campaign." Can you hear that collective "ugh" over in the Granholm inner circle upon hearing that?

We end this chapter where we began: back in the SUV after the debate headed for City Airport on Detroit's east side. DeVos and his wife arrive and jump into their six-seater, one-engine prop plane. DeVos, who also has a jet pilot's license, flies the thing back to Grand Rapids to make good on his promise to chaperone his daughter's prom soiree the next night. Turns out he was up all night making sure all the teenagers in the home stayed in the "right" rooms.

3
Meeting Mr. D.

The 2006 race for governor was unofficially launched the week of January 22, 2006. Governor Jennifer Granholm went first with her fourth, and the GOP hoped last, State of the State address. That was followed the next day at our public TV studios in East Lansing, where republican challenger Dick DeVos showed up through the back door to appear on the "Off the Record" (OTR) program.He came in the back door because a handful of young college democrats demonstrated, complete with anti-DeVos placards, at the front door. The only folks who saw them were reporters and TV cameras. For all we know, they may still be out there waiting for DeVos's white Lincoln SUV to roll in.

The DeVos appearance was a bit of a news event because it marked the first time he had formally met with anybody from the State Capitol Press Corps. Here-to-fore, all of his sojourns into the Capitol City had been below the radar screen to huddle with multi-client lobbyists and other power-brokers in town.

Prior to the OTR event, I had managed to "ambush" Mr. D. on the campaign trail on two occasions. His campaign, in the early stages, was not releasing his whereabouts, and so it was only by "hook and crook" that I was able to catch up with him in Oakland County and later at the Michigan Chamber of Commerce headquarters.

The Oakland County appearance was in the fall of 2005. I had notified the DeVos guys that I would be there. DeVos was slated to address a local chamber of commerce group, but before he got to the local eatery, he rode out to a dead-end road.

GOP State Senator Mike Bishop of Oakland County was ushering DeVos around and took advantage of the opportunity to cry on DeVos's shoulder about a dead-end road that the senator wanted open to traffic. That's where we headed to wait for them.

Here's the scene: My TV-10 cameraman Steve Coon and I parked the news truck along side the road. He sat in the air-conditioned car while I anxiously waited outside in the hot sun, looking for the DeVos vehicle. As we loitered, nicely coffered suburban housewives from an upscale subdivision drove their kids to school and checked us out. Ten minutes later they returned home, sans kids, only to see us still sitting there. "Can we help you?" one of them nervously inquired thinking perhaps we were on a stake out for an unscheduled terrorist attack. I explained who I was and got the ole, "Tim who?" look as they drove off. Finally, this black SUV rolled up. While this was to be our first interview of the premature campaign, DeVos and I had known one another for years. DeVos served on the State Board of Education, but I was hard pressed to remember one thing he had done during his two-year stint there. We had also met over the years because he was married to Betsy DeVos, who was once state GOP chair. Ms. Betsy was not with him this time, as he jumped out of the front seat with Bishop tagging along. "How you doing?" he inquired as he smiled broadly and firmly shook my out stretched hand.

There was an easiness about him. He was very approachable, even with some guy behind me with a 40-pound camera grinding away. We exchanged pleasantries but quickly cut to the chase, because he had all those well-heeled business types waiting to hear his words of wisdom. I wanted to talk about school vouchers.

For months, the Michigan Education Association and other

Democratic Party folks were shopping the story that DeVos, if elected, would endorse school vouchers. Recall that in 2002, Betsy and Dick ran a hugely unsuccessful, yet vocal, campaign to bring vouchers to the state's education system. They argued passionately that parents should get state tax dollars to send their school kids to private and/or religious schools. The MEA feverously fought the plan and won, but the residue from that campaign had now filtered into the 2006 race for governor.

My first question to Mr. DeVos was, "If elected, will you try to bring vouchers to Michigan?" He did not flinch. He did not waffle. He hit it straight on with an unmistakable, "No." During the rest of the "Q and A," he complained about all the negative attacks coming from Democratic Party chair Mark Brewer acting on behalf of the governor. That was not the last time we would hear that beef from DeVos. The whole exchange ran about two minutes. I got what I needed in my first TV interview with the man who wanted Granholm's job.

We walked back to his SUV with the camera still rolling. (You always try to get those shots of candidate and reporter together because it shows the audience that the reporter has access to those seeking office. All part of the image game.) As he got closer to the door, I joked, "Well that's the first ambush interview down, and 832 more to go." He smiled broadly, "Not if I have anything to say about that." It was a funny line. We laughed and off he went as we tailed him to the restaurant.

We pulled up just in time to get the "arrival" shot of him pumping paws with everyone in sight. I was thinking, "Man, this is just the beginning of an arduous campaign that will take forever to run. How many more handshakes will I see before this thing is over?"

I don't think many correspondents truly enjoy campaigns. They tend to degenerate into the same speech and the same corny jokes, with the same answers to the same questions over and over again. At least this day, I was getting a first impression. The TV interview was pretty good. His stump speech was awful. But before we heard his stilted message, we ran smack dab into some "official" with the chamber. She promptly announced that my cameraman, who was now inside the room getting more paw-pumping shots of the candidate, would have to leave the room. Leave the what? Was this woman nuts? We had driven all the way from Lansing to get some video of this guy running for office, and she wanted to kick us out? Where was my copy of the First Amendment?

We nif-nawed back and forth over her unreasonable demand and my unwillingness to budge. I ran the clock with her, because all the while my guy was still getting the video we came to get. Being in a good mood and knowing that this woman was on a mission from God to keep us out, I finally relented and asked Steve to head back to the truck. I went into the room to listen to the speech.

For three years, I had been been covering Jennifer Granholm. She consistently electrified the room with her charm oozing all over the joint. I could sense I would not be oozed on this day. DeVos began with the usual stuff about how grand it was to be here—wherever it was. Honestly, after months on the trail, some candidates forget where they are, but they do know that it is grand to be there. Then he launched into how he was a Michigan businessman and how the state was in dire economic straits and how all those good business folks needed one of their own to lead us to the "Promised Land." Frankly, it was pretty thin gruel, and I was glad I had gotten that earlier TV interview because this stuff was not newsworthy.

Two things struck me: First, he seemed uncomfortable as he stood behind the podium reading from his notes. Granholm, in strong contrast, was well versed in getting out from behind that darn podium, which is a barrier to communication. She wanders around in the audience ala Phil Donahue in a pantsuit and works the crowd up close and personal.

DeVos appeared stiff as he plodded along from his notes, including the section where he talked about his family. Geez, I thought, couldn't he chuck the notes and speak from his heart about his own flesh and blood? He did have a funny line about not being able to communicate with his teenage kids. Everyone in the audience could relate to that, but that was the only highlight as far as I could see. He was clearly a "work in progress." If he did not improve, I felt Granholm would make mincemeat of him. With the news watch ticking toward the 5 p.m. newscast, I could not hang around to say goodbye to DeVos. I did thank his handlers and reassured them that they would be seeing more of me down the road — that long and winding road to November 2006.

As we headed out to I-75, I thought about the day. I figured I could work with this guy. Often times, when you are dealing with a millionaire, he or she is not only aloof, distant, and egotistical (how's that for a cheap stereotype), but there is no common ground to boot. Senator Bishop, whom I debriefed days later, said he had those fears, too, but found DeVos to be down to earth with none of the "millionaire baggage" you might expect. "He talked a lot about his family," Bishop told me after he spent the whole day with DeVos. The senator reported the folks in his district liked what they saw as well. The Oakland County event was a mere fond memory as we return now to the studio in East Lansing just before the OTR taping.

Mr. DeVos and I meet again. He was quick to recall the other exchange we had had two months earlier in Lansing—the "litmus test" meeting. Instead of a warm sunny day, this one was on the eve of fall turning into winter. You know those ugly Michigan days when you are aware that the sun will never shine again? This time I sat in the news van waiting for DeVos again. He was holed up in the state chamber of commerce building with the chamber's CEO, Jim Barrett, and his guys. It was supposed to be a 45-minute session, which had now dragged into 90 minutes and counting.

Finally, some movement. The DeVos SUV was moving and so was Greg McNeilly from the campaign. As the candidate came out the door, I got out with cameraman in toe ready to do interview number two with the invisible Mr. DeVos. For months during my speeches at various events, I had opined that DeVos was running a rose garden strategy, which is political speak for avoiding the media. In fact, to illustrate how small the political world is in this state, I shared that observation in front of some group up in Traverse City, and by the time I drove home to Okemos, there was a voice message from the DeVos campaign taking me to task for making such a remark. The snitch in the audience was Jim Haveman from Grand Rapids, a member of the old Engler administration, who apparently had a new assignment: spying on me! Haveman was not being malicious. In fact, we joked about it when I figured out he ratted on me. He was doing his job, and I was doing mine.

We did our second DeVos interview on the single business tax, his relationship with Detroit Mayor Kwame Kilpatrick and some other issues. After it was over, in a very gentle and joking way, DeVos said something like, "So what is all this stuff you've been saying about me being unreachable?" For a half second, I was taken aback but quickly recovered while confirming I had said that, because it was true.

For months, DeVos had stayed away from the Capitol Press Corps and focused on local news media in every town across the state except Lansing. It actually was a smart move analogous to opening a play off Broadway where you work out the kinks before bringing the show to the "Big Time." DeVos, at that early stage of the game, was clearly in search of his political voice, and if he stumbled in Onaway while looking for it, nobody would ever find out. But as a reporter who gets paid to cover politicians, I want to see them. And since I was too lazy to drive to Onaway, I just griped about the fact that he was running a stealth campaign. To correct this, I blurted out, "You need to do our program." Now he is smiling, "Ah, so you have a litmus test, hey?!" "Guilty," I joked back. Recall that the GOP is famous for applying a political litmus test, usually on a candidate's position on abortion. And if that candidate flunks, he or she can't get anywhere in the party. So he was accusing me of applying a journalistic litmus test, and if he did not do our program, I would continue to say he was inaccessible. We laughed and left it at that as he drove off.

Obviously, this guy has a good memory because months later, he is standing in my studio and quips, "Now can we can stop all this crap about not being accessible?" I assured him he had passed the litmus test, and it was off the table. We both laughed again. It was the last time he laughed that day. It was time to play OTR.

Studio C was crowded with capitol correspondents as they hung around DeVos while the WKAR-TV crew got the joint ready for the program. Word came from director Dick Best that it was time to clear everyone out. Just the players remained: Veteran *Detroit News* correspondent Charlie Cain, Kathy Barks Hoffman from the

Associated Press, Rick Albin, who did politics for WOOD-TV 8 out of Grand Rapids, yours truly and DeVos's handlers John Truscott, McNeilly and I can't remember who all.

During a typical taping, we do about 14 minutes of correspondent "chit chat" on the issues of the day. Then we bring in what we affectionately refer to as the "pigeon" and/or "red meat" for the interview. But since this was our first true bite of the DeVos apple, we reduced the first segment to five minutes so we could have more time with the candidate. During that first segment the reporters talked about Ford laying off 30,000 workers, we did a couple of takes on the Granholm State of the State, and then it was time to call in DeVos.

Albin had provided me with a dandy segue. He finished his remarks about the governor's speech by commenting that she had said it was time to "bring it on." That meant she was ready to rumble with the republicans in the legislature. I picked that up and said, "Perhaps she was also thinking about our guest today: Dick DeVos." He briskly took the 25 or so steps from offstage to the center chair on the set. He took a little jump up the steps to non-verbally demonstrate that he was ready, maybe even eager, for the impending exchange. We shook hands. He sat down. I took my seat and the fun began.

Hoffman tossed out the first one. A question that sounded vaguely familiar to me. Sometimes folks who have an axe to grind with the guest call reporters on the eve of the program to "suggest" or "plant" a question or two or three. There is nothing unethical about it. Correspondents are under no obligation to ask them. When Hoffman asked her first stem-cell inquiry, I wondered if Chris DeWitt from the Granholm campaign had fed her that question just as he had spoon-fed me? It didn't matter as I listened for the candidate's response—or as in this case, nonresponse.

Embryonic stem cell research was one of those hot-button issues that Right to Life and, therefore, all good republicans opposed. Adult stem cell studies were okay, but research on embryos that were being discarded was verboten. I waited for DeVos, who was a Right to Lifer, to slug this one out of the park. But he surprisingly whiffed at it instead. "This is very complicated," he began. "We are looking at it very closely," he cautiously finished his answer.

As Charlie Cain asks the next question, I'm thinking, "I can't let this guy off the hook with a non-answer to the stem cell stuff." So I waited for DeVos to finish Cain's inquiry and announced I was bringing him back to the previous question. DeVos would not budge. He was not going to take a stance no matter what. Give him credit for sticking to his guns, but I couldn't help but think what the Michigan Catholic Conference (MCC) was thinking. The MCC had wasted little time denouncing the governor for embracing stem cell research in her speech the night before. DeVos said he was not aware of that statement from the lobbying arm of the Catholic Church. He ended his answer by saying he "respected" the church for its position even though he neither agreed nor disagreed with it. He did not look in command of the subject.

The topic shifted to the economy, which is what he wanted to talk about. DeVos got a chance to tell the viewers that he had been to all 83 counties in Michigan (logging more than 30,000 miles at that point), and folks were telling him they didn't know the contents of the governor's economy recovery plan.Up until this time, DeVos had not announced what his plan was either, and by golly, he was not going to reveal it to us. "She has had three years" to do something, he said as he warmed to the subject of criticizing her. He proudly announced it was time for a person with business experience to get the job done. "How can you go around the state and beat up on the governor for not having a plan when you don't have one yourself?" I interrupted his well-rehearsed sound bite. He suggested that he was not the one beating up the governor; he was merely reporting what citizens were telling him, and then in a vain attempt to insert some tension relieving humor, he added, "I'm just a reporter here, Tim." Yuk. Yuk. He smiled. The panel did not. (Unless a guest really delivers a funny line, reporters are supposed to keep their game faces on.) So his "humor" just sort of laid there as the questioning continued.

DeVos noted that Granholm did not have her economic plan in place when she ran in 2002 until several months before the actual election. He promised, "We'll be well ahead of that...I'll be coming forward with my plan," he reassured everyone. He justified this delay by saying the voters on this cold January day were not focusing on the race for governor, and when they got focused, he would have something for them to focus on.

The program clock was ticking, and I wanted to get his stance on tax increases. For decades, candidates for governor have taken the so-called "no-tax pledge." It was an ironclad promise that, if elected, they would never raise your taxes. Granholm had never taken the pledge because it was irresponsible, especially when you factor in unforeseen circumstances that might warrant some revenue increase. DeVos agreed with her. "I don't take any pledges, and I will not raise taxes. Period." I suggested he had just taken the pledge. "I won't sign a piece of paper. It's political gimmickry. That's silly, but I have no intentions to raise taxes." It was nice to finally hear a clear answer.

Albin jumped in with a question on the 51 tax cuts that the GOP legislature had passed and the democratic governor had signed: what did he think about that? DeVos noted that tax cuts were not the end all and be all to turning the economy around. Hoffman chimed in, hinting that maybe DeVos did not agree with the GOP tax reductions. Sensing perhaps that Hoffman was setting a trap, he demurred. He respected what the legislature did, but as a candidate, he was going to stay out of the day-to-day legislative debate. Former Governor John Engler told him to take that stance.

After the program, however, Truscott explained that DeVos had earlier "warned" the GOP legislative leadership about passing the governor's 21st Century Jobs program because she would use it for her own political gain in the campaign. That sure sounded to me like DeVos had stuck his nose right into the legislative game when moments earlier, he said he was not going to do that. Which was it?

The floor director signaled that we had under a minute left. This program had flown by, and I went in for one more shot. "If you were governor and Detroit Mayor Kilpatrick called and said his city was on the brink of bankruptcy and he wanted a bailout from the state, what would you do?" Republicans, especially those from West Michigan, have a history of not wanting to do much for Motown. I was told DeVos, on the other hand, had been working the streets of Detroit. He was making some inroads with some of the African American ministers there. Would he bite on this loaded question?

Instead of a bite, there was a punt. "That's a what-if," he began and carefully ending with the statement that he wanted to see Detroit be successful. Never one to toss in the towel, I tried again, "So you would not do a bailout?" He noted, "Bailouts don't sustain a city." But he made it clear he wanted to see Detroit sustained. He even pledged to do everything he could to see that happen. I promised him that we would sustain this debate over the next 284 days, and with that, I said goodnight to him and the panel. Fade to black. The program was over. The cross-examination was not.

4

DeVos Won't Answer the Questions

There was a huge pent-up demand in the Capitol Press Corps to watch DeVos in action and to quiz him. Nobody had much of a chance to do that since he informally announced his candidacy on Mackinac Island seven months earlier in June of 2005. The timing of his declaration, and the guessing game leading up to it, was a story in and of itself. Since I missed the story by a country mile, it was retold to me by the guy who did break it.

I remember getting a call on Thursday, June 2, 2005, from my radio station in Detroit. It was a cryptic call that caught me sleeping at the switch, to say the least. "Dick DeVos is announcing he is running for governor," the assignment editor on the other end of the line said as he ruined my Thursday afternoon. The dateline on the story was Grand Rapids, which could mean only one thing: my compadre Rick Albin at WOOD-TV (TV-8) had scooped me.

Truth be known, Ricky deserved it, because he had been

working the story harder than anyone else in town. TV-8 is the only other commercial TV station in the entire state, in addition to TV-10 in Lansing, that has made a commitment to covering Michigan politics, and Albin had done his homework. For this book, I asked him to walk me though his exclusive report, and he was kind enough to do so without rubbing it in.

That fateful day, Albin was on his way to Lansing to do an interview, when the cell in his news truck went off. It was a "well-placed Lansing source" who suggested, "You may want to be on Mackinac Island this afternoon." Albin trusted the source enough to stop the truck on I-96. Turn it around and head back to Grand Rapids where he hoped to charter a plane to the island. Man, nobody in the TV news biz does that anymore for a political story.

The airplane was the only option, however, since there was no time for TV-8 to get its huge satellite truck to the island in time for a 5 p.m. broadcast. So Albin's team convinced the good folks at channel 7-4, the NBC affiliate in Traverse City, to move their "sat" truck to Mackinac City. That way Albin could get the story on the air—if there was a story.

By this time, Albin had hooked up with his "Sky King" and was in the air making his way to beautiful Mackinac Island, where he hoped to nail down the exclusive he had been dogging for months. "The whole time in the air, I just kept thinking," he tells me after the fact, "If DeVos doesn't confirm this after I've chartered a plane and raced up here, I may want to have a fresh resume handy." That certainly was a legitimate fear. Up to this time, as reported earlier, the DeVos team had been very cagey about his contacts with the media. And one had to wonder, if he was really going to make the announcement, why didn't he hype it to every media outlet to maximize his statewide exposure?

Albin's plane landed, and he discovers that DeVos is already there. Albin is eager to get to the Grand Hotel, but the taxi service from the airport is, well, about as slow as a horse pulling a buggy—which it is. Albin gets on the horn to Greg McNeilly, who is riding in his own slow horse to the hotel and discovers DeVos is checking in at that very moment. If DeVos heads to his room, Albin may be out of luck. Albin's horse clops into the Grand, and he spies DeVos at the check-in desk. The reporter politely waits and then strolls out in front of the hotel to pop the question when DeVos comes out. DeVos confirms he is running. (Albin can stop worrying about a new resume.) He just smacked a home run, and as he puts it, "No other media was around." Ah, a reporter's dream come true.

But having the story doesn't count unless you broadcast it. Albin could not get the borrowed satellite truck on the antiquated and quaint little island, so now his "Mad, Mad, Mad, Mad, World"-like story shifts to, what else, a ferry boat. Since he can't walk on water, that is the only way back to the mainland. Now the news watch is ticking, as the boat bounces along. Albin takes to his cell phone to do a live "phoner" for the 5 p.m. newscast from the middle of Lake Huron. The phone gods are on his side. The cell holds up, he breaks the DeVos story and follows up with a live on-camera report at 6 p.m. thanks to the team from TV-7-4.

That would have been enough for one day, but now he jumps back on the next boat to get a comment from the woman DeVos wants to beat. Governor Granholm is also on the island at the executive residence with the glorious and panoramic view of the Straits of Mackinac. Albin is told "she is done for the day," which is governor-speak for "she ain't comin' out to comment on anything…especially this story." He does another report for the 11 p.m. show and then "heads for a drink." It was a hell of a day and one hell of a story. By comparison, I sat in our kitchen in Okemos and did the story live for the radio station in Detroit that afternoon. Bet they were glad I didn't have to charter a plane to do it.

In between the time of the Mackinac revelation and the time he showed up in our studio seven months later, DeVos had steadfastly avoided any formal meeting with Lansing reporters. It was my sense that the strategy was very much on purpose. However, all the time he was studiously avoiding us, he held a critical skull session on July 8, 2005, involving a "who's who" of modern-day state GOP politics. Obviously, nobody in the Capitol Press Corps was given a heads up on the all-day session in the Thornapple room in the Amway Plaza in downtown Grand Rapids.

Get a load of the heavyweights gathered around the table, which amounted to the John Engler administration in exile. There was Engler who was governor for 12 years; Lucille Taylor, Engler's former legal advisor and spouse of State Supreme Court Justice Cliff Taylor; House Speaker Craig DeRoche; Richard McLellan, a long-time Engler crony and legal eagle for the GOP; Mark Murray, who was then head of Grand Valley University and served as Engler's budget director; Jim Haveman, who ran the health department for Engler; Denny Schornack, who ran environmental issues; former Lt. Governor Dick Posthumus; Doug Roberts, who did treasury work for Engler and former Governor Bill Milliken; Kurt Anderson, a hired gun from D.C.; and fellow Washington insider and George W. Bush advisor Matthew Dowd. As we reported in Chapter 1, Dowd was an important figure, because he helped George W. Bush defeat a popular female governor of Texas.

Rounding out the impressive list was Bob Dalfdow, who did policy work for Oakland County executive L. Brooks Patterson; John Truscott, former Engler media press secretary; Tom Ginster, who did criminal justice issues for Engler; Greg McNeilly, the long-time DeVos devotee; and wife Betsy DeVos, who popped in for the last two hours. I didn't get whiff of the session until almost six months after the fact. Because I was writing this book, a source filled me in. Better late than never.

I originally thought the objective was to map strategy to beat Granholm. To be sure, that thread weaved its way in an out of the 9-to-5 discussion, but the real goal was to kick around policy issues. DeVos was not a policy wonk so once he got on the trail, he needed to appear knowledgeable, otherwise who would vote for him?

My inside source reports that the vast majority of time was spent on jobs and taxes. No surprise there since those topics had dominated the news agenda in Michigan for years ever since the state's auto industry went in the tank. There were two poignant moments that caught the illustrious attendees by surprise.

The group was talking about the so-called Michigan Civil Rights Initiative, which was an effort to ban affirmative action for college admission and government hiring. Remember the issue she hit him with in the Showdown in Motown chapter?

Conservatives in the legislature were falling all over themselves to get on the MCRI bandwagon. So the unspoken assumption in the room was that DeVos would "head to the head of the wagon," too. "Everyone was going in one direction," talking about how the candidate could embrace the anti-affirmative action amendment to score some badly needed points with the conservative base of the state GOP. Then my leak recalls there was an "audible gasp in the room when DeVos announced he was almost 100% sure he was against it."

The assembled "ad hoc think tank" must have been stunned and immediately went to work challenging DeVos on his convictions. "He was pushed and challenged."

"What will you say to a person in Macomb County?" (A blue collar and right wing county where the amendment was expected to pass with flying colors.) DeVos would not budge. Years before, his wife Betsy had complained as state GOP chair that the battle over the amendment would be racially divisive, and for that reason, it should not go on the ballot. Hubby Dick, however, went beyond that as he argued the state needed to work toward a "color-blind" society. He had concluded there was no way this amendment, if adopted, would help in that regard. The total discussion was not very long, as DeVos hung tough against virtually everyone else in the room. Opposing the idea was one of the few times he had something in common with his democratic opponent.

The other showstopper involved the GOP Speaker DeRoche and former Governor Engler. After those 12 years in office, "Big John" was term limited out in 2002, when the party picked Lt. Governor Dick Posthumus to take on Granholm. The DeVos brain trust was kicking around the reasons Posthumus had lost, and DeRoche blurted out, "The state was fatigued with you," he said as he looked Engler in the eyes.

Just pause here for a second to add context to DeRoche's incredible, yet true, observation. Engler had a bazillion more years in office than DeRoche, who at the time had a grand total of three years in the Michigan House. Engler did not suffer fools easily and cut a wide path when he felt he was right. Everyone in the joint who had worked with him knew that. They also knew Engler could blow his top at the drop of a hat. Needless to say, everyone braced themselves for a repeat of history now that DeRoche had "started talking before thinking," as one of the participants put it. To everyone's relief, instead of cussing out DeRoche, Engler laughed. DeRoche confirmed all this for me months later and was shocked to know that I knew.

As the session went on, only interrupted by a deli sandwich lunch at noon, there was plenty of back and forth over "what she will do to win." Posthumus, who had come within four points of winning, advised his friends that DeVos should not "make the mistakes I made." One of those miscues was not having enough money down the home stretch of the race. This would not be a problem this time out.

The group had charts revealing that Granholm was in worse shape than Blanchard when he ran against Engler in 1990. When voters were asked if the state was on the right or wrong track, the group saw that Granholm's numbers were lousy. That meant she was vulnerable, the group concluded.

A good deal of time was spent laboring over the state's single business tax, and there was a division over what to do. Former GOP candidate Posthumus called on DeVos to "be bold and embrace the flat tax." One of the persons sitting around the table thought that was ironic coming from a guy who sheepishly refused to concede there was a state deficit when he ran. Now Posthumus wanted DeVos to embrace a tax that would stir up a hornet's nest. DeVos ruled out the flat tax, but the skeleton of what he would eventually offer was hatched based on a wide "exchange of ideas." "Parts of it, we do know," this source confided months after the July confab. But as this portion of the book is written on April 9, DeVos has not given the voters or the media any peak at his SBT solution.

As the training session wound down, Engler had one bit of advice for DeVos that we discussed in Chapter 3, "Don't start to govern before you are governor." Put more directly, he suggested DeVos not get tangled up in the day-to-day, blow-by-blow, Granholm-vs.-the-GOP legislature stuff that would go on until the election. And while the Granholm camp feverously shopped the "story" that DeVos was up to his eyeballs trying to kill the SBT deal she had with GOP legislative leaders, this source says DeVos took Engler's advice and stayed out of it.

After the fact, my source confesses the daylong policy gig

"was murder," but if there was a DeVos upset victory in his future, one could make the strong case that the summit in the Thornappple room was the launching pad for that.

The early take on the GOP hopeful suggested he was no John Engler who was a policy geek. On top of that, DeVos had very little experience in front of the microphone, TV cameras, and the political media. So it only made sense for him to get his feet wet by staying out of the State Capitol and visit every little berg in the state instead.

Periodically, the DeVos campaign would send along press clippings from outstate newspapers, and, of course, most accounts were positive. With all due respect to outstate reporters, just having DeVos in the newsroom or at a local eatery was big news in and of itself. And more often than not, that was the storyline: "DeVos Sips Coffee with Mayor." Seldom was he confronted with tough questions. And even if he made a political gaff, it would largely go unnoticed in Lansing. Thus, he breezed along for those seven months not making any news but getting badly needed experience without having to worry about a misstep in front of the Lansing news hounds.

Only on occasion did the campaign notify us that he was going to be somewhere within range. One such instance was at the Ionia Free Fair. Jack Spencer from the Michigan Information and Research Service (MIRS) newsletter attended and explained afterwards that DeVos should not make any more appearances with the Rev. Keith Butler on the same program. Butler, at the time, was the frontrunner for the GOP U.S. Senate nomination and gave a barn-burner of a stomp speech. Spencer told me DeVos could not compete with the fiery pastor. So despite seven months of trying to clean up his act, DeVos was not much further along than when I nabbed him during that appearance in Oakland County. And to drive home the point, we return now to what unfolded after his not so sterling performance on OTR. The on-air interview was not that great as you recall, but what followed was...well, more of the same.

With the OTR taping in the can, the stagehands opened the big doors on Studio C, and all those reporters who had watched the show from another studio came rushing in to continue phase two of the program: the after-show cross examination. DeVos picked up where he left off—with a series of non-answers to very specific questions. The pack of journalists was getting restless. Somebody asked again about his decision not to release his economic game plan to eliminate the SBT. DeVos explained that he was merely doing what he had done in the private business sector. "You make these decisions, and you find solutions to deal with the reality of it." In my mind, it was rather like driving your car over a cliff and then standing there wondering how the heck you were going to get to work.

Yet there was precedent for what DeVos was suggesting. Years ago, the legislature and then-Governor Engler blew up the state property tax system for funding the schools and didn't develop a new funding source until long after the explosion. DeVos obviously felt if he was elected, he could pull off the same trick. But there was one huge difference. Engler was a wily and veteran chief executive, and the legislature was filled with seasoned lawmakers. Term limits had not yet kicked in. If DeVos was elected, he was neither wily nor experienced, and the bunch of term-limited legislators could not hold a candle to their predecessors, who fixed the school-funding void. Reporters asked again about the hole in the budget if the SBT vanished. DeVos stuck to his story saying, "I'm more concerned about people's jobs in Michigan than I'm concerned about Lansing's budget right now."

He was then asked about hiking the state's minimum wage. The night before in her speech, Governor Granholm had blessed that by taking a shot at lawmakers. "You who are working in minimum-wage jobs have not had a raise for nine years." (Pause for effect before whacking those sitting in front of her in the house chambers.) "Even the Legislature got a raise since then." You could hear the grunts and groans from the GOP lawmakers who did not enjoy being called out on statewide TV.

As was mentioned earlier, DeVos refused to reject the minimum-wage increase, but in the post-show session, reporters wanted to know why. "I've not read the particulars on that," he continued to dodge a direct answer. "We'll get to the details," he said as he tried to fend off the relentless inquisitors.

Cain asked if the DeVos pledge not to raise taxes extended to the gasoline tax. DeVos punted one more time, falling back on the line he used to duck from the stem cell question. "That's a very complicated thing again. This will be all part of a more detailed discussion as we go forward. Those particulars of that... we'll roll those out." What the heck was so complex? Either he wanted to raise the gas tax or he didn't. Despite the simplicity, he would not go there, saying you had to figure out where all the money was going. No duh.

Hoffman wondered if that meant no road dollars for Detroit. DeVos would not confirm that either. You could feel the frustration growing in the press corps over all these non-answers. And so it went until Truscott decided he had seen enough. To his credit, the post-show news conference could have been eliminated, but DeVos sat there and took another barrage of questions until J.T. tried to end it all with those dreaded words, "Last question." As reporters prepared to pack it in, DeVos indicated he wanted to say one more thing. With as much sincerity as he could muster, he explained that "The governor is a very nice person...a very fine person," and he suggested that if you followed him around you would likely conclude that "I'm a reasonable guy, too. So let's put that off the table." He explained that the two persons in the race were different and "came from two very different backgrounds with two very different visions for the future." He ended with, "We're going to have a very clear choice...in this state." And with that, the crowd broke up, and I walked with the candidate down the long hallway outside the studio to the front door. The student demonstrators were long gone, and I thanked DeVos for doing the program.

Back in the studio I re-emerged to chat with colleagues who were figuratively scratching their heads. They had heard the same non-answers I had heard. Everyone was wondering why he did the program in the first place if he was not going to be more forthcoming. Know that reporters get paid to ask questions, to get answers and then report what we have found. And when we don't get answers, that becomes part of the storyline, too.

I went downtown to find the state GOP Chair Saul Anuzis and his democrat counterpart, who were appearing on a local radio broadcast. After they were done, I pulled Mark Brewer to the side and explained what DeVos had said, or not said. "No surprise," he began as he smiled.

Brewer had spent the last seven months as the surrogate "pit bull" for the governor. While she stayed on the high road and ostensibly out of the mud, Brewer had been down in it, blasting DeVos every time he took a breath. This was just one more chance to do it again. "All he can do is criticize—Dick DeVos has nothing. He has no plan." Out of fairness I asked, he has plenty of time to lay one out, doesn't he? "It's long past the time when he should put a plan out there," Brewer said as he finished his analysis.

GOP head Anuzis had not seen the show but reflected there was plenty of time to trot out the plan. It was early, and he suggested that when Granholm was a candidate, she waited until the fall to release her plan. Hours later, after Anuzis watched the DeVos performance on the internet, in a private e-mail he suggested, "I think he did a good job...He gets better every day..." I thought that amounted to putting perfume on a you-know-what, but what else could he say?

With the Brewer and Anuzis reactions to the broadcast on tape, I headed for the studios of the Michigan Radio Network, which feeds about 65 outstate radio stations. Despite the fast-paced and hi-tech nature of the news biz, it still takes time for a story to flow into the mainstream of public awareness.

As I got my story ready for the radio stations, however, there were 525 "eager beavers" who could not wait for the natural flow to begin. These were the Lansing insiders who live and breath politics. They were consuming OTR on the internet. Usually, we get about 250 hits during the first hour the program is online, but this one had double the box-office pull.

Hoffman from the AP put the first story into play, reporting that DeVos didn't take a stand on the business tax thing. And shortly thereafter, the phone rang in the radio studio. It was Chris DeWitt on the horn. He was the governor's campaign mouthpiece, a role he was reprising from the first "Granholm-for-Gov" effort about four years earlier. He had read the Hoffman wire service story and wanted my take. I am guarded in my remarks when somebody asks me, "How did the show go?" Frankly, until I see it myself, I don't know. When you are doing the interview, that is not the time to sit back like the viewer at home and make an evaluation of how it is going.

It was clear that DeWitt was happy with what he saw. By the time he had spoken with me, he had seen it three times, as he dissected every nervous tick that DeVos demonstrated and sifted every word that was spoken by the opponent. Ironically, the one person in the state who had the most interest in seeing the program could not see it.

Days later, Governor Granholm confided that her home PC was missing some "thingamabob," so she could not view it. However, she did say she had "heard" the program. She offered no analysis, but it was clear she agreed with others inside her inner circle that the DeVos maiden voyage on the tube had run amuck. Even the man himself confided at dinner later that night after the taping, "I didn't do too well."

The *Lansing State Journal* the next morning jumped in with an editorial titled, "Tell us more, Mr. DeVos." "It seems silly for him to go on TV to blast incumbent democratic Governor Jennifer Granholm for failing to improve Michigan's economy, then afteward not offer much on what he'd do differently," the editorial started out. "For our money," it went on, "it's never too early early for a candidate to begin explaining why he is the better choice."

Once the story filtered out, there was one question I got over and over again: "Why the heck did they let him go on if he was not going to answer the questions?" It was a good question that I put to Truscott days later, and his response was sanguine. They just felt it was time for him to do the show, and even if he didn't answer all the questions, it was good for him to get in the game. J.T. was confident there would be plenty of time to answer all the questions down the road. I also heard months after the fact that it was John Engler who pushed DeVos to do OTR early on. The crafty former governor knew that if it did not go well, nobody would remember it when the campaign heated up. Indeed, but it still remains one of the more curious programs we have ever done.

By the beginning of the next week, word about the program was on the street, and even some stalwart republicans were scratching their collective heads wondering about DeVos. They did not badmouth him, that's for sure, but knowing that Granholm was a "star" on the tube, the unspoken message was, he would have to do better than he did on OTR to unseat her.

Two weeks or so later, DeWitt was back on the phone requesting a DVD copy of the program. I informed him that I did not control the release, since it was copyrighted by WKAR-TV. Being the inquisitive reporter that I am, I asked why he wanted a copy as I also explained it could not be used for political purposes.

I said that years ago when Candice Miller was first running for secretary of state against long-time democratic incumbent Dick Austin, she made a copy of the infamous program where Austin couldn't tell the difference between pro-life and pro-choice. The Austin meltdown was sent around to about 150 folks—just in case they missed it on the tube. Miller's folks did that without consulting the TV station and the WKAR crew was not very happy. I suggested that DeWitt take his request to Tim Zeko, the executive producer for the TV station. I hung up from DeWitt and immediately called T.Z. to give him a heads up so he was not blindsided by the DeWitt inquiry. Zeko says he made it very clear that the tape could only be used for "educational" purposes and was not to become part of any campaign strategy. A short time later, I discovered that DeWitt had ordered two copies, made 150 more and peddled them to a variety of folks, including influential editorial writers around the state. It was hardly an "educational" mailing.

Under the Michigan Democratic Party letterhead, party chair Mark Brewer told the newspaper editors, opinion writers, journalists, and others that DeVos was evasive. "As you will see, his lack of answers to reporter questions gives a clear insight on how ill prepared he is for the job of Michigan governor." Warming to the subject, Brewer goes in for the kill saying, "The campaign for governor is a job interview. If you can't answer even the simplest of questions, you shouldn't get the job." Along with the DVD, Brewer and company also sent along a two-page, side-by-side comparison of DeVos and Granholm on a variety of issues.

It didn't take long for word of this mailing to reach the ears and eyes of Dan Alpert, the affable guy who runs the Detroit Public TV operation. He called DeAnne Hamilton, the general manager of WKAR-TV, and it wasn't long before she was calling me. I recounted my chitchat with Zeko about the DeWitt conversion, and when she suggested this whole incident did not look good, I concurred.

Long story short: She eventually conferred with the legal eagles at Michigan State University about possible copyright infringements. But when all was said and done, the Democratic Party apologized for what it did, and the university took no action, even though it was clear to one source that "this was not a fair use of our copyrighted material...." Suffice it to say, however, the station will not be inclined to share its programming with either party in the future. Suffice it also to say, whenever a political party can exploit something for political gain, it will, and this time, OTR was the vehicle toward that end.

5
SOS

January 25, 2006, was a "mucho" important day for Michigan's first and only female governor. It was State-of-the-State time, and while nobody on her team would concede the point, it was also the unofficial launch of her re-election job interview. If the speech went in the tank, she would be getting off to a bouncy start for the 2006 election year, but if she hit a homerun, it would help to build some momentum for another four years.

This would mark the 35th State of the State (SOS) that I had covered for the public TV stations, dating back to 1970. To be honest, most of them were forgettable. But regardless of that, the broadcasts were always fun and usually attracted a respectable TV audience. Since the commercial stations were not interested, we had the live coverage all to ourselves, along with the folks at Michigan Government Television.

The format for the broadcast had changed significantly over those many years. When Bill Milliken was in office, the speech was always delivered at 11 a.m., and there was no statewide live coverage. That changed when Jim Blanchard came into office. Nobody thought it would work, but we suggested moving the thing to 7 p.m. at night, the legislature signed off, and that's the way it has stayed ever since.

This would be the governor's fourth trip down the center aisle to center stage in the house chambers. With so much riding on it, she worked for months fine-tuning her message, which turned out to be a little bit of everything for everyone. To its credit, the Granholm administration had reinstituted the pre-speech briefing for the Capitol Press Corps. There was the firm understanding that none of the information gleaned from the session could be used until after the address.

At 4 p.m. that afternoon on the ground floor of the Capitol, we all gathered for what was to become a controversial exchange. Liz Boyd, the governor's first and only media secretary, held forth, as the correspondents sought to dig out the details. It was pretty clear to everyone that this speech would deal with the economy. Granholm had been in office for over three years, and Michigan's economic story was pretty grim. I'm convinced that when she was elected in 2002, she had no idea that three years later, the ship of state would still be on the rocks. Oh sure, she had scored some economic points over the years, but the overall jobless rate was still among the highest in the nation. The auto industry was laying off workers left and right, and to borrow former President Jimmy Carter's adjective, there was an "economic malaise" hanging over the state. And all this lousy news was on her watch.

Republicans smelled blood. For months, they had decried her lack of leadership on the jobs issue, and for months, she was putting up her political dukes to prove them wrong. The speech tonight would give her a full 50 unedited minutes to make her strongest pitch that she deserved another term.

So I wanted to know in the briefing, how many jobs this administration had lost since coming into office. "I don't have that figure," suggested Ms. Boyd. She was darn sure, however, that they had created more than they lost. Despite repeated efforts to squeeze the numbers out of her and two other administration sources in the room, the jobless figures did not appear. In effect she was saying, trust us because we have a net job gain.

Suffice it to say, there was not a lot of trust in the room. It was not a tough question. All they needed were three lousy numbers. If she was right, the top number would be jobs created and below that the jobs lost. After you subtracted, bingo, you had her net job gain. Try as we did, they couldn't do the math. Frankly, they looked silly, unprepared, and even evasive, which is not the image you want to project as the governor prepared to address the entire state.

Turns out, Boyd had bumped into the jobs number story earlier in the day. On the front lawn of the Capitol, the state Republican Party had set up a so-called "Jobs-Loss" digital clock. Every 10 minutes that ticked off the clock, the GOP argued, Michigan lost another job. The clock was ticking merrily along as everyone went into the Capitol to hear the governor.

Boyd made several phone calls to Jerry Lawler, who is the Capitol building manager. She wanted to know if the GOP had filed all the appropriate paperwork to demonstrate on the front lawn. Lawler informed her, the party had dotted all the i's and crossed all the t's. The clock would continue to tick.

Interestingly, a month later, when the GOP clock showed up at the state Democratic Party convention in Lansing, somebody destroyed it. Party chair Saul Anuzis blamed the democrats with the "crime." But apparently, no one was arrested, and democrats, with a straight face, suggested there was no proof one of their own had tossed a monkey wrench in the clock works. Undaunted, Anuzis ordered two more clocks and continued to parade them around the state as they bird-dogged the governor wherever she went.

But back to the briefing. It ended with no resolution on the jobs number, and I headed to WKAR to change clothes and get ready for the 7 p.m. broadcast. I would be anchoring from Studio C, where we do the OTR broadcast, and would have three colleagues to help with the post-speech analysis. Live TV is always a hoot because whatever can go wrong usually does, but this night it didn't. The floor director shouted, "10 seconds to air," I took a slug of water and got ready to say good evening. We had it worked out so that the governor was already outside the big red doors leading into the house chambers. When I started to talk, she was cued to head to the podium. As I welcomed the statewide audience on public TV, a statewide radio audience at WWJ, and the Michigan Radio Network, the governor walked in to thunderous applause.

One of the first persons she hugged on the way down that

long aisle was the mayor of Detroit, Kwame Kilpatarick. I had written a column the week before suggesting the governor had all but ignored the mayor and Motown in her previous speeches. In three previous messages, she had never mentioned him by name and made only eight references to Detroit; eight references in over three hours of speech-a-fying.

There was a reason for that, as I explained in the column. If she was seen by outstate voters as doing too much for Detroit, it might cost her votes with them. But in a classic double-bind scenario, if she was viewed as doing too little for Detoit, then the voters there might take it out on her at the polls. The popular wisdom was, Detroit voters had done that before to Jim Blanchard, who got in Dutch with former Detroit Mayor Coleman Young. While Blanchard thought the notion was wrong, there were some in this town suggesting Granholm might be headed for the same fate.

So the hug for the mayor was noteworthy, and I said so on the broadcast, as she continued down the main aisle toward the microphones. She eventually got to the rostrum and hugged and kissed the GOP Speaker of the House Rep. Craig DeRoche and her Lt. Governor John Cherry. Then she extended a firm handshake to the Senate GOP leader Ken Sikkema. No hugs or kisses for him, since the governor confided he was "not a huggy kind of guy." No understatement there.

One acquaintance of Mr. Sikkema suggested that his idea of a fun day was "playing golf…alone." In reality, Sikkema was an O.K. guy, with a sense of humor, but he was coming to the end of his 20-year legislative career. He harbored grave concerns about this governor's leadership abilities, so he was not in a hugging mood.

After being introduced and another standing O, the governor began. I sat back in the anchor chair to evaluate what she had to say.

Viewers sometimes ask, what do you remember about the 35 State of the State messages you covered? I don't remember much about Bill Milliken's speeches, except they lacked a flare in delivery but had a lot of content. Jim Blanchard, who followed, had one notable speech where he called for an income tax increase and heard only one hand clapping in the back of the chamber. Ironically, it was that tax increase that led, in part, to his political demise. John Engler's last speech was different in that he actually allowed his emotions to show and came close to tears as he said goodbye to this town. As for Gov. Granholm, you always remembered her wonderful delivery. I always felt she gave the best performance of all the governors I've covered, and I assumed that her fourth would be the same.

After her obligatory acknowledgment of all the important folks in the audience, she picked up where former President Ronald Reagan left off. "The Great Communicator," as he was known, was famous for going around the Congress to get what he wanted from the American people. Granholm started out by telling her audience of politicians assembled in the Michigan House, "I ask your indulgence, as I speak more directly tonight to our employers...the people of Michigan." After all, they would either re-elect or kick her out of office.

She touched all the right buttons, referencing fathers who had lost jobs to China, a waitress who couldn't afford college tuition for her kids, and the woman behind the dry cleaners counter who is sick and can't afford medical care. The only ones she left out were the baker and candlestick maker. She wanted them to know that "our people feel that pain more than in any other state in the country" —a Bill Clinton "I-feel-your-pain" line if ever there was one.

And then she made her first major re-election point without, of course, calling it that. "I am here to tell you: we have a detailed and comprehensive plan to grow this economy. We are working the plan. And everything in that plan will secure the opportunity for a good life for you and your family." Cue the violins, wave the American flag and pass that apple pie.

Next, she took full advantage of the platform she had. The SOS is the one time every year that the governor gets to deliver a message that is not sliced and diced by the media.

At the end of 2005, the governor told her year-end news conference that her administration needed to do a better job of getting out the "positive" economic news, since the media was doing such a grand job of highlighting all the bad stuff. It was a good idea. She mentioned plants that had moved from other states into Michigan. Like Reagan, who started the practice of recognizing real citizens in the audience, she pointed to Greg Boll sitting in the balcony. As he stood, she reported he was actually moving jobs back here from…MEXICO.

The place went nuts as everyone, including the republicans, jumped to their feet. Who'da thunk anyone would come back here to work. And on it went, as she tried to put a positive spin on the state's sluggish economic news. She boasted that 99,000 "more people were working than when I first took office." For some reason, she left out how many jobs had been lost and just like her staff, she didn't do the math, either. She did not want to share that on the eve of her re-election bid.

Then came perhaps the most shocking line of the entire speech, which I was sure would be tossed back at her during the heat of the campaign. In all her exuberance about getting the legislature to create a 21st Century Jobs program to create jobs of the future, she told everyone, "In five years, you're going to be blown away by the strength and diversity of Michigan's transformed economy." I couldn't believe it. Here was a woman whose own job was on the line, and she was telling the audience to be patient because in five, count'em five years, "you'll be blown away." I thought the use of that line could blow her away and out of office. And sure enough, eight months later, the phrase magically appeared at the end of a DeVos ad. I remember laughing out loud the first time I saw it.

Next, we got a peek at her re-election strategy, which again, she did not identify as such. For months, she had been blaming Washington for trade policies that were hurting Michigan. Now, in the SOS, she drove home the point to her statewide audience, "The leadership in Washington must be our partner in responding to the crushing challenges of a global economy. A partner. Not a bystander."

Democrats in the room shot to their feet. Republicans remained glued to their seats. It was an obvious broadside at President George W. Bush, even though his name was not mentioned. She did not want to appear too partisan or self-serving by using his name, so she just went with "leadership in Washington." Well, who the heck could that be?

It was good for her to keep on that message, because it was

working. Bush was getting blamed for Michigan's weak economy by a two-to-one margin with the voters here. That was the best news this governor could have. She knew if she could perpetuate that impression, her own re-election bid would be easier. The GOP knew that as well, which is why they did not applaud.

To understand the next portion of her speech, let's stop the tape for a second. Five days before she spoke, as I mentioned before, I wrote a critical column about how this governor had basically ignored the City of Detroit in all of her other addresses. As I was prepping for the broadcast, I reviewed everyone and found only eight references to the city. That was eight references out of more than three hours of speeches. And I also discovered that not once had she even mentioned the name of Mayor Kwame Kilpatrick.

But ignoring Detroit over the years was nothing new. Whereas Governor Milliken often mentioned the city in his addresses and worked out a good relationship with then-Mayor Coleman Young, Jim Blanchard did not enjoy the same rapport. John Engler never made a big deal out of Detroit either—except the one where he called for abolishment of the Detroit Board of Education, which happened. Granholm didn't exactly ignore Detriot. In fact, when I gave her staff a heads up that the negative column was in the works and I wanted a response, they banged out a massive report on everything she had done for the city, and frankly, it was impressive. But she seldom listed those accomplishments in any of her statewide SOS messages. There was a reason for that, and it had to do with politics.

As noted before, there is a strong anti-Detroit attitude in various parts of the state, and if Governor Granholm were to talk a lot about helping Motown, she would run the risk of losing support from those anti-Detroit areas of the state. Consequently, she didn't, and I explained that in the column. For good measure on the OTR broadcast prior to the speech, the panel speculated on whether the governor would invite Kilpatrick to attend the speech, and everyone guessed whether she would introduce him if he showed up. I voted that he would be there. (Actually I already had inside information from a GOP source that he would be there.) And, I predicted the mayor would be introduced.

Roll the speech tape again, as we go back to the governor's message and the section on Detroit. "And let me pause on our largest city," she began. She talked about how Detroit had hosted the annual auto show, how it was about to welcome the Super Bowl and how "the entire state needs and wants Detroit to be successful. We all have to work together to see it happen." And then she did it, "Mayor Kilpatrick, welcome."

He stood and beamed his big and friendly smile for everyone to see. She led the applause, and after he sat down, she added for good measure, "To those who practice the politics of division, who would drive a wedge between the city and the state, let me say this: the only thing that should come between Detroit and Michigan is a comma."

Several days after the SOS broadcast, I ran into the Chief Judge of the State Court of Appeals William Whitbeck. "Hey Skubick," he called me over. "When I heard the governor mention the mayor the other night, I said, 'There's the Skubick portion of the speech.'"

Back to the speech itself. She went on and on about the need for stem-cell research, better schools, protecting families, health care. You name it, it was in there, as she finally came to her conclusion. "So my friends, as I've said tonight, we have much to do…let me be clear: there is certainly a lot to love about Michigan just as she is." Then she takes another page from the Reagan playbook. Recall his "Morning in America" theme, where he waxed on about the beauty and uniqueness of this country. Her segment, I scribbled on my notes, was Morning in Michigan.

It was sappy but vintage Granholm, and you could see the fingerprints of First Gentleman Dan Mulhern in there, too. "The Lenten fish fries and church BBQs. The kids in the neighborhoods across the state holding lemonade sales for tsunami victims they will never know. Fishing on a quiet lake at dawn. Going to a cottage…and lazing in an Adirondack chair on the porch with the sun on your face." Man, it was getting thick, but she wasn't done.

She smelled the white pine trees and talked about "once in a while" going to a Wings or Pistons game and celebrating the return of a Michigan soldier with potluck dinner and yellow ribbons. "We love the Michigan that is and the Michigan that will be." Then, she wound down with the traditional call for bi-partisan cooperation. "I invite you to join me in believing in that next chapter in Michigan's history. And then join me in writing it. God bless you all. And God bless Michigan."

Five minutes to 8 p.m., just before the tip-off of the MSU and U of M basketball game, it was over. She did not dare run into the game because she would lose her audience. By going as long as she did, she accomplished two political objectives. Her audience would move to the b-ball game and miss the GOP response to her speech. And, as a bonus, the OTR panel's "insightful commentary and analysis" of what she said and didn't say, would have no audience either. And her cute strategy worked like a charm.

When the overnight ratings were handed to me, it was good news for the governor. She started the broadcast with a meager 1.3 share of the audience. But due to her star power, she proceeded to build the audience. At 7:15, the rating was 1.7. Then it climbed to a 2.0 share at 7:30, and she ended the broadcast with a very respectable 2.3 share, or about 72,000 viewers in some 45,000 households in the Detroit area. Those numbers did not include the outstate public TV markets, because there were no overnight surveys. But suffice it to say, she had an audience in excess of 100,000. However, at 8 p.m. when she said goodnight, the audience did, too. The rating dropped to .07 for the GOP response and .06 for the correspondent segment. That meant the audience heard exactly what the governor wanted it to hear without anyone else spinning her story after the fact. I sent a note congratulating her on stiffing us.

The box score that night was a clear win for her: Granholm: one. GOP and reporters: zero. That's just the way her team wanted it. Nonetheless, for those who were left in the TV audience, the question was, did we just see her last State of the State?

I finished the broadcast with Bill Ballenger from *Inside Michigan Politics*, Jack Spencer from the MIRS news service, and *Free Press* Editorial Page columnist Ron Dzwonkowski. And even though my mom Eleanor, wife Gayle, and daughter Carly were the only ones left in the audience by that time, I told the trio of reporters they had done a great job dissecting the speech both pro and con.

It had been a long day, but it was still not over for me. As I drove home to Okemos, my next assignment was to bang out a column on the speech, but on what aspect? I searched for the answer during the short five-minute drive. Normally, by Wednesday night I have the column in the can for the 22 statewide newspapers that run it. But because of the SOS, I gave everyone a heads up that this column would have to wait until after I saw the speech. So, there was added time pressure to get this one done.

I got home about 9:30 and anxiously awaited the analysis from the person that counted the most, my wife. She religiously watches all my stuff and continues to be my best critic. She liked the speech, liked the reporters, and thought my hair and tie looked nice. (We have an inside joke that the only things viewers really notice are my hair and ties.) We kissed good night. She dozed off to sleep. I headed for the P.C. I am using right now.

I was looking for some angle that nobody else would cover. I settled on the 99,000 jobs statement that the governor had proudly trumpeted in her speech. There was some meaty controversy there given the earlier exchange in the day with Ms. Boyd and her seemingly unexplainable inability to prove they created more employment than they lost. I started to write, "If you do not have an advanced degree in math, by the time this race for governor is over, you'll need one. Without it, nobody knows who is telling the truth on jobs created and jobs lost." I pointed out that the administration couldn't produce the equation to show how they got to 99,000. "Come on gang," I lamented. "somebody must have the silly number…[or] could it be that the job loss figure was so astronomical that it would have thwarted the governor's attempt to put on an economic smiley face for her radio and TV audiences?" I stopped just short of accusing them of deliberately withholding the number for political purposes. I couldn't prove it, but it sure felt like it.

The GOP jobs' clock was dragged into the piece. I credited them for at least having a formula to arrive at the "one job lost every ten minutes" equation, even though it was convoluted as all get out. And several weeks later, GOP Party Chair Saul Anuzis had to admit that his numbers were wrong. It was one job lost every 20 minutes, not ten. I explained that readers should get used to the back and forth between Granholm and DeVos, as the jobs thing was the only thing they would hear for the next ten months. The column on who was creating or losing jobs ended with, "You will have to decide who is right, so grab your handy dandy calculator and start work on that math degree before you do." At about 11 p.m. I finally pushed the send button and the column was done. I had just enough time to flip on the tube to watch the story I had done for TV-10 and to catch the SOS coverage on all the other stations. I finally hit the sack not knowing that in two days, the administration would be all over me like a cheap suit.

The column appeared in the *Lansing State Journal* that Friday morning, and the first call on Friday morning was from Ms. Boyd. She was not as charming as she usually was. "How come you didn't call me before you ran that article?" she started out in third gear. To be honest, I had thought about it, but I had already talked to her about the subject in that briefing and got no answer. I concluded another go around with her would be a waste of time. She made it clear she did not like the article one bit. No surprise there. It was not meant to be complimentary. I told her if she wanted an apology for not getting in touch, she could have it, but that did not mollify her one bit. I stood by the column. She didn't concur, so we agreed to disagree. I thought we were done with it. Not by a long shot.

The same Friday that the column ran, I had been invited to attend the annual luncheon sponsored by the Michigan Press Association (MPA). Mike MacLaren, who runs the group, was kind enough to invite Gayle and me, since I was speaking to the membership the next morning. The MPA gig is always accompanied by a late January blizzard, but on this day, the sun was shinning, the roads were clear and we were in the Amway Plaza—built by the DeVos and VanAndel families of Amway fame—about a half hour before the lunch.

Truth be known, I am not overly fond of "working" a crowd, but it goes with the job, so the two of us waded into the giant room filled with publishers, editors, and other newspaper big wigs from all over the state. The joint was also filled with local lawmakers from around the state who were dining with the newspaper crowd as well. Several joked that now that I was there, they would leave. I caught a glimpse of the governor as she worked the crowd and gave every impression that she was having more fun then I was.

We finally made it to our table, and before I got settled in, there was Ms. Boyd—this time in person and not on the phone but in my face. "Your column is getting out of hand," she announced to me before I could get my napkin on my lap. She requested the names of all the papers that carried the thing, and I tried to remember them. Finally, I asked her to contact my editor at the *Oakland Press*, Susan Hood, who I was sure could provide all the names. Boyd warned me that she was going to compose a rebuttal to my words of wisdom, and we left it at that. I looked forward to that. Obviously, I had gotten her attention and ruined her Friday morning to boot. Sorry Liz.

Gayle and I settled down to lunch, and I shared Liz's comments with my wife, and explained that I needed to talk to the governor about this. As I chomped away on the salad and whatever else we had that day, the governor returned from conferring with her security detail just to the left of our table. As she walked toward her seat, I got up and walked over to her.

"I hear I am on your list," I began as we stood in the front of the giant hall.

"You're always on my list," she quickly retorted. We laughed.

"No. The other list: the sh__ list," I tried to explain.

She apparently had no idea what I was talking about, which surprised me. This governor, more than any other I've known, has a knack for correcting flawed reporting. After all, she was a copy editor of the *Harvard Law Review*. On several occasions, for example, after I have done a live shot on WWJ radio in Detroit, the phone would immediately ring at home. Liz would be calling to say this or that was wrong with my story. I knew Liz wasn't the one listening, so it must have been the Boss.

Anyway, I reminded the governor of our agreement when she first came into office. I explained that whenever she had a gripe about my work, I wanted to know about it. And in this case, I gave her a quick thumbnail sketch about what I had written. The governor didn't seem to be upset. But perhaps with both of us standing right in the front of the room with 500 newspaper folks looking on, she was not about to unload on me just then. "You know," she told me, "Liz may be upset because it involves her." At any rate, we ended the conversation, and I thanked her for listening. We shook hands and went back to our respective corners. I figured if the governor was not upset, Liz would eventually chill out and drop the whole thing. I waited for her to compose a column taking me to the cleaners, but it never materialized. Maybe they knew I was right. After all, journalists always are.

6

The First TV Commercial

Dear Diary: Yesterday, February 16, was one of those freaky days when all the planets aligned to produce a weird news day. Governor Granholm got all tangled up in a child murder case. Her challenger, Dick DeVos, launched the first commercial of the 2006 campaign—a whopping 264 days before the balloting, and the weatherman turned the state into a mish mess of sleet, freezing rain and even a tornado watch in the dead of February. The stage for what unfolded on that date was set the night before. I was moderating a legislative panel in front of the Lansing Regional Chamber of Commerce audience of about 150 business types. The task was to cross-examine two members of the House and Senate and try to make some sense out of the continuing debate over how to turn the state's economy around. I decided to pick first on Senator Mike Bishop from Rochester.

"Senator Bishop, let me begin with you. Isn't it true that whatever the problem is—be it bird flu, juvenile delinquency or the lousy weather—you republicans have the same ole answer: cut taxes." The audience erupted in laughter. Bishop, the showman, correctly paused for a moment to let the laughter die down and answered, "Yes." Even a bigger laugh.

Later on, the grilling turned to Detroit democrat Senator Buzz Thomas. He and I were going back and forth on some issue when he conceded defeat, "Tim, I don't want to argue with you. Your microphone is bigger than mine." Now the audience is in total stitches with the obvious double entendre. I, the showman, waited for the joint to quiet down and added, "I have a million lines, but I will not go there." More laughter.

When the event was over, I was chatting with Chamber leader Bill Sepic. The great thing about the news biz is, you never know when you're going to get a tip. Sepic was lamenting the fact that the group had wanted to land Governor Granholm for an event the next day, but she declined the offer because DeVos was going to be at the same gig. I made note of that but asked, "DeVos is going to be here?" Yep. I decided I would be, too.

That night at home, one of my GOP sources called. "You didn't get this from me, but DeVos is going up tomorrow." "Going up" is campaign lingo for running commercials. It was 264 days before the voters would decide the next governor, and here was Mr. Money Bags shelling out who knew how much to launch his first commercial of the early campaign.

Now I really needed to interview the candidate, since this was a great story and nobody else knew he was going to be in town. Cameraman Steve Coon from TV-10 and I arrived at the Lansing Sheraton Hotel, scene of the "your microphone is bigger than mine" event the night before. DeVos was gabbing with some chamber types waiting his turn to go behind closed doors to make his pitch for support. The last thing I wanted to do was wait around for 45 minutes to get an interview, so I made eye contact with his advance man Nick and requested a bite with DeVos right then and there. The answer was no as Nick moved DeVos into the room, closed the door and left me cooling my heels.

With time to kill, we drove across the street to the DeVos campaign headquarters on the west side of Lansing. They had scheduled a 12:30 news briefing to unveil the first commercial, but I didn't want to hang around for that either. Unannounced, I walked into the office and requested a copy of the commercial. I figured they could hand me a VHS copy, and I would be on my way back to the hotel to flag down the candidate. Another dead-end. The campaign was sticking to its guns that nobody would see the spot before 12:30, and besides, there was no VHS copy. It would be shown on the internet instead.

Zero for two, we headed back into the news van and planted ourselves outside the room where DeVos was doing his thing with the Chamber. One of the participants came out and said that DeVos was taking questions from the audience and told everyone he was happy to converse with them given "the kind of questioning I'm going to get from Skubick, who is waiting outside."

Five, 10, 15 minutes ticked off the clock and finally a burst of applause. He was done, and now it was my turn. He came out of the door, acknowledged me with a head nod and chatted with Jim Barrett, who runs the Michigan Chamber of Commerce. When they finished, with Coon grinding away, I moved in. This would be what we call a "run-and-gun" interview, whereby the candidate walks to his car, and we walk along to save time. The picture is often a little bouncy as the cameraman has to walk along, too, but it's a good action picture. For some reason, I started talking about the weather and suggested it was just like spring outside. He said he thought it was winter, and I added I was an optimist, even though I was a journalist. "That would make you unusual," he fired off the first of two zingers in the unfolding exchange.

I finally got to what I was after. As you recall, when he did OTR several weeks earlier, he observed that he was not answering a lot of questions because voters were not paying attention at this early stage of the game. So I wanted to know, "If the voters are not paying attention, why are you running commercials?"

He wanted no part of the question and lapsed into his standard crapola about traveling all over the state and meeting the people and telling them, blah, blah, blah, blah. I vainly tried the same question again, trying to coerce some comment that would tie into my story on his campaign ad. He would not budge, and as we got closer to his car with the motor running, he suggested, "The campaign has a briefing in which they will answer all your questions." I didn't want the campaign guys in my story; I wanted him but was striking out. "You can't answer the question," I asked out of total frustration and added that I wanted a response so that I would not have to attend the 12:30 news conference.

Then came zinger number two. "It is not my job to make your life convenient." Pow, right in the kisser, and he laughed. I did, too, but it was a line that caught me off guard. However I knew I would use it in the TV story that night because it showed a side of the candidate viewers had not seen before. In fact after it appeared on OTR, somebody actually emailed me and said DeVos had been disrespectful. I did not agree.

Stepping into the front seat now as he prepared to leave me high and dry, he said he looked forward to seeing me down the road. I returned the overture, and with that, the door closed, the automatic running board on the SUV disappeared and so did he. I turned to Coon, "That was weird." He agreed as we headed for the news briefing at DeVos headquarters that I had hoped to avoid.

Running the first commercial in any race for governor is a newsworthy event. It signals a new phase, and in this case, it was pretty clear that DeVos was eager to boost his name identification with the voters, two-thirds of whom referred to him as, "Dick Who"? Walking into the viewing room, I expected to see DeVos and his family on the tape talking to the audience about how they were a Michigan family, how they had grown jobs here and how they wanted to help Michigan be great again. Instead, the spot began with some sullen music as DeVos did a voiceover video of manufacturing plants for rent, of padlocked gates outside a plant parking lot and grim photos of empty factory floors. The only thing missing to make the image more gruesome were a few dead bodies. "It's an injustice when there are people in this state who are willing to work, and they can't find work here," he began in a slow and almost painful voice. "The next governor of Michigan has got to change that," he went on and then he used a more upbeat voice with a faster pacing, "I'm Dick DeVos. A Michigan manufacturer. I'm a job-maker. I haven't spent my life in politics."

The 60-second spot continued, suggesting that he was ready to "work for change." And then, the final scene involved DeVos walking briskly out of his office, his sport coat flung over his right shoulder as he marched into the camera. He was ready to "take Michigan in a new direction." Fade to black.

DeVos was not at the briefing, so campaign manager Greg McNeilly and press secretary John Truscott took the barrage of questions from the 10 capitol correspondents in the room. How much are you spending on the spots, and how long will they run? "We don't disclose strategy information such as that," they seemed to say in unison as if the release of the data would determine the outcome of the election. The questions continued. We learned that the workers in the video that DeVos was walking with, shaking hands with and smiling with were employees at the Alticor Company in Ada, formerly known as Amway. "All of them were paid for their time," McNeilly volunteered, just in case the democrats tried to make an issue out of it.

Several things were missing from the ad. There was no mention of the fact that DeVos was a republican, and the name Jennifer Granholm was not used either. The only oblique reference was this line: "Unfortunately we're not putting it together right now." "This is a positive ad...it is a vision ad not a bio ad," McNeilly told us.

The other amazing thing was that they did not show the commercial to a focus group before it ran. The usual drill is that you produce the spot, call in about a dozen "typical" citizens, play it for them and get their reaction. Many an ad has been scrubbed based on what the "average Joes" had to say. Or sometimes, part of the script is rewritten to make it more effective with the audience.

Truscott reported that a couple of folks in the campaign saw it and liked it. So much for trying to figure out if the darn thing would work. Not using a focus group was not unique. When Jim Blanchard ran for governor, one time he ran a spot with a white drill sergeant shouting at a bunch of black kids at a reform school camp. White folks made nothing of it. The African American community took offense and let Blanchard know it in no uncertain terms. By comparison, the DeVos ad was truly benign, but would it work? Would it make more voters aware of the candidate, and would his upbeat message break through? The DeVos folks sure hoped so.

Meanwhile back at the ranch on this same "weird" day, the press corps had a chance to interview the person whom DeVos wanted to replace. She was about to have a bad hair day. It was a photo op, as Governor Granholm was having her picture taken with four of the original "sitdowners." These were elderly United Auto Worker union members who participated in the historic sit-down strike in Flint in the mid-1930s. The sometimes violent work stoppage against auto giant General Motors was historic and a major turning point in the labor movement.

"Me and my brother went from 52 cents a hour pushing a broom to $1.04 an hour," recounted Olin Ham who smiled with his three union compadres as they and she posed for the cameras.

There's an unwritten protocol to these events. Reporters never shout out questions to the governor. You won't believe this, but it is out of courtesy to those who come to see the governor and have their 15 minutes of fame. But when the last participant was out the door, then she was fair game.

The governor moved closer to the TV cameras as we moved in on her. Press Secretary Boyd had warned us that the governor was "on a tight schedule," and there would be time for only one question. She was always on a tight schedule—especially with rabid news hounds ready to take her on.

Some context for the first question. For days, the local Lansing and Detroit newspapers had been filled with the tragic story of little Ricky Holland. The seven-year-old boy had recently been found, buried in a plastic bag in a field outside of Williamston, which is some 25 miles east of the capitol. Despite a massive manhunt, his body was never found until his foster father lead the authorities to the burial sight and informed the cops that his wife had killed the boy. The wife had made the same accusation about her husband.

Obviously, the governor had nothing to do with the crime, but she was about to find herself dragged into the story nonetheless. Court records revealed that the Department of Human Services, which is part of her administration, had worked on the Holland abuse case. Reporters wanted to know if a shortage of Child Protective Service (CPS) caseworkers may have indirectly contributed to

Ricky's death. In other words, did his case fall through the cracks; could his death have been avoided, and if so, would the governor take responsibility. The governor did not flinch as she carefully began her answer to the timely and provocative inquiry. Ignoring the thrust of the question, she noted that in her most recent budget, she had requested 51 additional CPS caseworkers. Still sluffing off the question, she said there would be an investigation by the department into the death, and she reassured everyone that her administration was committed to protecting the lives of young children. What else could she say?

It was a nice answer but still not on point, so I came at her from a different angle, suggesting that if she was requesting 51 new workers, perhaps that meant there were not enough CPS workers to investigate the case, and therefore that could have contributed to the child's death. She conceded that her agency had been "understaffed for a long period of time" and "there is no doubt we need additional personnel in that department in those areas." Apparently realizing that her answer might leave the impression that she was at fault, she attempted to deflect the shortage to whom else? The GOP-controlled legislature. "And we've repeatedly asked for additional resources" from lawmakers, and she finished by promising that no budget bill would be signed this year unless it had money for those employees.

End of interview. Well, almost. She was asked to comment on the fact that neither she nor DeVos was going to take public tax dollars to run their campaigns, which meant a ton of money would be spent. "Um, I'm not going to comment on anything that has to do with the campaign," and she headed for the exit when I jumped in, "Have you seen the DeVos TV ad?" Press Secretary Boyd told the governor with a chuckle, "Keep walking governor." And she did and ignored the question, even though I shouted it out again for good measure.

It was clear on this February day that this woman did not want to be dragged into a back and forth with her opponent, but within hours she had another problem to cope with. What she had told the media about the caseworker story was dead wrong.

The Associated Press ran the story that morning, and

Representative Scott Hummel, who chairs the House Budget Committee, heard it and immediately called Ms. Boyd. He informed her the governor had never made a request for any new CPS workers—never. Uh-oh. Boyd did some checking, and sure enough, Hummel was right and her boss was wrong. To make matters worse, Senate Majority Leader Ken Sikkema got into the act. He fired off a blunt statement accusing the governor of trying to "score some kind of leverage in budget negotiations," which he argued was, "in poor taste and unacceptable."

And just to make sure he drove home the point that the governor had screwed up, he went on, "The governor has never asked for additional funding...despite the lack of a request, the legislature did increase funding two years ago to provide for 14 additional caseworkers." Not only did the governor not know that she never requested an increase in the employee ranks, she was unaware the GOP had done it for her.   Double uh-oh. This is why Boyd was on the horn to me just as I was preparing to do the story at the Michigan Radio Network for our 60-some out-state radio stations. "The story is incorrect," she reported.

And a short time after that, the front office issued a three-paragraph statement. It is human nature, when caught in a mistake, to sort of dress it up so that it doesn't sound so bad, and the statement tried to do that. However, it still amounted to slapping some lipstick on a pig—the statement still oinked. It began by restating that the governor had requested more funding this year, and then it said, "While the Granholm administration has taken a number of steps to protect Michigan's children, the administration has not asked for additional resources for Child Protective Services in the past." It concluded by suggesting "this is a matter that should not be used for political gain...."

Republicans could argue she was the one who was trying to gain some political advantage by incorrectly fingering the GOP legislature for not fulfilling a request she never made. We ran the story on the radio network, but somewhat amazingly, the rest of the media ignored the governor's miscue in their reports the next day. Instead, what was reported was the fact that the governor called for an investigation and wanted more workers. I firmly believed that her screw up of not being conversant with all the facts was newsworthy as well. But the next morning, when we went into the TV studio to tape the weekly "Off the Record" series, none of the guys on the panel felt it was a big deal. Larry Lee from Gongwer did say that perhaps I had a point, but we did not discuss it on the program.

Think about it.The governor's department was under a cloud: it may have contributed to the death of a young boy. The governor clearly did not know what was going on, and that is not news?

The episode in my little mind seemed to fit the GOP criticism that this governor often got a bye from the media because she was well liked. I don't believe that for a second, but I did conclude that sometimes the media did get sucked in by the governor's uncanny ability to downplay the bad news by attempting to find something positive to say instead. And in the Holland matter, it worked. Instead of a story that reported she had no idea what was going on in the CPS ranks, she got the more positive coverage that she was calling for an investigation. At the very least, both angles should have been shared with readers.

Two days after all this, the *Detroit News* editorial writers did check-in: "Granholm's knee-jerk blame game is offensive."

As I write this a couple of days after the story got out, you have to wonder: is this the end of the Holland story or will the GOP try to keep it alive to make the governor look bad as the campaign moves toward the finish line? I was guessing the latter.

As indicated at the beginning of this chapter, the day was not only full of juicy political news, but the weather got into the act, too. Former *Detroit News* columnist George Weeks got up early that morning to head to Lansing where we would all celebrate and bemoan his recently announced retirement. After 22 years of covering Michigan politics, he was hanging it up with the *News*. He quietly started on his normal three-hour journey from Glen Arbor to Lansing. Seven and a half hours later, he pulled in.

Weeks ran into sleet, snow and slush that jammed his windshield wipers. He also encountered an ice storm, and when he got within 70 miles of town, he heard thunder and lightening and ran into a tornado watch to boot.

George finally made it to the local eatery, and the party was a total hit, but while everyone imbibed inside, the monsoons continued well into the night. Everyone got drenched running for their cars as the thunder clapped in the dead of February. It seemed like a fitting end to a very unusual news day.

The night was also prophetic in that it signaled some stormy weather for the incumbent governor, who in February of 2006 sure looked like a shoe-in for another four years; but looks can be deceiving.

7

Can We Talk?

On balance, writing a book is not the chore you might think it is. Sure, there are times when it reminds of you of high school. Remember when some term paper hung over you, and the nagging call of the typewriter rang in your head as you dashed out the door on Friday night? But on balance, banging out a book is sort of fun—except for now.

The clock just struck 5 a.m., and my wife just shouted down from upstairs, "What are you doing?"

"I'm working on the book. I can't sleep. This won't take too long, and I'll be back."

Without a doubt, waking up in bed, in the middle of the night, and composing a chapter in your head is one of the more disconcerting aspects of this "term paper." It came as no surprise to me, because it happened on the first book. In fact, writing at this ungodly hour allowed me to finish that one in a record three months. So here I am again. The chapter I was writing in my brain, then putting down on paper, had to do with news events that seemingly on the surface have no relationship to one another.

There are two ways a journalist views a campaign: you take it one day at a time in an isolated manner. But then, every once in a while, you step back to see if there is a mosaic emerging that might give some hint as to how this whole thing will shake out.

One of those little mini revelations is what this chapter is all about. I'm beginning to seriously think the current governor may be in trouble as I talk with you on March 25, 2006, and here's my proof. Yesterday was a fun day. We did the OTR broadcast, which is always a hoot. Then I ran over to a local middle school to watch the governor do one of her "round-table" community "touchy feely" exchanges. This one was on beefing up standards for high school kids. She was dialoguing, as they say, with educators, parents, business guys and school kids. They were the poor suckers who were going to get hit with the state's continuing efforts to make them smarter.

In these forums, the governor plays the role of interviewer as she attempts to, ala a TV talk show host, draw everyone into the conversation to share their innermost thoughts on the subject at hand. While she labors away on that, the cameras grind away, hoping for some morsel of news to drop on the floor. It hardly ever happens.

Frankly, the Capitol Press Corps was really there to quiz her after the event on subjects we wanted to chat about. And there was plenty. As it turned out, she wanted a piece of me after the event as well. She was not pleased with me and was eager to bend my ear.

As I watched the governor do her thing with great ease, I keep wondering, what the heck good does all this accomplish? The legislature at the time was on the edge of finalizing a rather historic package of bills that would force all high school grads to take a ton of English, science, math and social study courses.

But yet, here she was on an 11th-hour, fact-finding mission that probably would have zero impact on the eventual outcome. There was no way she would extract anything from this town hall session that would alter the soon-to-be-enacted bills. But she gave it her all as she always did. First, she got all the adults around the table to embrace the need for students to compete in the global economy. Man, stop the presses.

That was easy, but dragging the middle school students into

the conversation was like pulling teeth. DDS Granholm ventured in nonetheless. Her first attempt failed as the kids clamed up. Nothing unusual there. Try interviewing a pre-teen sometime and see what you get. But being the competitive person that she is, the governor came back for another bite of the apple as she turned to the diminutive little eighth-grader sitting to her right.

"So, what do you want to be?" the governor inquired sounding like Art Linkeletter on the old TV show "Kids Say the Darnest Things."

"I want to go into broadcast journalism," came the one-sentence response.

Pay dirt for the governor. She advised the student to look around the room at all of us. There were three TV cameras and a bunch of bored-out-of-our-mind reporters leaning on a bookshelf waiting for this thing to get over.

"You could talk to them for advice," the governor suggested to the little girl, and at that point, I woke up just long enough to blurt out, "Find another career." Funny, but totally inappropriate on my part. The unwritten rule is reporters never become part of the conversation, but the devil made me do it. The governor took the opportunity to tell the student, "Ignore him. He is too cynical." More laughter.

About 40 minutes into this thing, thankfully, the governor's assistant press secretary, Leslee Fritz, gave her boss the silent high sign that the dialogue was over. Thank you, Lord. There was the usual shaking of hands as the governor profusely thanked everyone for being her props for this media event.

During this time, I spied the student who had professed interest in reporting and went up to the aspiring Katie Couric. I told her broadcast journalism was a great career and that if she had the passion to do it, she would be successful. She smiled and said thanks.

Now it was my turn, as the smiling governor walked up to the cameras. I was working on a story concerning a state lawmaker who wanted to lower the state income rate by 10%, and I wanted to get the governor's reaction. I got in two questions and was ready to ask number three when the governor just turned her head away from me and looked into the eyes of another reporter. She did that almost every time I had her on camera, and she did it for good reason: too many follow-up questions can get a governor into trouble.

The governor found safe haven with the reporter from TV-6 in Lansing, who started out her hard-hitting cross-examination of the state's chief executive by announcing, "Governor, I used to be a foreign language teacher." (Thanks for sharing.) Wow. This was more than a safe haven. It was manna from heaven. Not only was this going to be a softball question, it was on target with what the governor wanted to talk about.

Ms. Granholm did no head turning with this reporter, as she could have talked with her until the cows came home. Finally, the TV-6 person ran out of questions, and Larry Lee from the Gongwer news service got us back on track. He wanted to know, as did the rest of us, what the governor was going to do about the bill to eliminate the state's single business tax.

For well over a year, she and the GOP legislature had gone back and forth on this one, and at this point, she was seen as being on the defensive. The R's were ready to blow up the tax without any plan to replace the lost dollars. The governor was fixin' to veto it. She explained that she wanted to sign the bill. "I'm eager to make this happen," she suggested, but she warned that the GOP had to replace the $1.8 billion the state would lose if the business tax was scrapped. However, she quickly added, "I haven't seen anybody else propose a way to restructure." There was a reason for that. Nobody, including her, wanted to weed into this mess with the election eight months away. That's because to replace the SBT, some other tax would have to be increased to get the job done.

Figure it out. Who in this town wanted to talk about raising taxes in an election year? The answer is nobody, but that didn't stop the governor from offering some advice. "People need to get a spine in this election year in terms of offering an alternative." Ironically, I had written basically the same thing in my Friday morning column that very day. But I, in no uncertain terms, had blamed her for fiddling while the SBT burned. I didn't suggest that she needed a spine, although it was a great line, but I did say that she needed to call in all the players and get this job done. After all, she was the governor.

The line of questioning next moved to the high school graduation standards. There was a legislative disagreement on whether algebra II should be in the final package. On this one, the governor was clear. If we are going to compete in the global economy (geez, I am sick of that term), we need the "problem-solving mentality" that algebra II can provide.

Warming to this subject because it was not nearly as dicey as the SBT stuff, she suggested "it was different when you went to school, [as she looked at Rick Pluta from public radio], and when I went to school and certainly when YOU [looking at me] went to school, algebra II was not required." Picking on me got a great laugh, and then she said, "Sorry I just had to do that," and then I jumped back with, "Did you take it?"

Nope. "I didn't take Algebra II. It wasn't required," the non-math-major-turned-governor responded. Turns out she is not the math wizard in the First Family, but hubby Dan and daughter Kate are.

By this time, all the reporters had enough and after a few more goodbyes to school officials there in the library, the governor walked over to me. I recognized that look, having seen it before on every other governor I had the privilege to cover. I had been placed in the barrel by Milliken, Blanchard and Engler. It was not a lot of fun, and now she was on my case.

She had read my unflattering column that morning and wanted to chat. Oh yeah. She wanted to chat all right. Here's what ruined her first cup of coffee: When this governor first came into office, she made it clear that she wanted to emulate former moderate GOP Governor Bill Milliken both in tone and style.

Milliken made a 14-year career in town of demonstrating how a republican chief executive could work with a democratically controlled legislature. Granholm, the democrat in this instance, confronted a GOP-dominated house and senate, and she was pretty good at playing "Bill Milliken in a pantsuit," as I often described her during my speaking gigs.

The article that day that she didn't like started out by suggesting that instead of doing her Bill Milliken imitation, she was acting more like ex-Governor John Engler, who seldom called in the loyal opposition to talk about anything. I noted that Granholm had not talked to the GOP Speaker Representative Craig DeRoche in over a month. She was angry with him, and I'm convinced whatever trust the two of them enjoyed, that had dissipated over time. Now she had slammed the door and was shutting him out at this critical juncture in the SBT debate. In a word, I opined that was wrong.

She was not hacked at the Senate GOP Leader Ken Sikkema, but Sikkema confided to me that just like DeRoche, he had not talked with the governor, either, in over a month. The governor's office denied that. Regardless, it was clear to me and, I said so in the column, that she needed to suck it in and call the two boys in. "It's not as if the three have nothing to talk about," I wrote. With the impending elimination of the SBT, I reported that the "Three Amigos" needed to talk "with" and not "at" each other. As if that was not enough to get her dander up, I further criticized her for being "Jenny One Note" on her solution to the SBT budget deficit. It clearly was not, and I wrote, "She needs to get off the dime and offer a different solution to that problem."

I ended the piece by taking a whack at the trio by saying, "The failure of these three to commence serious and face-to-face discussions on this issue means that their definition of leadership is this: do whatever is necessary to get re-elected and worry about good public policy later on. Governor Milliken would not be impressed."

There was passion in my words, because I truly believed what I wrote. I recalled the advice of that wonderful former *Free Press* political scribe and dear friend Hugh McDiarmid. When I asked him in 1989 how to go about writing a weekly column, he wisely suggested, "Timmy, find something you feel strongly about and just write." Now you get a sense as to why she wanted to chat. "Let's have an off the record talk," she said as she came up next to me. We moved to the back of the room away from the crowd, and I could hear her passion, too.

She started with her complaints, but after a minute or so, her handlers said she needed to get out of there. The bell was about to ring, and they didn't want her caught in a crush of middle schoolers stampeding to lunch. So out the library doors we went, well ahead of the throng of pubescent starved kids. In a very animated way, we exchanged views as we continued to agree to disagree all the way to her SUV. Since all of this was OTR, I can't share the content, but know that it was not a heated exchange. She made her points on what was wrong with the piece, and I parried back on why she was wrong to think I was wrong.

We made it out the school door just in time, as the bell blasted in the background. As I walked with her to the vehicle, I said, "Well thanks for buying the paper." Always the gamer, she shot back, "I'm going to cancel the subscription." We both laughed. And with that, she was off to another event.

And I was left to ponder. I was glad that she had shared her objections. Early on with every governor, I have made it clear that if they had a beef, I wanted to know about it. She was not bashful about fulling my request. I liked that about her. But as I reflect on it now, it was pretty clear to me that none of what I had written had sunk in with her. She was on the defense, as she often was when the media did not report the story the way she wanted it, which meant our exchange was a classic example of "Don't confuse me with the facts; my mind is made up."

I had not been the only one ragging on her to start leading on the controversial issue. Legislative democrats, all off the record, had been whispering in my ear that they were frustrated with their inability to talk strategy with her. Even some republican sources confided that they had swiped the SBT issue right from underneath her nose and were surprised she let them do it. After 35 years of watching powerful leaders try to govern, I had concluded one sign of leadership is the willingness to admit you may have screwed up and then learn from that. The popular wisdom in town was that somebody continued to tell this governor that she could walk on water, when in fact she showed signs of sinking out of office. I'm not saying my column was perfect, but there were nuggets in there that she could have acknowledged as being right on the money. Maybe she knew that but would not concede the point to me, or maybe she figured it out afterwards, but it was nowhere to be found in our little OTR exchange.

But the day was only half over. I got in the news van and headed to the Michigan News Network to file a couple of stories

with the statewide radio network. I ran one on her "spine" comment
and then headed home to write a news article for the *Oakland Press*
on the income tax story that the governor talked about. It was a republican from that county that had introduced the rollback, and the
paper wanted the story for the Saturday papers.

Now it was about 2 p.m., and I was set to do a speech at 2:
45 on the MSU campus. For about the past 11 years, I have spoken to a great group of local government beancounters/accountants
from around the state. After sitting through a whole day of fellow
accountants droning on about municipal finance policy, the spon-
sors wanted to end the day on an informative, yet entertaining, note.
After the introduction, I started out with a new joke that a source had
just e-mailed me before I left home. "Hillary is at a cocktail party
and spies Arnold Swartzenegger over in the corner. She goes over
and says, 'You know if you were my husband, I'd put poison in your
drink.'"

Swartznegger replies, 'If you were my wife, I'd drink it.'"

Boom. Bang. And we're off to the races. I absolutely love
doing speeches. It really is a chance to find out what is going on
in the real world, and today would be no exception. As I rattled on
about the race for governor, two interesting points emerged. I told
the group that the latest polling data had suggested Dick DeVos and
Jennifer Granholm were tied at 41% each for the female vote.

If true, and there was some doubt about that, it was not only
unusual, but also it could mean she could lose the election, since she
won last time with a good bump from female voters. I reported that
I had detected some discontent among female voters over the performance of the state's first woman governor, and one woman in the
audience confirmed it. "I'm getting tired of all her charisma stuff,"
this person started out. The message to me was: this woman wanted
to see more accomplishments and less of the image stuff. I called
for a show of hands of how many others agreed, and I would guess
about 30-40% of the hands, most of them female, went up. Then another woman on the right side of the audience chimed in, "I'm getting tired of the governor's whisper voice." Others in the audience
agreed. This was nothing new. From the day she took office, part
of the backroom chatter in our town focused on Granholm's use of

a soft and very feminine low voice to make a point in her speeches. She didn't do it all the time, but enough to drive some women nuts.

Notice I did not use the adjective "sexy" to describe it, but that was the terminology some women used. And I had been told, the Granholm inner circle was not only aware of this, but also had urged her to knock it off.

Think about it. As I write this chapter, we are in the early stages of a very contentious and important race for governor, and some folks are worried about her whisper. But there was more to learn from these number pushers. Another female in the audience recounted a recent visit by DeVos to her offices.

"We've had a lot of candidates for governor come through our office," she began, "but no one has ever done what he did. He stood there and talked with each of my employees." She was clearly impressed and noted that he had more charisma than she had anticipated. And then she shared this postscript, which brought the house down. "After he left, many of the girls said, 'He's better looking in person than he is on TV.'"

There's one more tidbit I picked up from this event. You'll recall our discussion in an earlier chapter about DeVos's first performance on OTR. I asked for a show of hands of how many person had seen it. Not one hand went up — well there was one. My wife was in the audience. But not a single other person had seen it, which was good news for DeVos. His strategy was exactly right. Maybe they knew he could do a lousy job and no one, other than the press corps, would notice.

As Gayle and I headed home, I weighed the criticism about Granholm and factored in the fact that many of the municipal folks were a pretty conservative lot and predisposed to dislike the governor. Nonetheless, when you hear voters express doubts, you wonder what is going on especially when you hear the exact same groaning from democrats who want to see her win but have their concerns as well.

Recent polling data that I shared with the group was in play, suggesting for the first time that the race for governor, with nine months to go, was a dead heat. Where the heck had her 20-point lead gone, and more importantly, why was it but a fond memory?

8

Polls Don't Vote, People Do

Former State Attorney General Frank Kelley's right-hand man, Leon Cohen, had a funny line whenever the media asked about polls.

"Mr. Cohen. Do you have any polls?"

"Yes. And we also have Czechs, Romanians and Serbs in addition to the Pols."

To write this chapter on the polling in the governor's race, I need to disclose my bias: I think polling is the worse thing to ever happen to politics. Many pols use the polls to govern, which is not only wrong but dangerous. Polls have replaced personal convictions. Years ago, before you had data on what everyone was thinking, elected officials had to make gut-wrenching decisions based on what they thought was the right thing to do; based on the best thinking they had in their inner circle. And while the decision may have been wrong, at least it was grounded in their belief they were doing the right thing.

Now, at the flick of a computer screen, a politician doesn't need any convictions. He or she can see what the citizens want them to do, and they often do it. Only problem is, that public opinion can shift, and when it does, the original poll-driven solution may no longer apply and could turn out to be wrong. We pay our elected leaders to make those tough decisions, not to read polling data and act on that alone. End of rant, but unfortunately, there will never be an end to polls.

Before we sift the intriguing polling data about Ms. Granholm and Mr. DeVos, let's get the trite polling disclaimers taken care of first.

1. A poll is only a snapshot of public opinion at a particular point in time.
2. A poll's only as good as the questions asked. Or put more bluntly, depending on how your phrase your inquiry, you can get just about any result you want. For example, if you could have a beer with Jennifer Granholm or Charles Manson, whom would you choose? If you want to show the governor in a favorable light, you ask slanted questions such as that.
3. Citizens sometimes lie to pollsters. "Are you a racist?" is likely to produce some dishonest answers.
4. Citizens sometimes deliberately mislead a pollster just because they hate polls.
5. Polls don't vote; people do.
6. The media loves polling stories, because somebody else does all the hard work. Plus, the so-called "horse-race" aspect of a campaign is easy to write and easy for readers to understand. Polls, however, are not a substitute for gritty and in-depth reportage of what candidates stand for and what they would do if elected.

Having said all that, here is the first poll in the early race for governor that sort of turned this town on its ear. All the others up to this point were ho-hum, showing Granholm with a more-than-comfortable lead. But the one survey that changed that notion was concluded on March 20, 2006. It declared the contest was a dead heat. Granholm had 43% and the challenger, DeVos, scored 41%. That made it a statistical draw.

We were called into the conference room at Marketing Resource Group (MRG) in Lansing that glooming pre-spring day, where the firm's pollster Paul King and *Inside Michigan Politics* editor Bill Ballenger were holding forth. Ballenger paid for the survey, which is why he was there. The first finding they disclosed was that 75% of the residents in Michigan felt the state was on the wrong track: the highest that number had ever been since MRG started asking it in 1987. Traditionally, this question was a good indicator of the mood of the people regarding their optimism or lack of same on where the state was going. The numbers were not pretty.

Compared to a year ago, 63% of the respondents felt the state's economy was worse. Thirty-two percent said it was about the same, and 5% felt it was better. (They all lived in Harbor Springs.)

Asked to project to a year from now, 26% felt the economy would get better, 32% felt it would be worse and 33% saw the status quo. The most pessimism around the state was found in the Tri-City and Thumb region of Saginaw, Midland and Bay City, where 49%, or almost one out of every two persons on the street, predicted an economy that would get worse.

Next came Northern Lower Michigan, where 40% didn't have much hope. This was followed by Wayne County, excluding Detroit, where 39% were not optimistic and 37% in Oakland County, where the feelings were mutual.

If you are an incumbent politician running for anything, those numbers would give you a headache. And if you are running for governor, it could give you two. But interestingly, there seemed to be a disconnect between those economic "feeling" numbers and the electorate's feelings about the incumbent governor.

The survey asked about her job approval and her favorability rating. Early on in her tenure, the numbers were mind boggling, as she hovered in the high 60s. Now 47% said they approved of the job she was doing, while 48% did not. She was in trouble in Wayne County, where 48% felt she was not doing a good job. That is significant, because Granholm needs to do well in Wayne County, and she won last time by taking Oakland County. This data revealed for the first time that she had problems. Fifty-five percent of those Oakland folks were not impressed with her, and next door in Macomb County, the negatives came in at 49%.If you buy the popular wisdom in this town that anyone running for governor must win in Wayne, Oakland and Macomb Counties, then she had some work to do.

There were other precursors of potential problems in the so-called head-to-head match up. Most of us in the room that day concluded that DeVos had moved up as a result of his massive media buy. If you watched any TV, you could not avoid DeVos briskly walking and putting his blue blazer on and off as he marched to create jobs. So in some respects, the dead heat was not a real shocker. After all, Granholm had no commercials, and he had the whole field to himself. And public opinion being so susceptible to advertising, it's perhaps more shocking that he did not have a lead.

The survey conveyed several conclusions in my mind. You can "buy" your way into the polls. And voters were forming impressions about the challenger without knowing a single thing about how he would create jobs, how he would run state government or what leadership qualities he really possessed. In other words, the numbers moved in this survey because he projected the kind of image that some voters liked.

Image. There is that awful word again. Voters had no substantive knowledge about his guy, yet some were getting on the bandwagon. And not all of his 41% supporters were republicans. In fact, only 28% told MRG that they were from the GOP. That meant DeVos was successful in reaching out to others. He had cobbled together 13% from democrats and independents as well. And those two groups he needed to defeat Granholm. She, by comparison, held her 34% of self-disclosed democrats but got only 10% of everyone else in the electorate, which she also needed to win.

Granholm had problems in seven out of the 15 regions of the state where DeVos beat her. That included his lead in Oakland, the Tri Cities (remember their pessimism about the economy), Cadillac-Traverse City, Northern Lower Michigan and the Mid-Michigan area including Lansing. Consistently in recent polls the governor was not winning in the Capitol City. King suggested that the voters were a little more attentive to what was going on in state government, and there was, comparatively speaking, more media coverage of the governor's coming and goings than say in the Upper Peninsula.

Crassly put, the folks in the Capitol City who knew the most about her, didn't like her. They favored DeVos by a 49% to 36% margin, and recall that Ingham County is fairly rich democratic turf. To be sure, no election is won or lost in Lansing, but it was a finding that registered in my mind.

Conversely, the same could be said about DeVos. Where he was well known, he had problems, too. He did not have a commanding lead, as you might expect, in the Grand Rapids market. He had 43% support. She had 44%. Another dead heat.

Granholm needed a good bounce out of Detroit and Wayne County, and here the numbers were mixed. She led in Detroit by an impressive 68-17% margin. She led in Metro-Detroit 44-39% but in the rest of Wayne County, yet another tie at 40-40%.

I won't bore you with all the stats, but we do need to look at two subgroups to get a feel for where this race might be headed. Based on previous elections, I was from the school that argued races for governor in this state often turned on the female vote, the older vote, and the ticket-splitters, or those who vote the person, not the party. And if these MRG numbers were correct, DeVos had made some inroads.

Stay-at-home moms, who supposedly watch a lot of TV when they are not chasing the kids around the yard, gave DeVos a commanding 62-24% lead. Females between the ages of 35-54 also liked DeVos by a 10% spread. Granholm had only a 5% lead with woman over the age of 55. And if you looked at the female vote in total, the two were tied at 41%. She held a slight 2% lead with men, but that figure was within the margin of error, so in essence, they were tied there, too.

Older voters, who vote in larger numbers than anybody else in the state, are critical to the outcome. Here, Granholm had a comfortable eight-point lead, as she got 48% of the senior vote over 55 and half of the retirees. DeVos received 37% of the retirees, and he won all the younger voters between 18 and 54, but many of them don't show up on Election Day.

And finally, the all-important independent folks who often are the most intelligent voters in the electorate. They do their homework; they try to get up to speed on what the candidates stand for, and most critically, they are not sucked in by all the commercials and image-creation efforts. In March of this early campaign, this survey again suggested a tie with DeVos getting 39% and Granholm getting 36% of the independents, which was within the 4% margin of error. And since many of the independents also tend to be moderates, we need to sift those numbers as well. There was some good news for the incumbent as she racked up 51% of those folks compared to his 27%.

I generally hate writing about so many numbers, because they can be numbing. But to get a feel for this 2006 race for governor, you can't ignore them. If the respondents were telling the truth, I came away thinking this was a competitive race. It was not like in 1990, when everyone in town felt John Engler could not possibly beat incumbent Jim Blanchard. Not one of the polls even hinted that Blanchard was in trouble, and in fact, it was not until the weekend before the vote that democrat Blanchard woke up and found himself losing to republican Engler.

Two years ago, the prevailing winds in this town suggested Granhholm was also unbeatable. Flying high in the polls just after she beat Dick Posthumus, the media was filled with Granholm-for-president stuff, even though, by birth, she could not run. The expectations for her first term were off the charts in the early and heady days of her first few months in office. I was thinking those days are long gone. Even her team privately admits this is going to be close. They take nothing for granted, which is why this governor is working night and day to nail down a second term. If the March numbers are accurate, she better have a big hammer.

The MRG poll was the lead story on OTR that week. I started out asking Kathy Barks Hoffman from the Associated Press if the numbers produced an earthquake or merely a tremor in our town. She confessed she was not sure the figures were right. Chris Christoff from the *Detroit Free Press* seconded that emotion.

There were some doubts, unfounded or not. MRG is a well-known GOP polling firm with deep roots that go back to the early days of then Representative John Engler. Tom Shields, who formed the company, does survey work for republicans, and the governor's backers knew that Ballenger, who paid for the March poll, was not a big Granholm fan. I am not suggesting the poll was slanted because of those two facts. I'm only reporting that inside the loop, that kind of chatter tended to cast some doubt about the findings. Plus, the poll had omitted one critical question that I noted on the broadcast. They had failed to ask if the Michigan electorate continued to blame President George Bush for the sorry state of our economy.

In previous surveys, Granholm had dodged the bullet on the state of the economy, and she was overjoyed that Bush was getting the blame. And whenever she was "going anywhere, at anytime" to promote her accomplishments, she let everyone know that the problem was in Washington. But yet, this survey left out the Bush-blame question. Had they asked, and had he still been the bad guy, the dead heat between DeVos and Granholm would not have been as dramatic a story.

Because of those factors, my final take on this poll was iffy. The race was clearly not over, but DeVos was making some headway. Granholm had not really begun to fight, and most of the electorate was worried about something else and not the race for governor.

Yet there was stuff in the data that suggested this could be an upset year, and EPIC-MRA pollster Ed Sarpolus told me privately, if his next poll showed Granholm under 50% and in a tie with DeVos, "the race is over." That was enough to peak my interest in his survey that was finished on April 12, 2006.

Between that last sentence and this one, it is now May 7. Lots of fun stuff happened between April and May that "prevented" me from writing; namely a wonderful two-week stint in Siesta Key, Florida. I did take the laptop along on the vacation, as I thought I might add a chapter or two, but alas, I did nothing on this project for two reasons: one, I was afraid I would lose some chapters on the laptop and two, I really didn't want to. There is something about 14 consecutive days of sunshine with 80-degree-plus temps that can lead you astray. However, I must confess that the research that pro-vides the basis for the next section here was completed in the Tampa

Bay airport.

In the midst of the vacation, I had accidentally scheduled a speech back in Lansing for a group that wanted us to put on another edition of "Off the Record, On the Road." Since Rick Pluta of Michigan Public Radio, Bill Ballenger the editor of *Inside Michigan Politics* and Dawson Bell of the *Detroit Free Press* would have missed me, I left my wife Gayle to soak up the rays while I headed back to the cloudy environs of Michigan for this one-day gig.

I had four hours to kill in the airport. So I grabbed a seat at gate 46 where nobody else was sitting. I methodically pawed over the new data from the EPIC-MRA survey that Eddy did for the *MIRS Newsletter* gang and the *Detroit News*. I looked up periodically to see everyone in his or her shorts and tank tops strolling by on that beautiful Monday afternoon in Tampa.

It was like déjà vu, as much of this new data echoed what the MRG folks had uncovered in March, with some exceptions. First of all, this April information confirmed that the race was indeed a dead heat. The MRG stuff was no fluke, and Tom Shields and company were obviously relieved to have their data confirmed by another polling group. The credibility of the Shields findings would have been suspect had Sarpolus not found the same thing. But he did: Granholm 43% and DeVos 43% with 14% undecided.

Since at this read I am still convinced that women and independent voters will decide the outcome of this close contest, I surfed through those numbers first. Granholm continued to hold a lead with the independents with a 43-33% lead, although she was down about three points over the March survey. Independent female voters had increased their backing of the governor, as she got 51% of their vote while he got 33%. She was up a little from one month ago. She also beat DeVos with independent men by a smaller 38-33% margin, which was an eight-point drop.

Looking at gender alone without the independent label, Granholm continued to lead with college-educated women by a hefty 27-point margin. However, her lead with noncollege educated females in March had flip-flopped by April. DeVos was now beating her 48% to 36%, which was a 17-point drop for her. The female vote based on age continued to be revealing and made for interesting reading as the jets came in and took off behind me. Granholm was slipping in both columns. DeVos actually upset her with younger women. Granholm lost seven points from the earlier survey. He beat her by a 49-42% margin. She held onto to her lead with older women, but there was significant—and I mean significant—erosion here. She dropped 13 points. She was still ahead, but her support had dropped below that magical 50% plateau.

There were signs that republicans who had flirted with the Granholm candidacy in March were having second thoughts. The governor had a respectable 23% of the GOP female vote in March, but it fell to 11% one month later. However, most of the GOP woman who left her did not move to DeVos. They hopped into the undecided column instead. Traditionally, once voters move to undecided, many end up with the challenger. This was bad news for her and good news for him. Granholm won in 2002 with a good chunk of the female republican vote.

Another critical category that deserves attention is the senior voter. For those 65 and older, the two candidates were virtually tied with another 17% on the fence. That represented a whopping 18-point fall off for her in that group. Not good news, either.

However, DeVos saw his substantial lead with younger voters evaporate into thin air, too. He once enjoyed a hefty 62% to 38% edge over her but was now looking at a 51-38% deficit with those between the ages of 30 and 35.

The trouble with so many numbers is each side can pick and choose the figures that make their candidate look the best. If voters don't see all the data, they can be misled. For example, in the vital tri-county region of Wayne, Oakland and Macomb counties, both sides could put a positive spin on the findings. DeVos could say he was ahead in Macomb, closing the gap in Oakland and inching up in Wayne. And all of those statements are true. Ah, but Granholm could counter she was boosting her Macomb County support, while holding onto her lead in Oakland and continuing to beat him in Wayne. Again, all of this is true.

But here are the numbers they don't tell you because it changes your opinion of what each is saying. DeVos's Macomb lead had dropped by 9 points. Her lead in Oakland had dropped by 11 points, and her Wayne County edge was down by 12 points. So instead of being in good shape, as their press releases might lead you to believe, the real story is they are fading.

One final note on the EPIC-MRA findings, Granholm managed to tie DeVos in Lansing, where she was behind earlier. She gained 10 points while he dropped 5. She continued to win in his backyard of Grand Rapids, but he took over the lead in the Saginaw-Midland-Bay City corridor. I had a chance to do a speech in that area weeks after the polling data was out, and I got an earful. "Saginaw is now ground zero," one local republican with a smile. The region was in turmoil due to the so-called Delphi problem, and the issue was front and center on the race for governor stage.

As I journeyed up I-75 to do the speech there, on the right-hand side of the freeway was the giant Delphi sign on the plant next to the smaller, but still noticeable, UAW logo. Even though the two signs were side by side on the front of the factory, the two sides were embroiled in a nasty, and very public, battle over all the issues that had dogged the Granholm administration from day one. In fact, Delphi, the automotive supplier, was the living and breathing medifore for the mess Granholm was desperately try to cope with: wage and benefit givebacks from workers; top company officials sweetening their own paychecks while at the same time ordering the outsourcing of jobs and the downsizing of the workforce, which was a nice way of saying workers were being kicked out the door.

It was no accident that the night I arrived in town for the 7:30 a.m. (ugh) speech the next morning, DeVos was at the local GOP hangout on his "Get it Done" bus tour. He knew this area was distressed, which is why the bus stopped. To make sure he found those folks, he headed to a local bowling alley, where I am told he did quite well, both on the lanes and with those he met. I talked about the DeVos visit with 200 business types at the early morning speech the next day.

"What was he like?" I inquired from those who raised their hands to confess they had seen him the night before.

"He was down to earth," a local banker suggested. That was not news to me. I had heard it hundreds of times on the speaking circuit. DeVos was not coming across as an aloof millionaire or a stuffed shirt. In fact, his very unstuffed, casual and open collared shirt reinforced the image his team was trying to create: He was "one of us." Remember, the Granholm side said she was "one of us. And he was rich."

I asked the group how many had seen the DeVos commercials that had blanketed the airwaves. Ninety-five percent of the hands went up. There was one guy sitting near the front who did not put up his hand, so I picked on him. "What planet have you been on?" I asked while gently sticking the mike in his face. He confessed he had never heard of DeVos and to make matters worse, he had never heard of "Off the Record" or some clown named Tim Skubick, either. I laughed along with the audience and pointed at him and said he was in good company. Nine million other folks in this state didn't know me, either.

I continued to be amazed at how DeVos was moving the polling numbers when in effect, the only thing citizens were responding to were his TV ads. I told the assembled business folks the ads didn't reveal what he would do if he was actually elected governor. That launched me into my rant about how he was still refusing to dish out specifics on what he would do to replace the single business tax, which had now become part of his commercial message. "DeVos has a plan to repeal the SBT," his commercial drones on. But what is the plan? What specific business taxes would he raise? What state services would he slice and dice to fill in that almost $2 billion hole the repeal of the SBT would create? Rest assured, none of those answers were within five 500 miles of his commercials, and they were left out on purpose.

Just the day before when the bus tour trekked through Lansing, DeVos did tell the Capitol Press Corps that his "plan" would include replacing the majority of lost revenue with another business tax. DeVos said he also expected economic growth in the state to replace some of the money, too.

Anyway, I told the crowd I thought a candidate had an obligation to the electorate to tell us what he would do—before he was elected. I even reminded everyone that DeVos had told columnist George Weeks in Traverse City that he might not reveal his details until AFTER he was elected. In other words, he was saying "trust me." Elect me, then I'll tell you what I will do. Hog wash. Most of the audience seemed to agree, but one elderly republican in the back of the room got on my case for making such an unrealistic demand.

"He's never been in government," she began her feeble defense of his unwillingness to come clean on what he would do. "He's a businessman and has the experience to create jobs, so just let him alone." Good grief.

"Do you really believe that?" I not so gently stuck the mike in her face.

She stared back at me and said yes. The audience applauded. None of this dodging was new to me. DeVos was doing the exact same thing candidate Granholm did when she ran in 2002.

Asked about what she would do about the blooming state deficit, she suggested she could not provide any details until she did an audit of the state books—AFTER she was elected. It was a dodge with a capitol "D." She knew it. The press corps knew it. The public bought it, and after she was elected, there was no audit. Now DeVos was engaged in the same strategy, but of course, the governor was calling him out demanding to know what his plan was.

Eight hours after I departed Saginaw, the governor showed up at the Delphi plant. She met with a bi-partisan group, including someone from Congressman Dave Camp's office, GOP lawmakers Mike Goschka and Roger Kahn, along with Saginaw Representative Carl Williams, a democrat. "Consider us part of your team," she said as she commenced the half-hour confab. My source reports she wanted to find a buyer for the Chassis Plant run by Delphi. She offered "tools from the MEDC (Michigan Economic Development Corporation)." She also tried to reassure the locals that when the Electrolux vacuum cleaner management cleaned out the town of Greenville with thousands of layoffs, she had been successful in bringing a high-tech industry to create new jobs. This source confided in an e-mail afterwards, "she looked a little tired and stressed."

Reflecting on the polling data about female voters we discussed earlier in this chapter, this source added an interesting postscript, "Women like to support other women when it's a first [first woman in space, etc.], but I believe women are the first ones to throw another woman out on her ass if they perceive she's not living up to what they think she should. Men are more forgiving of other men, I believe."

It was a prophetic statement, and it was not the first time I had heard it. I wondered, with six months to go, was it coming true. Would she lose her female support? And that was underscored when a third survey came out in early May once more showing the race tied. Sarpolus did a poll from May 1st through the 8th and gave DeVos a slim one-point edge over the governor, 46%-45%, which made it a dead heat—still.

I won't bore you with more numbers except to say there were a couple of changes. The ground that Granholm made up in the Lansing market earlier was now gone, and DeVos was beating her by an impressive 63-31 margin.

Her lead over him in Grand Rapids continued but by a much smaller margin of 48-45. Most of the other findings remained about the same. However, Eddie did one thing I asked him to do: Ask the Bush question, "who do you hold responsible for the lousy state of our economy?" The findings, as far as Granholm was concerned, were exactly what she wanted to hear. The blame question was broken down into 87 different subgroups of the electorate, and in 92% of those categories, Bush got more blame than the governor. The only folks in the state who felt she was at fault included GOP men and women. No surprise there, as 44% of the men and 41% of the women held the governor accountable. So did voters between the ages of 30 and 40. Reflecting her apparent weakness in the capitol city, 30% blamed the governor and 29% blamed Bush. Interestingly, for those earning over $100,000 a year, it was a tie at 33%-33%.

The bottom-line was clear: the GOP message that she was not a leader on the job front was not working. Former Governor Jim Blanchard made note of that when he appeared on "Off the Record" just after the poll was released. His historical take was interesting, as he compared the Bush unpopularity in 2006 to that of former President Richard Nixon in the aftermath of the Watergate scandal in 1974.

Blanchard spoke from fond memories, since he was running for Congress at the time. While he never mentioned the Watergate mess on the stump, he privately knew he was benefiting from the problems in the GOP. Jumping back to the here and now, Blanchard believes the GOP funk in 2006 mirrors that of 1974, and that was good news for his friend Ms. Granholm.

"The GOP faces a democratic tsunami. Bush's problems will energize the democrats to vote and demoralize the republicans to stay home, just as they did over 30 years ago." He says he shared this theory with Granholm, who said she hoped he was right. His optimism not withstanding, Blanchard was reminded the current race was tied. He shoved that aside and boldly predicted a 4- to 5-point win for Granholm, suggesting that she was not in trouble.

Which is almost exactly what she said the day before, when the Capitol Press Corps finally got a chance to cross-examine her on the latest polling. It was a bit ironic that we caught up with her as she toured the construction sight of a new emergency room at a Lansing hospital. She had on a hardhat and was taking about health insurance. I sort of smiled said to myself, "This is appropriate. She may need that hardhat and emergency room care, given her less-than-stunning performance in the polls."

Anyway, everyone waited for her to complete her comments about her universal health care program. The GOP had earlier dubbed it "Hillary Clinton Lite." (Recall former First Lady Clinton's ill-fated stab at a national health care plan.) When Granholm was done, I was standing next to the podium, with camera running, eager to get into the good stuff.

Earlier that morning on the way to the event, I was trying to think of an opening question to sidestep her worn-out response to polling questions: polls are polls. The only one that counts is the one in November, etc., etc., etc. I had one. She finished glad-handing some doctor and turned her face toward the cameras. I asked, "As a highly competitive person, you must be elated that this race is a dead heat?"

She took the bait. "Actually, I'm thrilled," she began. I thought to myself, "Thrilled?" I wondered what she had for breakfast. She explains that the general public is not tuned in on this contest, so there was no need to panic. I followed up with, "Explain to me why an incumbent would be thrilled to be tied?"

"Remember how much money has been spent in this race so

far, and there has been nothing from me up on the air, yet. This is way, way earlier—earlier than at any point in Michigan history—that a gubernatorial race has seen this kind of expenditure." She had that right but was sanguine about it all. I reminded her that some have suggested if she did not get her ads on the air by June, the race would be over.

"All I can say is: remember Debbie Stabenow." (In her race with incumbent U.S. Senator Spence Abraham in 2000, current U.S. Senator Stabenow held her resources until the tail-end of the race, even though Abraham had an early lead.)

"So, you can sit on your pot of gold until August?" I tried to get more out of her.

"People are worried about putting food on the table. They're worried about insurance. They are worried about their jobs. They are not worried about a governor's race in May. We'll go up when we're ready," she said as she moved toward the exit. I moved with her. I love talking to politicians when the camera is off. Sometimes, you get a better story. As we moved toward her SUV that was running, I noted that some of her supporters were getting antsy about her ignoring DeVos and not getting in the fight.

"Can I report, not for attribution to you, that you will start your ads in June?" She dismissed the question with an air of confidence and the Granholm smile. There was an "echo chamber" in Lansing, she explained, which was her polite way of saying none of the political back and forth between candidates and the media was reaching the unwashed in the hinterland. She confided, as the state trooper revved up the engine, that she was not going to run any commercials until she felt the time was right and when the voters were listening. Implied in her answer was the realization that only political reporters were on this story and she would not be stampeded by us, or anyone else for that matter, into spending her precious money before it was time.

I thanked her for the chat and went inside and found an elderly woman who confirmed what the governor just said. "Did you know there's a governor's race going on?" I asked her on camera. Her eyes shifted to the heavens looking for divine guidance but got none.

"No."

"Do you know who is running against the governor?"

"No," again.

"When will you get engaged?" I went on.

"When Granholm is out of office," she blurted out.

9

Building Japanese Cars Here

Having chronicled the comings and goings of Michigan politicians over the years, one unmistakable trait emerges about all of them: each is a control freak. If they could, they would take total control of every event. If they could, they would eliminate any outside forces they could not control. That would include controlling reporters who rebel at doing stories when they are told to by those control freaks. But alas, no one has that much control, and the reality of that makes politicians very nervous. It's the stuff over which they have no power that could end up controlling them and their careers.

History is replete with governors and would-be governors who bumped into uncontrollable events such as the widespread human consumption of the fire retardant chemical PBB, which almost did in former Governor Bill Milliken in the middle 1970s. John Engler was confronted with a General Motor's decision to mothball a plant in Willow Run and ship those jobs to Texas. Little did we know in 1994 that would become a common-day occurrence around here. Engler floundered at the uncontrollable nature of that event back then. Jennifer Granholm and challenger Dick DeVos could be the victims or the beneficiaries of an outside and uncontrollable force this time out. It's hard to believe, but Japanese carmakers could determine who wins this race.

You read that right. The winner could be aided by two critical decisions now under review by Toyota and Honda. If one or both come to Michigan, the governor would score big. But as she aggressively goes after those plums, if she loses, it could be the final nail in her political coffin driven in by DeVos.

I first got wind of this story in November of 2005. While working on a routine story with then Department of Labor and Economic Growth director David Hollister, I innocently bumped into some startling news. Hollister told me on the Q-T that Toyota was actively considering building a new engine plant in Michigan. That had never been reported, and I asked Hollister if I could run with it without using his name. He agreed but warned me that the whole situation was extremely delicate. Dealing with the Japanese was not a walk in the park, and he did not want anything to upset the delicate talks that were underway.

I waded into the story in my column that week noting that in previous years, if any politician had anything to do with Toyota, it amounted to a political kiss of death. To wit, I reminded everyone of the former astronaut Jack Lousma, who was the GOP nominee for the U.S. Senate. He was a delightful chap who made one huge miscue: he had a Toyota parked in his garage. The second mistake is that he allowed some democrat to take a picture of it.

Lousma's opponent took it from there. Once democrat Carl Levin let the entire state know that Lousma owned a foreign car, well let's just say it was sayonara Jackie-poo. For you non-Michigan types reading this, recall that Michigan was, and still is, a Big Three state, and the United Auto Workers union was a force with which to be reckoned. Owning a foreign car was considered an act of treason, as Lousma found out.

But now it was possible that Toyota could actually save the Granholm candidacy rather than destroy it. As I reported in the piece, if the company decided to build that engine plant here, it would help to eradicate the notion that this governor was clueless on the job creation front. To be sure, she could get the facility and still lose, but given the choice between landing the plant and not, I was sure Granholm would give her right arm for the former.

The column ran and then slowly filtered out. By the time the governor was set to make her first visit to Japan in August of 2006, reporters wanted to know what she was doing about the Toyota deal.

If you believed what everyone was saying, Michigan was in the hunt. I contacted the car company, in what I knew was a wasted call, and got the usual corporate clap trap about "We don't talk about plant location decisions." But the Toyota P.R. person took extra steps to underscore the point that the governor had made a favorable impression on the car company officials. One of them was even quoted as saying she was very attractive.

In the debrief with the media on the Japan trip, the governor was careful not to be too optimistic, but reading between the lines, you could tell she felt Michigan had a chance.

There were two problems: Michigan was home to Ford, GM and Chrysler. Plus, the UAW had a strong presence and had an anti-Japanese attitude to boot. Example, if you drove a foreign car, you could not park it in the Solidarity House parking lot where union officials parked their very American-made vehicles.

The governor acknowledged those factors were a potential barrier to Toyota coming to Michigan, but she reported that the union, now embroiled in an all-out war for jobs, had changed its tune and was willing to welcome Japanese employment. She also told reporters she reassured the Japanese that coming to the home of the Big Three was really a plus, not a minus.

The story after the news conference sort of bobbed and weaved in and out of the media. When new Michigan Economic Development Director Jimmy Epilito came on board, I recall chatting with him, and he reassured me that the Toyota thing was being dealt with "on a daily basis." He tipped me that the company had already started a tentative search for land in West Michigan far way from the headquarters of the Big Three and in a region of the state where carrying a union card was not a prerequisite for breathing the air.

I went to State Senator Wayne Kuipers from that side of the state with the news that his area might be in play. He was shocked to find that out and promised to check with some local real-estate types for any inside scoop. Silly me. I assumed that might produce a nibble, but come to find out, Toyota does not search for land by telling the locals who they are. By hiding their identity, they prevent a land rush and higher prices for the property they might want to buy. Bottom line: I was drilling a dry hole, but the potential impact for the governor was alive and well.

"You've got a real shot at this Toyota deal, don't you?" I quizzed her as we walked to a public radio interview one day. She acknowledged that but again was careful not to tip her hand or to lead me to believe it was a done deal. However in her own optimistic manner, she ended the chat by saying, "If we don't get it, it will not be because we didn't try."

I knew that was true. She understood the gravity of the story. If the soon-to-be-number-one carmaker in the world picked Michigan, her chances of four more years would skyrocket. In fact, as I noted in the column, if she accomplished that objective, she would not object to driving the kids to school in a Toyota SUV. Heck, if she won, even Jack Lousma could now buy one without fear of retaliation from the UAW.

Now we are in May of 2006, and as I write, guess where the governor is? Yep. Japan. But now the stakes are even higher. Following her first trip to that country, the GOP criticized her for waiting three years into her administration to make that first sojourn. That was a fair criticism. Perhaps the governor did not go earlier because she and lots of other folks in town felt the state's lackluster economy would be booming long before she had to run for re-election. Wrong. It was a misplaced hope. So yes, she was a governor come lately to the Japanese courting game.

As she prepared to leave for her second journey to the land of the rising sun, GOP state chair Saul Anuzis dismissed it as a publicity stunt. He predicted that she already had some Japanese jobs lined up for Michigan, and there was no need to go there to announce that. That was a cheap shot. You can't blame her for not going and then blame her for going, but that did not stop ole Saul from doing it anyway. To no one's surprise, Saul was right. The very first day she was there, she notified everyone back here that about four companies were ready to sign a deal and outsource to Michigan several hundred jobs.

Nice touch, but no earth-shattering announcement, and it was made even less impressive by the news the next day. The state's jobless rate was well above 7%. But after that hit the newsstands, there were more headlines that moved the political earth in this town and took the rest of the shine off the governor's announcement that she had found 200 new jobs.

On day two of her visit in Japan, the Honda Company told the world that it was looking for a state to build its sixth auto assembly line. This was unprecedented: two Japanese auto giants both hunting for new plants with a combined 2000-plus jobs on the line.

If the governor could pull that off, it would have a tremendous impact on the race for governor. But more on that in a moment. As the Honda news entered the news cycle, it looked as though fate was on the governor's side. She was already in Japan. She could knock on Honda's door and make a personal pitch for that plant, too. But amazingly, she did not knock. And she said so during an early morning interview with WWJ NewsRadio 950 in Detroit. In a smart political move, the governor made the rounds on all the morning radio shows, but now the anchors wanted to know about the Honda plant. Anchor guy Joe Donovan wanted to know if she would meet with them.

"We made a pitch to them when I was here the last time, but we don't have them on the list for this trip." Her honesty was admirable, but man, what a lousy answer. Even if Honda was not on her list, put it on; show up in the lobby and talk to the guard if she couldn't get in to see anybody higher up. Instead, she sent the wimpy message that they were "booked."

Anuzis hit that one out of the park. He ranted that the governor was "booked talking to companies that bring two or three hundred jobs whlle ignoring the real challenges and/or opportunities with Honda. Indiana and Ohio have folks talking to them," he wailed on. He was right. In a feeble defense, it was left to the governor's media secretary Liz Boyd to spin this explanation aimed at the GOP chair.

"He obviously doesn't know anything about how business is done in foreign countries," she told the MIRS newsletter. "That means she'd need to cancel one meeting to try to meet with Honda...so what Mr. Anuzis is talking about would be rude on many counts." And whenever it was on the ropes, the Granholm gang always lashed out at the last GOP governor. Boyd lamely suggested, "John Engler failed to bring auto plants like Honda and Toyota to Michigan. Under Engler, we lost out to Mississippi and Alabama," she labored on. The only thing missing from that was the school yard taunt, "Na, Na, Na, Na, Na, Na!"

One legislative democrat who wanted to go nameless said he "bemoaned" the missed opportunity to court Honda. Reminded that there was a delicate protocol in Japan, this lawmaker suggested, "That doesn't mean anything in Michigan...She should have gone to Honda headquarters anyway."

Back to the radio interview, the governor noted that Honda had a "predilection" to build plants in states where they already had car facilities. That is why Ohio and Indiana were given a better chance of winning the Honda sweepstakes.

Nonetheless, the governor boasted about Michigan's 10,000 well-trained auto industry workers who had cars "in their DNA," and she said, "This is not a done deal...We will give it our best shot."

"We're hungry," she told the Detroit radio audience.

She also described another mitigating factor. Japanese companies wanted to "respect" the Big Three by not coming here. She was hoping she could convince them to set aside that "respect" and give her some by choosing Michigan.

Even the specter of Granholm landing one or both of these projects must have given some pause in the GOP camp. For months, candidate DeVos had been broadcasting his claim that he was a better leader on jobs and that "Lansing was not getting the job done." That, of course, was a euphemism for saying Granholm was a flop, but he did not want to attack her directly, so he did it my innuendo instead.

After I did my radio piece with WWJ at 7:05 on the political impact of all this, I figured in three hours, when I would cover DeVos, it might be fun to get his take on these latest developments. The campaign had given the press corps a heads up that he was slated to address the Michigan State Medical Society at a downtown Lansing hotel. I was there in the lobby, camera in toe, waiting to greet him. His staff had alerted him that I was there, along with about six other colleagues.

He was late, which always means there's a chance he would delay any questions until after the event. I hate that, because it means you have to sit around and listen to a speech you've heard a thousand times before you get a chance to pursue the story you really want. This time, his handlers said we could have a few minutes before his speech.

He walked through the automatic doors and said good morning. Dressed in his pressed blue shirt, black suit and, I think, a red tie, he looked dapper as always. I, on the other hand, was not going on camera that day, so I wore a turtleneck with a grey sweater.

"Thanks for getting dressed," he chuckled as he fired the first shot before I could fire mine.

"If the governor were to land either the Honda plant or the Toyota facility or both, how would that affect your message that she is not leading on jobs?"

He did not take the bait, but said that everyone would applaud if that happened, because Michigan needs the jobs. Then he came up with an off-the-top-of-his-head answer that was pretty good. He said that no governor, including him, could survive on "one-off deals," as he called them. In other words, landing the auto plants was nice, but it did not solve the overall economic woes the state was facing. Then in a backhanded manner, he took a mild shot at her: "One deal in four years is a wonderful thing." Translated, even if she got one or both plants, what the heck had she been doing over the last three years? And then he closed by saying, "Jobs that come by the thousands, unfortunately we have come to see in this state, can also leave by the thousands." It was a good bite.

He proceeded upstairs to glad hand the docs and tell them about his health care ideas, which were pretty thin. One person asked DeVos what he would do about the Medicaid problem. That's the indigent health care system that was running amuck. "We need to change it," was his not-so-brilliant response. He later recovered and cobbled together some stuff about needing to get rid of the abuse and fraud in the system. That was nothing new, nor would it save the financially strapped system from bankruptcy. He looked weak, and the docs knew it.

I left the hotel after his speech and walked over to the Capitol. On the front lawn were a bunch of RV owners who were serving a free lunch to lawmakers. Standing over on the south side of the capitol lawn was the Lt. Governor John Cherry. I had two stories to ask him about. The first one was a hoot.

Driving into work that morning, I ended up behind a bright golden-colored SUV with a bumper sticker. The name Granholm was visible in bold white colors against a blue background. Nothing unusual there, but as I got closer to the car, and I mean really close, underneath the Granholm name was one that was much smaller. It read Cherry. It was pretty obvious she got top billing, and his name looked like an afterthought. Cherry confirmed that he had seen the stickers.

"So, it doesn't offend you?" I asked as he started to laugh, knowing full well where this exchange was going.

"We're a team, but she's the quarterback. She's the captain. She's the coach." And you're chip beef on toast, I should have said.

He re-asserted that his ego was not bruised, and now he is in a hearty laugh as he goes on, "I'm pleased to have a little spot on the bumper sticker."

I joked, "Yeah you could have been left off altogether."

"Exactly right," and now we are both laughing.

Cherry had worked for three long years in the legislative trenches to push and jam her legislative agenda through the GOP legislature. And this is the thanks he got: second billing on a bumper sticker, and an invisible billing at that. But Cherry was loyal to the boss noting, "It's the governor's name that needs to be prominent."

The funny stuff out of the way, I sought a response from

him to balance out the DeVos semi-attack on the governor on car jobs. "The story that he is ignoring is how much Michigan has been very aggressive in bringing business here," he argued. And then he added that if DeVos was minimizing the possibility of new auto plants, "that would be disingenuous."

I killed the camera, and then as we were saying adios, Cherry in an aside said, "I almost sent you a box of candy." That caught me off guard.

He explained that a column I wrote almost four years ago helped him to get the lt. governor's post, and the last time he appeared on OTR several months ago, he was asked about wanting the job again. He said he was not campaigning for it but would be "honored to be asked." Apparently, the answer played well in the Granholm inner circle, and there he was on the ticket again. Hence the "candy" statement.

There was one postscript to the Japanese auto story, and it was not one the governor liked. The *Detroit Free Press* and *Detroit News* both ran the Honda story in their business section, and ironically, right above that story was this: "Delphi strike authorized: UAW could walk if pacts change." If the Japanese read those two headlines, it would merely underscore that Michigan, with it's aggressive labor union movement, might not be a friendly place to do business. Since Honda and Toyota were already nervous about the union thing, this kind of labor turmoil could not be a plus for the governor's sales pitch. I figured all the hard work in the world by her could not trump those Japanese fears.

10

Governor's First Ad

When's she going up? When in the heck is she going up? Jesus, when in the hell is she going up?

Ever since challenger Dick DeVos launched his unprecedented barrage of TV ads in February of 2006, Jennifer Granholm supporters have been asking the above questions with more intensity, and the answer is always, "When we are ready."

For four arduous months, the Granholm campaign was not ready and would not budge. The criticism in the democratic ranks became increasingly audible as the DeVos ads droned on while she remained on radio and TV silence. It was maddening to groups such as the Michigan Education Association that feared she could lose the election without making a peep. Recall the governor tried in her best den-motherly way to have everyone chill out. In due time, she told the media and all those nervous backers.

Well, today those backers got what they wanted. June 8, 2006, she's up, up and away. Her first TV ad in this historic contest began its media run on the morning news shows statewide. Citizens sipping on their first cup of coffee, saw a black-and-white, 30-second spot that featured the governor with workers—lots of workers.

And the announcer told them, "With Jennifer Granholm, Michigan comes first."

The Capitol Press Corps knew this was coming, because the State Democratic Party notified the gang that chairperson Mark Brewer would unveil the thing at a news conference. Before I left for the Brewer gig, I got an e-mail from a source in the DeVos office sharing with me the script of the Granholm commercial. Let me repeat that for emphasis. I got the script for the governor's ad from the DeVos campaign. I was pretty sure she did not send it along out of kindness, so that could mean only one thing. DeVos had a mole buried somewhere within the Granholm campaign.

I looked over the script and discovered it was not an attack ad, nor did I expect it to be. It would have been an awful miscue for her to come out swinging at DeVos. She needed to state her case, and the ad attempted to do that.

The commercial started out with a blast at George Bush instead of DeVos. "Outsourcing. Bush Economics. Corporate profits and jobs shipped overseas," the spot begin in a male announcer's voice. Then this: "It's time to stand up and fight." That's what the red-meat crowd in the governor's corner has wanted to hear.

Next, the ad suggests that she has ordered the state to buy Michigan's products first, and she is putting money into Michigan businesses that hire Michigan workers. Those are good points, but they obviously have done nothing to slice into the state's near-record-setting jobless rate hovering at just over 7% as this chapter is written.

And then a line that seems a total waste: "Because if they (the workers) can't count on their state government, who can they count on?" Wow, state government to the rescue. That will play well, I thought, with the anti-government crowd of which there are legions. For years, the GOP has so effectively bad mouthed government that if you took a vote, most folks would vote to eliminate it altogether, and here's the governor trumpeting the virtues of government and how you can count on it. I thought it was a disconnect. Instead, why not say, "If you can't count on Jennifer Granholm, who can you count on?"

Brewer was unphased by those suggestions and criticisms

when they arose in his news conference. He thought the ad was great. So great that, just like the DeVos campaign, he did not bother to focus group it before he hustled it onto the airwaves.

I recently started reading the Joe Klein book *Politics Lost,* and in it, he regretfully reports that before any major candidate goes to the bathroom, they focus group it to see how the viewing public will respond. He writes about how each word in a commercial is run through a slicing and dicing machine to see if it evokes the correct audience response. For example, savvy office seekers never say "estate tax," because they got more bang for their advertising buck by saying, "death tax." Or, it was not good enough to say "tax relief" but much better to get your arms around a "tax cut."

So the focus group is the norm, and here were the dems floating out a spot that they had no idea would work. If you were shelling out over $250,000, wouldn't you want some guarantee the message would hit home?

Brewer sloughed off the focus group question saying he was putting his money on Joe Slade White from Upstate New York, who put the thing together. When in doubt, cuddle up to a media guru to give you political cover from an obvious mistake. However, a couple of days after that denial from Brewer, one of my Granholm folks broadly hinted without selling the farm that perhaps the statement was misleading.

"Do you think for a second with all their money that they would not run it by a test audience before putting it on the air?"

I wondered if they used a different term other than focus group to avoid telling me a lie. They could have called it a test audience, and while that is, in reality, a focus group, they could say it wasn't when I asked the question. I could hear the chuckle on the other end of the line as this source all but confirmed that's probably what happened.

And months later, I discovered that was exactly the case. "You asked the wrong question," Brewer blurted out one day. We didn't use a focus group, and that is what you asked. We used 'dial-turners.'" That's when you round up a bunch of folks and give them a dial. When the ad comes on and they like what they see, they turn the dial up. Conversely, when the image on the screen is unpleasant, they dial down. Based on those reactions, the ad wizards go to work to clean up the ad to reflect those feelings from the test audience.

As for the commercial content, if I had had a dial, I would have turned it down so low all you would have gotten was a fat goose egg. There was too much info in the thing. Brewer told us it was not an attack ad. He wanted to tell the voters that the governor was doing something to combat those nasty "Bush Economic" policies.

And there was another well-hidden underlying theme that Brewer also sloughed off. When the ad says, "jobs shipped overseas," it was a clear reference to the democratic theme that DeVos had done just that. While it was clear to the six reporters in the room and Brewer, I figured the general public would miss the subtle point. And Brewer conceded the point.

Give me a break. You are spending a quarter of a million dollars, you want the voters to know that Granholm's nemesis was supposedly farming out Michigan jobs to China, and you don't tell the viewers that and leave them to figure out. What's wrong with that ad?

Brewer argues the spot provides a "nice contrast to DeVos, without mentioning his name." What, were they afraid of giving him more free advertising? "The contrast will become more explicit as time moves on," he defended the ad once more.

The party chair was quizzed on why his side waited so long to finally go up. Brewer says he reached that conclusion after seeing the governor perform so well at the annual Detroit Regional Chamber of Commerce event on Mackinac Island the week before. He rejected out of hand that pressure on her to do something had finally reached the boiling point. EPIC-MRA pollster Ed Sarpolus had a different take. "Her supporters told her to do it...she had to do it."

In an interview with Big Ed prior to the ad premier at the democratic headquarters, he waxed on about how "most voters make up their mind by the end of June," so it was imperative that she get off the bench and onto the airwaves. He warned that Granholm was "severely in trouble." Her supporters had told her they were losing confidence in her ability to win this thing if she did not act now. Sarpolus has been a pain in the campaign's behind for his steady drip, drip, drips of criticism about how she was not getting her message out. In fact, at the aforementioned Mackinac conference, some folks from the Granholm campaign leaned on him to lighten up. Sarpolus was not amused when he was summoned to the woodshed, where they blasted him over and over again. He had no choice but to defend his company as an independent polling firm. The fact of life is every time a survey comes out, the credibility of his shop is on the line. Clearly, the Granholm defenders thought his credibility stunk.

Obviously, the verbal tongue-lashing he got had no impact. In my interview, he continued the criticism, contending that politics is a "blood sport," and the governor was acting like she was in some corporate boardroom trying to be collegial when she needed to be a fighter. As for the effectiveness of the first ad, Sarpolus contends, and others agree, before the viewing public starts to understand the message, it has to see it at least seven times—that's right seven times. The word from one local TV station in Lansing revealed the commercial would run for one week. Sarpolus argues, "One week doesn't get it done...it will be a blip on the screen."

Brewer would not confirm any of that and would only say that viewers would see it "several times." I concluded that did not mean seven. Here was the analysis from deep inside the DeVos campaign to that ad: "It's weak." It did not connect the dots and left too much to the viewer to figure out on their own. This source concluded the intent of the ad was to "retard the growth of the wong track [numbers.]" Translated: the ad was designed to make sure the 78% of the voters who believe the state is headed in the wrong direction would not blame her for that.

The DeVos folks did not take the spot laying down. Even before the Brewer newser, reporters were handed a press release announcing that at 2 p.m. that very day, the DeVos folks would have a new ad of their own. It was tit for tat and a rapid response to the nth degree. By putting out a counter ad on the same day she did hers, the DeVos message would get into all the news stories the next day. And get a load of this: the DeVos rapid response machine was so well oiled, they had a stockpile of commercials to cover every conceivable issue she might lob at them. At one point, there were reportedly about 15 commercials sitting on the shelf ready to be shown at a moments notice.

The DeVos spot focused on unemployment with lots of complaining jobless workers. One woman lamented, "One day I came into work, and they told me that my position was eliminated." Another guy bemoaned his fate, "I've been unemployed for approximately the last 11 or 12 months."

So what did DeVos have to say? He reminded us for the millionth time that he's been "traveling all over Michigan." Goodie for him. He knows that, "We have a crisis. It's not about economic theory. It's about people's lives."

Nobody caught this, but that line about economic theory was in direct response to Granholm's reference to Bush economics in her ad. Think about it. They knew she would blast Bush, and they were ready to counterattack, but I'm sure the nuance was missed by most folks, including me, until I studied it and got it confirmed by one of his insiders. The ad ended with the announcer saying, "Dick DeVos. Governor."

So what did we learn from this commercial? Not much. Viewers never heard what DeVos would do to help those poor souls. But then, not getting specifics from this candidate was becoming the norm.

Although, in the morning paper on this date, DeVos actually told an audience in Detroit that if elected he would wipe out the governor's "Kool Cities" program, he'd mothball the First Gentleman's office now occupied by Dan Mulhern, and he would fire the state's surgeon general. The article noted that, by golly, this was the most specific he had been in a long, long time.

There was one other time that he got specific about an issue and got whacked over the head for doing it. For months, there had been a simmering dispute over the governor lowering the flag for Michigan veterans gunned down in Iraq. The "flag police" had taken her on for "violating" flag protocol that says you can only lower the stars and stripes for "high-ranking" officials, and that's it. That apparently meant a lowly private who gave his or life for the flag could not have the flag flown in his or her honor. Only in America would we have a public dispute over something so inane.

Well for some reason, Mr. DeVos got into the fray and first suggested he sided with the "flag police." But then, according to the smiling Granholm troops, he got some flak. That prompted this letter to the editor to un-do what he had done. Granholm folks gleefully labeled him a flip-flopper.

"In recent weeks," DeVos began his mid-air conversion, "my position on displaying flags at half-staff has been misrepresented." Oh, those dastardly misrepresentations. DeVos went on, "We can never do enough to pay tribute to those who have died serving our country." (Cue "America the Beautiful.") And then, he endorses the governor's decision without, of course, mentioning her at all.

The Granholm folks shopped the story and must have been pleased to have at least one flip-flop on his ledger to go with the numerous ones on hers. Hold it. What flip-flop, the DeVos campaign asked? It noted that DeVos was not on tape supporting his first position in support of the flag cops. Therefore, there was no proof he had said that in the first place, although his media press secretary had told everyone he had. It was a flimsy excuse, because it is generally assumed that when the media secretary states the position of the candidate, that is the position of the candidate. Period. The DeVos team finally admitted to a screw up but steadfastly denied it was a flip-flop. Most observers disagreed.

But back to the first Granholm spot. The day after it hit the airwaves, we hit our own airwaves on OTR to take the thing apart. The dissectors were Rick Albin from TV-8, Mark Hornbeck from the *Detroit News* and Jack Spencer from the MIRS newsletter. After we ran the ad to open the broadcast, I turned to Jack with, "Alright Jackson, grade it A to F."

He gave it a C. Albin gave it an A, Hornbeck a B and Skubick a C-, but I said it was probably closer to a D+. Albin's high mark was based solely on the fact that she was finally on the air. On content, he felt it was an O.K. spot, as did Hornbeck, but Hornbeck concedes he was "confused" by the line about trusting the government. Albin reflected, and correctly so, that the line reflected the attitude of the Granholm shop, "We can take care of you from cradle to the grave." That stood in stark contrast to the DeVos philosophy of getting government out of your cradle and off your grave.

The panel agreed that the spot did not lead with its best product, which was the woman herself. She did not talk to the viewer. However, my source in her camp says consultant Slade White did the same thing in 2002. He started with the low-key spots in which she said nothing and ended the campaign with her talking to the voters.

That may have worked against a weak opponent such as John Smietanka when Granholm ran against him for attorney general in 1998. And it may have worked against challenger Dick Posthumus when she defeated him for governor. But DeVos was no Smietanka or Posthumus or the two put together, for that matter. His massive media buy had changed everything. Albin agreed that, "You better lead with your strength if you want to win."

I was troubled by the use of black and white in the commercial. There was not one drop of color, even at the end when she flashed her patented toothy smile all over the screen. Black and white to me is depressing, and if Granholm wanted to send a message that she could help the state, that was hardly the color scheme to use. I contrasted that spot with the first one from DeVos. He opened with the shot of padlocked plant gates, and those pictures were in black and white. But then, when he came on the screen, there was the color. It was a striking contrast that created an air of change and maybe even some optimism.

Albin disagreed with my color analysis. We contrasted this limp commercial with her stunning performance on Mackinac Island the week before. She dazzled the captains of industry with a brilliant display of media savvy, a grasp of the issues and the Granholm charisma. You saw none of that in the advertisement, which led Hornbeck to suggest the governor should pull a Ross Perot and do a series of televised town hall meetings where she could be Oprah and Dr. Phil all rolled into one.

Jack closed our discussion with a darn good point. Just one day before her appearance on the island, her corrections department announced the firing and reassignment of several employees. These workers botched it when they paroled a guy who should have been behind bars, and while he was out, he popped three people. That came out on the eve of her gig, which meant in the morning paper on the island, there was this huge screw-up story on the front page, just as she prepared to reassure everyone that she was the type of leader Michigan needed. Perhaps maybe, just maybe, somebody should have put a lid on that prison story until after the governor's show. Another governor named Engler would surely have done that.

Next on our OTR show, we moved to the flag thing with DeVos. The consensus was it was a flip flop and an issue in which he should never have gotten involved. Hornbeck nailed it: "Up to this point, they had run a fairly flawless campaign."

Weeks after the broadcast, the governor staged an event with the flag center stage. It was wonderfully scripted. She had in the audience several Michigan families who had lost loved ones in the war in Iraq or Afghanistan. Veterans were everywhere in the audience on the eve of Flag Day, which allowed the governor to wrap herself in it. She was signing two executive orders concerning the proper use of the flag, but she did not raise the flap with DeVos. I did. "Isn't it ludicrous that there is a political debate over the flag?"

She answered, "There should not be a political debate over flag protocol."

"So when your campaign complained about the other guy's change in position on that, doesn't that politicize the issue?" I asked.

She did not take the bait, saying, "This issue should not be a political issue."

And then, as media secretary Boyd sought to end the exchange, one last bite of the apple, "So it is wrong to drag it into the political arena?"

"This is about honoring our soldiers. It is not about politics."

One thought to close this chapter: word has come this way that the DeVos insiders are amazed that the governor has waited so long to get into the advertising air war. A source put it this way, "We're not going to make the mistakes with her that she made with us." I asked for clarification and got this, "We factored everything they could do into our plan. They have always had the dough to retard our progress and chose to let us into the game."

What this person was saying is that they had wiped out her commanding 20-point lead by being on the air all by themselves. And now that Granholm showed signs of getting in the game, they were going to respond to everything she said in her commercials. DeVos would not make the "mistake" of allowing her to have a monologue with the electorate as she had allowed him to do.

And the game was getting more interesting, because shortly after the Granholm ad hit the airwaves, a new poll came out suggesting the statistical dead heat was history. DeVos now had an eight-point lead.

11

DeVos Snares First Lead

DeVos 48%. Granholm 40%. The heretofore statistical dead-heat was itself dead. The latest statewide survey results from EPIC-MRA produced quite the stir in this very poll-sensitive town. In an unprecedented twist, both camps claimed the numbers were wrong. "Mark down this day," Chris DeWitt from the Granholm side advised, "I agree with Greg McNeilly [from the DeVos campaign]. The poll is wrong." The two advisories would agree on very little else for the rest of the campaign.

That aside, let's just assume that Eddie Sarpolus's numbers were correct. That meant that DeVos had taken a Granholm 20-point lead in February and turned it into mush. And having done that, he amassed an eight-point lead on top of it. That says a heck of a lot about the electorate, and none of it is very good.

On the stump last week, I was in the intellectual center of the universe and tried a new audience grabber. The professionals that night in Ann Arbor were obviously more than a cut above the typical citizen, but they were as uninformed as the typical citizen, too.

Take out a piece of paper and a pencil," I requested of the 50 startled folks in front of me. Even after being out of grade school, that phrase still instinctively produces a wave of anxiety.

"Name the two republicans running for the U.S. Senate," I began, " and if you don't know, write down a zero."

I didn't see a lot of hands writing. In fact, only 27 played the game while the rest safely sat on their hands.

"Now write down the names of the two democrats running for state attorney general, then the GOP incumbent attorney general, and then the incumbent secretary of state."

What did all this have to do with the contest for governor? The results will demonstrate how detached the electorate is from political news, which makes it susceptible to political advertising. For too many voters, those ads turn out to be their only sources for "facts" about the candidates.

I asked the folks to turn in their answers and, "Don't put your name on them," as I sought to cushion them from what I knew was about to happen. You never saw so many zeros in all your life! Fifty-nine percent in the crowd didn't have the foggiest idea about who was running for all those offices. Sure, the election on this June 13th night was still months away, but they did not know the new candidates and many could not even identify the two persons who had been in office for the last three years. Ah, but that doesn't mean they didn't give it the old college try.

One poor and confused soul thought the secretary of state was Candice Kelly. They get an "A" for creative thinking, having combined the name of Candice Miller, the former secretary of state, with the name of former Attorney General Frank Kelley.

Nine persons did correctly identify Mike Cox as the attorney general, five knew that Terri Lynn Land decided what color to make our license plates, and only one knew that the Rev. Keith Butler was running for the U.S. Senate. Another did write down Sheriff for the U.S. Senate, but that didn't do Oakland County Sheriff Mike Bouchard any good.

The survey results were appalling, wrote one of the professionals the next day in an e-mail to me. He was correct. The findings revealed that the IQ of the electorate was in minus numbers, which meant politicians, with their image-only ads with no substance, could exploit that ignorance.

Referring to the Joe Klein book again, on page 223 he quotes Pat Caddell, who helped engineer the first and last election of former President Jimmy Carter in 1976. That insightful pollster wrote, "The public wouldn't be paying all that much attention to details." The group in Ann Arbor that night was exhibit A of that point.

This brings us back to the poll and the ads that produced the DeVos eight-point lead. Remember, he was not laying out his specific agenda for how to turn the state around. He was just telling everyone that he could do it, and apparently lots of folks were buying it hook, line, and sinker.

"DeVos ads, economy take toll on Granholm campaign," the *Detroit News* headline read on June 13, 2006. Capitol correspondents Charlie Cain and Mark Hornbeck wrote, "A steady drumbeat of TV ads and the state's continuing economic doldrums have helped catapult Republican challenger Dick DeVos to a substantial lead over Jennifer Granholm for the first time this year...."

But it was more than that. It marked the first time in state history that a sitting governor was not sitting on a lead. It may have happened in those pre-polling days in the Dark Ages, but there was no way to prove it.

Granholm pollster Mark Mellman, who crunched the numbers for defeated presidential candidate John Kerry, stated the obvious to Cain and Hornbeck. "People have heard $7-million worth of one side of the story. They're just beginning to hear the other side [Yeah, with that D-plus Granholm ad]. It will take a lot of time for us to catch up."

When the governor did finally enter the air war with her spots, I expected her to get a nice four- or five-point bounce in the polls, but I was wrong. John Truscott checked in on the DeVos take on the numbers. He dismissed them as being "a more optimistic view than anything we're seeing internally."

So, was the data right or were the campaigns right? Either way, the governor could use the bad numbers to turn up the heat on her contributors to get out their checkbooks. "Come on guys," I could hear her saying to her supporters, "This guy is outspending us, and here we are eight points down. I need your help now." In fact, I asked her about that very point just before the poll came out. I knew she would avoid a specific response to the lousy numbers, so I came at it this way, "If a candidate is down in the polls, what impact does that have on fund-raising?" She suggested it could cut both ways. It could dampen the enthusiasm of the troops, or it could energize them. "If you are referring to this campaign…just a guess," she said as she smiled on camera, "people are extremely energized and are looking forward to a good fight." And then, her eyes got bigger and her eyebrows went up as if to provide a non-verbal exclamation point to her "good fight" line.

On the other side, DeVos did not want to be winning the race in June when it didn't matter. There had always been a fear among some DeVos supporters, including House Speaker Craig DeRoche, that the candidate could peak too soon. And here was DeVos with a supposed eight-point lead, not on the eve of the election, but on the eve of summer.

Without going into all the cross tabs, some danger signals emerged from the findings. The *Detroit News* article had a graphic above the headline that showed 48% of union voters going for DeVos and 40% for Granholm with a margin of error of 4.9%. In other words, DeVos had a lead there.

As I sifted the data, I went back to the two main sub-groups I had been following, based on the assumption that they would determine the outcome. The female vote was divided but leaned toward DeVos, and he had a clear victory with independent voters. Women over 40 went with Granholm by a slim five-point margin. However, females under 40 liked DeVos by a hefty 30-point edge. Independent male voters by 27 points preferred DeVos, while it was much closer with independent women going 39% for DeVos and 35% for the incumbent. There was one other troubling finding for the governor. When asked if they would vote to re-elect her, 30% said yes, 27% were willing to look at someone else and 33% wanted to replace her.

Part of the challenge of writing this book as the campaign unfolds is to identify what factors might determine the final outcome. This latest survey was a bit troubling in that it came out just as the Granholm ads were beginning. Mellman was correct, the numbers would move back toward her. But yet, she did not have the female or independent vote sewed up and that was dangerous from her point of view.

And those facts were confirmed in the next EPIC-MRA poll, which brought the race back in line with previous results. After the Granholm ads hit the airwaves, her numbers went up to 44 and his numbers dropped to 46. It was another statistical dead heat.

But once more, DeVos demonstrated some staying power, as independents went to him by a strong 17% edge. He captured the female vote by four points, which was within the margin of error and was tied with her for the male vote. The governor tied DeVos for women over 40, and he beat her with the under-40 female set by a commanding 21-point spread.

As June moved toward July, DeVos made a splash with the release of a polished and multi-colored document he titled, "The Michigan Turnaround Plan, Volume One." It had more jams and jellies than a county fair during a Michigan summer. It was chocked full of ideas, but just because you call it a "Turnaround Plan" doesn't mean it will turn the economy around. But at least DeVos was making a head-fake in that direction.

To underscore one of the tiny differences between the two camps at this point, when I got wind that the DeVos piece was coming out on a Friday, I called the campaign and explained my predicament. I wanted to discuss the "Turnaround Plan" on the OTR show that week, but I could not pick up a copy. I wondered if someone could shuttle it over to my home so I could review it that night. When I got home that night, the booklet was waiting for me.

Contrast that to the state democratic party. It was issuing a brand new ad on behalf of the governor. I asked headquarters to send a copy to the TV station so we would have it for the morning taping. I got to the station about 7:15 a.m. and found the tape in my mailbox. I had not seen the ad and was obviously anxious to view it. We got in the studio, and I opened the show with a tease about the ad, and then they rolled the tape. Wrong tape. It was the old black and white commercial we had seen weeks ago. Somebody had screwed up, and I said as much during the show. We were forced to discuss the new ad without showing it to the audience.

We got an apology from the party and a request to show it the following week. By then, it would be old news. It's a minor point, but still it was a missed opportunity to get the new Granholm message out. Like the old song says, "Little Things Mean a Lot." It also underscored another point: DeVos had a cadre of worker bees to do grunt stuff such as dropping off his booklet at my house. The Granholm camp did not appear to be as sharp or as large.

But back to the DeVos economic plan. I breezed through the slick 65-page document. Several things struck me. He was promoting some of the very things the governor had embraced. He wanted to push the federal government to enforce trade agreements. So did she. He wanted to eliminate red tape in state government. By golly, so did she. He wanted to diversify the economy. Hey, every governor way back to Milliken had said exactly the same thing. And on and on the list went. DeVos and Granholm want to make health care affordable, increase funding for tourism, sell more Michigan products overseas, etc., etc., etc. DeVos even chimed in on the running battle between the Big Three automakers and their ill-fated efforts to meet with the "Big Guy" in the White House. GM, Ford, and Chrysler were zero for three in attempting to talk with the president about foreign trade policies. Every time the White House offered an excuse for not meeting, Granholm took another swipe at "W" and berated him for ignoring the carmakers. The White House stiffing of the auto executives played right into her hands, as she paraded around the state beating up Bush, and she continued to do it in her TV commercials, too. This is why DeVos suggested he'd be happy to make a call to see if he could stop the president from beating around the bush. Pun intended.

Even though DeVos and Granholm shared some common ground, he did break some new ground by endorsing the elimination of the income tax for folks earning under $14,000 a year. That was a huge tax cut for about 197,000-plus families, which would drain the state treasury by about 40 million bucks and some loose change.

He also called for merit pay for teachers, which went over like a lead eraser at the Michigan Education Association. And, he invented a new power for the governor. He called it a "Governor's Bureaucracy Override." It would give the governor the authority to cut through all the claptrap that sometimes surrounds the issuance of business permits by the state. In theory, if some company was crying uncle because the bureaucrats would not budge, the governor could step in and relieve the pain by issuing the permits.

As I read on, another thought struck me. This guy, whose party was loathed to embrace anything that had to do with government, was actually using the government to advance his turnaround agenda. Former President and Mr. Anti-Government Ronald Reagan would have had a cat.

There were 15 governmental tax breaks or incentives that covered everything from supporting alternative fuels to giving future teachers more money to teach math and science. Heck, if you closed your eyes, you would swear a democrat had composed many of his proposals, and some from the conservative media made that very point.

Perhaps it was an attempt by DeVos to reach beyond his conservative GOP base to attract those independent and female voters he was doing so well with in the polls. But here was the point I made on OTR that week about his plans: there was no price tag on any of his stuff. Not a single penny was allocated to pay for the R and D tax code revisions, the increased funding for higher ed or the tax cut on farm machinery. He wanted the pop for suggesting the breaks but refused to do the heavy lifting by suggesting a way to fund them. If this guy was such a hot shot businessman, how come he didn't have a bottom-line cost on his turnaround agenda? I told colleagues Dawson Bell of the *Free Press*, Mark Hornbeck of the *Detroit News,* and Kyle Melinn of the MIRS newsletter that a good businessman would never issue such a document without a dollar sign attached to it.

Bell disagreed. "This guy is not governor yet."

Melinn agreed with Bell. "This is like my Christmas wish list when I was a kid," he recalled. I asked if that meant he believed in Santa Claus? Hornbeck sided with me, noting that it would be "kinda nice" to know how he would pay for all of it.

In a briefing with the DeVos campaign later that day, they quickly dismissed the "Where's the money?" argument by saying it was a "campaign and vision document and not a state budget."

Oh, I get it. When you have a "vision," you don't need to pay for it. Come on.

DeVos had smartly gone around the state during the week doing editorial board meetings with the major newspapers prior to the formal release. Following that, some of the papers trotted out editorials, and a familiar theme I had been talking about emerged from the conservative *Detroit News* of all places. "Where's the beef?" to borrow that old line from the Wendy's commercial was the focus of their editorial. In reference to his plan to wipe out the SBT, the paper noted, "Critics will argue that DeVos has not spelled out exactly how he will do this. And that's fair." But then the paper quickly provided some ground cover for their guy by contending, "He is setting out goals and directions, not an exact blueprint. It is, after all, early in the process."

The *Free Press* was more blunt and not quite as forgiving. It's editorial headline read, "DeVos Plan Falls Short of Specifics." It noted that DeVos wanted to shrink the government, lower taxes, encourage job creation but "everything has a price, and DeVos doesn't yet know how he's going to pay for it all."

In his defense, however, his team did show some areas where the budget could be cut, but there still wasn't a bottom line on how much would be needed. And, oh yeah, DeVos also counted on "growth in the economy" to provide new money to pay for some of his programs, too. Right. The same "growth in the economy" that Granholm had been banking on for the last three years that never materialized.

The *Freep* concluded, "He's asking voters to accept half a plan and 'trust me.' With Michigan at an economic crossroads, that is asking a lot." I don't know about you, but when a candidate invokes the "trust me" mantra, I turn and run.

That said, the DeVos booklet was a clear effort by the campaign to demonstrate that he was more than just talk. Here was his plan with 134 bullet points to prove he could also walk the talk. He told us in January on OTR that he would have a plan, and here it was. And to prove that there was substance to it, the media briefing to explain the whole thing commenced at about 11:30 a.m. When I walked out to file my TV story just after 1 p.m., it was still going on strong. The briefers seemed to be saying, without saying it, "You guys want details. We'll give you details until you are blue in the face." At one point, it had been dragging on so long, I offered a motion to order lunch but then noted we couldn't do that because the DeVos guys were unable to cost it out just like they could not cost out his blueprint. Everyone laughed.

There was one crucial element that emerged in the briefing, and I had to sit on some privileged information that I had gathered while on a speaking tour earlier in the week. On the Monday before the meeting with the DeVos guys, I gave a speech in Boyne Mountain, a resort Up North, as we say. On the same program was the chair of the House Taxation Committee Representative Fulton Sheen. What happened there underscores the quirky nature of this news game, i.e., you just never know when you're going to learn something that may seem insignificant at the time but turns out to be mucho important down the road.

Sheen, in his talk to the conference, revealed that he had recently met with the new State Treasurer Robert Kleine. The GOP House Speaker and the treasurer's office had been embroiled in a heated debate over the release of Single Business Tax information. Before Kleine took over, the former treasurer Jay Rising would not release tax tables showing how much taxes were paid by each segment of the economy.

Speaker Craig DeRoche demanded the info to help rewrite the state's business tax which he was helping to abolish. As long as he could not get the data, he had a convenient excuse not to draft a replacement mechanism. Sheen disclosed for the first time that in his meeting with Kleine, the information was released.

"It was great," Sheen told me afterwards. Since I was the only reporter in the room and since this was a new development, I informed the chair that I was going to do a story on it. He asked me to hold off, because he did not want to get Kleine in trouble with the governor for releasing the tax data. I agreed to sit on the story until I had a chance to confirm it with Kleine.

By the time I went to the DeVos briefing, I had not fulfilled my end of the agreement. But you can imagine my surprise when reporters started to question the DeVos brain trust on why it could not release a specific plan for replacing the SBT revenue. Greg McNeilly, John Truscott, and Todd Anderson all echoed the Speaker. How could they develop a plan without the tax data? "Dick does not want to fake one [a plan]. Dick is not going to commit to a program without the data." There I sat knowing that the data was already out, and a prominent republican had it. Either these guys knew that and refused to confirm it, or they were unaware. But I couldn't ask any pointed questions, because I didn't want the other 10 reporters to know what I knew. Plus, I still had that commitment to Sheen not to move on the story until I talked with the treasurer.

Anticipating that the story would eventually come out, I asked a set-up question, "What would you guys do if you got the data?" McNeilly blurted out, "We would model it." That is, they would run the numbers through a computer, and that would form the foundation for an SBT replacement scheme — something the media had been harping about for weeks. I knew at some point I would reveal that the tax data was already in republican hands, and then what would the DeVos camp do? I figured they really didn't want to offer a replacement tax before the election, but now I had them on the record saying they would do just that, once they got the data they wanted. Either way, the story I stumbled into up in Boyne was going to produce another story that could affect the race. Once they got the data, would they really craft a proposal to increase some business tax, or would they recant from the McNeilly promise to model a plan? I wondered what they would do. It took me awhile, but I found out. They would do nothing.

I finally bumped into Kleine at a governor's news conference, and I put him on camera, where he confirmed what Sheen had told me at the conference. Not only had Kleine shared the tax data with the chairman, but he sent along a 55-page memo to Speaker DeRoche with the same information. That was enough for a column that I wrote that week. In it, I suggested that if Mr. DeVos could scrape together 50 cents for the phone call, all he had to do was phone Kleine, and DeVos could proceed to draft a substitute for the SBT. Something, of course, he did not want to do.

Well the column ran, and Speaker DeRoche got on the horn to inform me that the Kleine data was so confusing and in error that nobody could draft anything from it. So the DeVos folks had a convenient excuse to ignore the pledge that McNeilly made when he said, if you give us the data, we will do the modeling. It never happened.

But back to the marketing of the DeVos recovery document. In a not-so-surprising next move, the DeVos campaign amplified its turnaround message it had given to the media by now giving it to the voters. Another DeVos commercial was launched on the same day a new Granholm spot went up.

Titled the "Engine" ad, this one was also underwritten by the state democratic party. In a release, Party Chair Mark Brewer noted the ad, "demonstrates how Gov. Jennifer Granholm has a proven track record of creating new high-paying jobs for Michigan despite Bush Economics that promote outsourcing jobs to Communist China." Same theme as ad one but a totally different feel.

This one was not in depressing black and white. Somehow, Brewer found colored photos of the governor, when he told us earlier none could be found for the first commercial. The spot tells viewers that when Chrysler wanted to build a new plant to make engines, Michigan was competing with other states. But, with dramatic music underneath the announcer's voice, the ad says, "Jennifer Granholm took action, made Michigan's case and won." Later, there is stark white lettering on a black background with the phrase, "George Bush's trade policies are hurting Michigan." But, the announcer says, "They can't stop Jennifer Granholm…300 hundred high paying jobs" were created.

She put "Michigan first," the spot concludes. What the ad didn't say and only implied was this: The democrats believe DeVos puts China first and Michigan second when it comes to jobs. I was sure that a more direct bang over DeVos's little head on that point would come later on in an attack ad.

While 300 jobs are nice, the ad did not disclose how many jobs had disappeared on her watch. But compared to the lousy first ad, I gave this one a B plus, but I still wanted to hear her talk. All she did in this ad was smile, which is what DeVos often did in his.

Obviously, the anti-Bush strategy was still working, as the governor continued to run against three men: DeVos, President

Bush, and former Gov. John Engler, who left her that nasty structural deficit that she has been unable to eliminate. GOP State Chair Saul Anuzis stayed on his message, contending that Granholm continued to blame everyone but herself. He noted that Bush was not on the Michigan ballot in November. But if the Granholm folks had anything to say about it, they would act as if Bush was running. As long as voters blamed him for the state's worrisome economy, the governor had a better shot at re-election.

Over in the DeVos camp, however, they were scratching their collective heads. They were totally amazed at the race Ms. Granholm was running.

12

Another Ann Richards in the Works?

I could hardly wait to get home to read this document. It had been handed off to me just outside the house chambers on June 28, 2006. The source was a Granholm supporter and this person, along with tons of other democrats, feared she was losing a grip on this race, and the data given to me confirmed it. There was a pervasive attitude among legislative democrats that she was in trouble, but the governor showed no outward signs that she shared those worries.

I jumped on the treadmill and started to paw over the 20-page report from the Greenberg Quinlan Rosner firm. If you didn't know these guys were democrats, their analysis of the race read like some republicans had put it together. Granholm came out looking awful. "The mood in Michigan is ugly...voters are turning away from Granholm...Granholm's dissipating job approval has created a desire for change...Perhaps the most telling finding is voters' difficulty in articulating praise for Granholm." This May 26 survey had a sense of urgency that Granholm needed to get in the game. As the researchers put it, "She cannot afford to wait any longer to try to strengthen her image."

In the DeVos camp, they were scratching their heads, wondering why the governor waited so long to fight back. Talking with chief campaign strategist Matthew Dowd he observed that, "They allowed us to have a one-way conversation with the public for so long."

And Stan Greenberg, who did polling for former President Bill Clinton, reflected that in his early findings. "Voters find DeVos's background as a successful CEO appealing rather than disconcerting" despite the public resentment of CEOs from Enron and other companies who appeared to be all about greed and nothing else.

They also noted that DeVos was seen as doing a better job on the key issues of jobs and the economy, while she was viewed as "pretty distant and not particularly engaged in the economic situation." Dowd expressed his surprise that they "didn't start earlier" to get her in the fight.

Granholm, you'll recall, had said that voters in the spring were not engaged and were not listening. Dowd and the DeVos folks had just the opposite take. "They [the Granholm team] were operating as if it was four to six years ago in a media environment" that no longer existed, he asserted. Dowd believed voters were tuning in and starting early to gather information from Web sites, radio talk shows, and a host of other diverse media outlets. DeVos was suited up, while Granholm sat and sat and sat on the bench.

Greenberg-Quinlan did give Granholm credit for eventually becoming more engaged, but even so, they noted that voters wondered "if she is the right person for the job," and they have begun to "question her leadership in general."

While Granholm continued to pound on President Bush and ex-Governor Engler, Dowd said that was playing right into their hand. "We're fine with her playing the blame game," he disclosed during a half hour phone conversation with about 130 days to go until the election. "Blame is not going to solve the problem with the voters."

Both camps agreed that citizens admired Granholm, but

Dowd postulated from the opening bell that it would not translate into votes. "It's O.K. for people to like her," he went on to explain, but "you can fire somebody who you like from a job," and he clearly hoped Michigan voters would do just that.

Back in 1990, just hours before the voters turned him out of office, then-democratic-Governor Jim Blanchard enjoyed a healthy 67% likeability factor.   Former Texas Governor Ann Richards was sitting on a 58% approval rating just before Dowd's candidate, a guy named George W. Bush, toppled her from office. And Michigan's own Mitt Romney overcame the likeable candidacy of the Massachusetts female lt. governor and beat her for the top job.

The DeVos strategy concluded it was O.K. for voters to like Granholm, and he would do nothing to dampen that impression by blasting her. None of his ads took her on, per se, and when the democrats argued they were attack ads in disguise, McNeilly was direct. "This bull--- about our ads having a subtext that attacks her is horse----."

I asked Dowd to clue me in on the Detroit strategy and how many votes they wanted out of Motown. At first he laughed and explained he did not want to share that strategy, but I reminded him none of this info would come out until after the election. He opened the door ever so slightly for me to peak in. He recalled that Engler had gotten about 20% of the Detroit vote at one point and that President Bush came in at about 10%, while former Governor Milliken scored about 14%. Dowd finally confided their target was somewhere in that range, but he did not expect to top 20% or even hit it.

The Greenberg-Quinlan memo noted that in Detroit, Granholm had a daunting challenge. While about 64% of the entire state felt Michigan was on the wrong track, the number in the Detroit metro area was 75%. The pollsters called it a "deadly" number for her. And to top it off, her job approval rating, in this May document, fell from 51% to 37% in the Metro area, "the biggest drop in job performance."

Dowd reported that in Detroit, the campaign was signing up lots of volunteers, and his candidate was overcoming the stereotypes that DeVos was a rich guy from that "other" side of the state, i.e., West Michigan. It was also amazing to me how both sides had the same data with regard to women. Greenberg-Quinlan found the same thing other pollsters uncovered: woman under 50 had problems with the governor. And she was losing among married woman by 13 points.

"What's going on?" I quizzed Dowd.

"I've always said, 'Watch the women.' They are like the canary in the coal mine. They are the first ones to get concerned."

Dowd reflected what others had explained to me earlier. When she first ran, women were excited to give her the vote. But now they were the "first to bail." They had high expectations, but now the second time around, some females had emerged as some of the governor's harshest detractors. In fact, as the campaign moved into October, some of those women appeared in ads saying they voted for the governor the first time, but would not do it again. It was powerful stuff. I also picked McNeilly's brain on their big picture strategy, and he conceded their advertising message was out of the ordinary. Typically, with an unknown candidate, you start with the "family" ads.

Here's Dick playing ball with the kids, chaperoning that prom night party for his daughter, and hugging his wife on the beach as the sun sets slowly in the west. What they ran instead was what McNeilly labeled "value spots." They introduced DeVos as a "guy that had certain values, not morals, but values of characteristics like getting it done, moving, action, hopeful, understanding Michigan's problems. A guy who has done turnarounds before." In his June 18 memo to me, McNeilly boiled the campaign down to two points: (1) convince voters to change, and; (2) convince voters to hire the challenger. McNeilly concluded that the first objective had pretty much been accomplished and Dowd had to concede, "It's better than we expected to be in June."

The internal polling stuff that had been slipped to me by that democratic source raised a red flag. "The data in the survey is stunning, demonstrating that voters are quickly losing confidence in her ability to turn the state around." Once again, both sides singing the same tune from the same hymnal, but reacting differently to it. Tomorrow, we would see what new tune the governor was singing to drown out all the negative choruses. The third commercial on her behalf would be premiered on OTR on the eve of the Fourth of July weekend, 2006. But first, the headlines in the newspapers on June 29 revealed that one of Governor Granholm's hopes that we talked about in Chapter 9 had been snuffed out.

A brand spanking new Honda car assembly plant was going up in Hoosier land and along with it some 2,000 jobs that would not be coming to Michigan. State GOP chair Saul Anuzis did not miss a beat. He blasted the governor, while the DeVos campaign, at the outset, said nothing in keeping with their strategy of not attacking her. They did put a link on their Web site with a copy of the wire service story out of Indianapolis. "Honda Motor Co. has chosen a site in Indiana for its new North American auto plant...." Anuzis wrote a harder lead, "Today the people of Indiana were rewarded for the hard work put forth by their governor, Mitch Daniels [a republican of course.]" The chair noted that the eleventh-hour pitch by Granholm while she was in Japan was "too little, too late." "It's ironic," he went on, "that Granholm's democrats are running TV advertisements proclaiming the governor's fight for the Michigan people. This, clearly, is a prime example of how she failed to provide effective leadership."

The executive office did try to slap a smiley face on the Indiana announcement. It was left to media secretary Liz Boyd to say this was good news for auto suppliers in the Midwest that would benefit from the plant nearby. Boyd missed a chance, however, to buttress her statement by pointing out that five of those Honda feeder plants were in Battle Creek. In one of those errors of omission, nobody in the administration shared that data with her. She also advised that it was a good thing the project did not end up in the South. Suffice it to say, that was not the statement Ms. Granholm wanted. She wanted to announce the plant was coming here, but it was now one down and one more to go. She could still pray for the Toyota engine plant, and that candle was still burning.

The panel on this day's OTR was Chris Christoff from the *Free Press*, Kathy Barks Hoffman from the Associated Press, and *Inside Michigan Politics* editor Bill Ballenger. None of us had seen the new Granholm spot proclaiming her job creation prowess. The

Democratic Party, after giving us the wrong ad weeks earlier, got it right this time, as the correct tape was in our hands the night before the taping. And this commercial was much better than the first one. It's amazing what a little color will do for a viewer. And credit OTR for the switch from black and white.

State Democratic Party chair Mark Brewer privately confirmed that after hearing the stinging criticism on the program regarding the very first B and W commercial, he went to the ad mogul Joe Slade White and suggested he find some color photos of the governor, and lo and behold, they were used in what the party called "The Plan" commercial.

According to the Greenberg polling data, remember, the folks in TV land were beginning to doubt the leadership capabilities of this governor and that was certainly addressed in the third spot. "To see a plan in action is to see a leader, taking charge" the spot began as the panel intently watched it unfold in studio C. The voiceover pointed out that the governor had been to Japan on two occasions and was successful in "bringing home 22 companies and 1,000 new jobs to Michigan."

Christoff noted during our analysis that it was ironic that the Honda story, jobs going to Indiana, broke at the same time the commercial went up. And Hoffman chimed in that most of the 22 Japanese companies were already in Michigan, but the typical viewer would never know that. She also correctly stated that the 1,000 jobs were the proverbial drop in the bucket compared to the 87,000 jobs lost on her watch. The ad concluded "There's more to do, but the plan is beginning to work. Because a leader [there's that word again] is standing up, fighting back, and putting Michigan first."

There was no reference to President Bush in this one, and a DeVos aide suggested that the anti-Bush angle wasn't working, which is why it was omitted. If that was indeed the case, the governor did not get the message, because on the stump she continued to stomp on Mr. Bush.

Nonetheless, this spot was a marked improvement, and the panel, including yours truly, gave it higher marks. I indicated that finally, we got a warmer feeling about what the governor was doing, but still, she spoke not a word.

For what it is worth, Christoff said she needed to get rid of the safety glasses in the spots. Hoffman noted that the governor was using her reading glasses, which made her look like she was hard at work.

Once the panel was done with its critique, the state GOP swung into action by issuing a two-page, 32-paragraph critique of its own, and as you might guess, it was all negative. It was overkill with a capitol "O." It took right off berating the governor for waiting three and a half years to "take charge." The GOP analysis repeated that she had not done enough to win the Honda plant, and even DeVos got into the act, as he ventured very close to criticizing the governor. He told the A.P. "I probably would have found time to visit Honda," he reflected. The governor volleyed back that, "I met with them one year ago, and we also presented them a proposal...my team did [meet with Honda] when they were in Japan." So there.

To be honest with you, I didn't bother to consume the rest of the GOP piece, as it droned on and on. I was sure I would hear the same stuff, packaged and repackaged, for the next five months. Actually, as it turned out, it was much sooner than that. It happened within two days.

With the program in the can, I had some packing to do, because I was off to the Island to do a gig with two of the big hitters in this little game: Mark Brewer and his counterpart, Saul Anuzis. Gayle and I arrived on Mackinac Island late Thursday afternoon on June 29, just in time to change our duds to meet the 6 p.m. dress code. You know the "coat and tie for men and no slacks for women," which is the drill at the Grand Hotel.

The venue was the Michigan Hospital Association summer to-do, and there must have been 600 hospital executives and doctors in the dining room when we walked in. Nobody offered to take my pulse or temperature. We headed for a table near the back of the joint and settled in for a nice dinner—alone. I mean, really, who would want to sit at the same table with a journalist? We returned to the same banquet room the next morning for breakfast. It was one of those rare and beautiful Michigan morns with the sun beaming across the Straits of Mackinac with that huge bridge just off to the right of the dining hall standing tall and picturesque.

But there was precious little time to soak it in. The party chairs awaited my smiling face in the other room. They both quickly ribbed me that I was getting paid and all they got was a free meal. I reminded them that there was that outstate college tuition for our daughter Carly, and I thanked them both for helping to indirectly pay that bill.

Each gave a five-minute opening monologue on all the races this year, and then I started off with an inquiry they were not expecting. "Mr. Brewer, let me start with you. Tell me something about the DeVos campaign that has impressed you."

A little gasp raced through the audience of about 100. "I'm impressed with how much money he is willing to spend," Brewer began. It was a point he made several times during the one-hour exchange. Anuzis, of course, had a snappy retort when Brewer postulated that DeVos would shell out $60 mil.

"He's not going to do that," Anuzis began his defense and quickly ended it saying, "Besides, he is Dutch."

The audience laughed with the exception of those from the west side of the state, where the Dutch population is, shall we say, omnipresent and quite sensitive about their wealth. Anuzis offered that he was impressed that Granholm had run such a great "Rose Garden" strategy to date. And he marveled at how she was attempting to "nationalize" the election by bringing in the war in Iraq, by blasting the president on trade policies, and doing everything she could to deflect blame from herself.

Brewer would have none of that. He parroted the governor's mantra about the need for the president to level the playing field in foreign markets on behalf of American manufacturers, and he took another shot at Bush for not meeting with the Big Three. Anuzis reminded the crowd that, after all, the president was a "busy man." That went over like a lead balloon.

One of the objectives I take into a session such is this is to keep the audience awake. It was 9 a.m., and who knows how late they had been up the night before or what they were waiting to do after this. It was working, since everyone was still in the game, including a woman from Alma who fired off a great question aimed at the GOP leader. She took the microphone and reported that Alma was on the verge of landing a new industry and hundreds of jobs, and she had heard that local republicans were trying to "delay the project so that the governor would not get any credit for it on the eve of the election. Did that kind of thing go on?" she asked with a straight face.

Anuzis, of course, had no personal knowledge of the situation but tried to reassure her that such sabotage was not likely. Brewer laughed, and so did some in the audience. To be totally candid, I snickered a little inside, too. Sabotage was nothing new to this governor, who complained to anyone who would listen that she had struggled for three years to push through her programs only to be stymied by the GOP along the way. Ironically, however, on that very day, while we were having fun on the Island, the governor and the GOP leaders were actually cooperating, and by days end, they forged a respectable compromise on the new state budget. Each side gave a little to get a little, and they deserved high marks for getting it done. But back to the action with Frick and Frack.

One of the ways I keep an audience awake and engaged is to pop questions on them, and the one I used next was an eye opener. "How many in here, by your applause, believe that any governor can turn the state's economy around?" Dead, and I mean, dead silence. Not one hand clapped, and I nailed home the point. "Isn't it interesting that both of the candidates are telling voters they can turn the economy around, and this race will be decided by who does the best sell job, but in reality, neither of them can do much about the state's job picture."

Anuzis, who had the most to lose by conceding the point, offered that governors can contribute to the economic climate, and being a businessman and all, DeVos was the guy to do it. And he added, "If we had a job for every time the governor smiled into the camera, there would be no unemployment in this state."

Brewer, never at a loss for a retort, suggested that DeVos did not have a plan to get the job done. "But what about that 65-page 'Turnaround booklet?'" I reminded Uncle Marky.

"It is all glossy pictures and charts," he observed. He had a point. I later counted them and found 52 graphics. She had 37 pics and no charts in her 22-page "Jobs Today" brochure. By this time, the group was getting anxious to hit the golf course, which is of course why groups have conferences in the first place, so I moved to the wrap-up question: a reversal of the one with which we started. "Please tell me what has not impressed you about your opponent's campaign so far."

Brewer stayed on message, again griping about the "lack of substance" coming from Mr. DeVos. Anuzis noted that the "governor had made a mistake by waiting so long to respond" to the onslaught of DeVos ads. Brewer would have no part of that, either, adding his spin, "They tried to draw us in so that we would have nothing [no money] at the end."

Interestingly, the day before on the OTR show, I polled the OTR panel on the very same, "Was it a fatal flaw to wait to respond" question. Hoffman thought not. Ballenger noted there was a long way to go, but he did not rule it out. Christoff and I both agreed: when the votes were counted, and if she lost, that would be a major miscue.

As the Island thing ended, I reluctantly agreed to stand between Anuzis and Brewer for the perfunctory group picture. We did one for real and then another so Saul could put his two fingers behind my head like we used to do in elementary school. Before Gayle and I headed back to Traverse City to begin the Cherry festival with the grandkids, I pulled Brewer aside to get some inside stuff I needed for this book. He and I chatted about the so-called "Amway" issue. As you read earlier, I had uncovered this wealth of anger about the sales techniques used by the Amway salespersons.

"Have you focus grouped that issue?" I asked. Brewer said he did not have to. He knew the anti-Amway sentiment was out there, and the party would use it against DeVos. And, he also filled in another blank. DeVos had made a big deal about how he came in and saved the company. Brewer believes what happened is that the buying public "got tired of the Amway approach and sales fell off....There is no need to explain how people hated Amway. The name itself invokes that—when people are told DeVos was with Amway, it's a plus for us. Link DeVos to Amway, is all we have to do," he suggested. To cement his point, he did disclose there was polling data on the Amway image, and the best it ever got was a 50-

50 split with the public.

Just to be fair, weeks later I ran the same idea past David Brandon, who was chairing the DeVos campaign. Brandon, who has done a little selling of his own as CEO of the Dominos Pizza empire, predicted the anti-Amway dog would not hunt.

Since nobody on this July 6 evening has played the Amway card, I don't know who is right, but I do anticipate that in a later chapter, before this is put to bed, we will know the answer. Either way this was still a first in Michigan politics. Never before has a political party tried to moved the numbers against an opponent by coupling his name to a product. It would be a calculated risk that may or may not work, but I came away from the chat with Brewer convinced he was going to find that out—one way or the other.

I was on the road out of Traverse City bright and early on the Fourth of July to beat the massive traffic jam on the freeway that would develop later that day. I came home to an e-mail that the governor was marching in five, count'em, five parades that day starting at 7 a.m. and ending that night at 6 p.m. in Grand Rapids. I do not know how she does it, and her hectic pace reminds me of a story one of her aides shared with me when she first joined the executive office. "My first day on the job, the governor warned me that working with her would be like drinking water—from a fire hose." A perfect metaphor for Jennifer Mulhern Granholm.

The next day, after all the fireworks had died down, I got an e-mail from a GOP source. He or she had been at some of the parades, and this person reported, the crowds did not seem to whoop it up for the governor. This source says the DeVos staffers outnumbered her crew, and "it appeared they [the Granholm team] were disorganized." I considered the source, but just to test it out, I covered the governor the next day as she delivered her campaign chalk talk to a bunch of junior college kids in Lansing. One of her aides was there, and I asked about the crowd reaction. This person sort of confirmed what the GOP source had indicated without saying exactly that. "There is some discontentment out there," this person suggested, and there were even some concerns within the inner circle about somebody doing something stupid during future public events to embarrass the chief executive.

One of those events was coming up this weekend. I would be back in T.C. to cover the annual Cherry Festival Parade. I would have a chance to judge the crowd reaction for myself, as the governor was slated to walk the gauntlet on Front Street in this very republican little town. Would anybody be so rude as to boo the smiling governor?

13
Cherries, Hitler, and Tigers. Oh My!

My attempt at eyewitness reporting at the Traverse City Cherry Festival turned out to be a feeble attempt at best. You would think after 35 years of doing this stuff, I could get it right, but I got it all wrong from top to bottom. The Saturday for the parade was picture perfect. My game plan was to catch up with the governor about halfway through the parade, and then attend the news availability at the end of the parade route. During the middle of the night, I even came up with a pretty good question to lay on her: what percentage of Michigan's lousy economy can be blamed on the president and what percentage is your fault? But first my assignment was to judge for myself the crowd response to her when I showed up at 13th and Union on T.C.'s south side.

According to the governor's schedule, she was going to enter at the mouth of the parade at about 12:15 and end up about 90 minutes later at the end. I waltzed in about 12:30 and started to walk counterclockwise to the parade, which went by on my left. The sidewalks were lined with folks enjoying the sunshine as they loudly applauded the octogenarian walking along Union Street.

The crowd adored former Tiger broadcaster Ernie Harwell, and they let him know it. I figured this would make a good benchmark for my story as I wrote it in my head: Harwell gets cheers. Governor gets ho-hums? Ernie faded into the distance, and I waded deeper into the crowd looking for the lady in red. The governor always wears her red jacket, blue pants, and white tennies to these grueling forced marches. But as I dodged the baby strollers and kids along the sidewalk, I got this instinctive and uncomfortable feeling. What if I had missed the governor?

There was only one way to find out. "Madam, has the governor gone by already?"

"Yes, about ten minutes ago," a woman with a soft drink in her hand said. I stopped in my tracks. I did an immediate about-face and started to march with the parade but at a much faster clip. I could see this story fading into nothing. As I zipped along, I reassured myself that at least I would have a chance to quiz the governor at that media availability at 1:45. So the day would not be a total loss.

I continued my brisk walk only to be interrupted with a, "Mr. Skubick." It was the voice of an unfamiliar staffer for the governor. "The governor is waiting at 14th Street. She got in the parade early." Wonderful.

Sure enough, as I approached, the giant Coast Guard chopper that dots the summer skies of Traverse City was lumbering along on the ground, and there, standing alone in her patriotic getup was the governor.

"How ya doing?" I blurted out.

She said fine, and there, off to the side, was campaign aide Chris DeWitt. He apparently had drawn the short straw, and instead of being on White Lake or some other fishing hole on this great day, he was on the clock. "So this is a campaign event," I ribbed him.

The two of them quickly reported that she had gotten a "good response" along the way. Like I expected them to tell me she got booed off the street. "Did you do better than Ernie Harwell?" I made a stab at getting a quote for this chapter.

She laughed saying she did not know but conceded no one

could top Ernie.

"Do you have a camera?" DeWitt inquired.

The governor answered for me. "When DeWitt said you were coming to the parade, I knew you wouldn't be working. Everyone knows Skubick doesn't work on weekends." She had that right, but I was working this gig because I wanted this stuff for the book.

The whole scene for me was surreal. This marked the first time that I had any extended face time with her for months. The governor's handlers were more comfortable when she was at arm's length from the senior capitol correspondent, but there I was right next to her having a friendly chat.

"Did I send you a note on the Milliken show?" she started in.

I told her I had not gotten one, but she said she did contact the former governor. In fact, come to find out, she had actually met with Milliken earlier that morning in T.C.

"It was a great show," she offered.

About a month earlier, we taped a one-hour interview with the popular former GOP governor at his home in T.C. We'll talk more about that later on. She made no mention, however, about the comment he made about her lacking some political courage.

We both noted that the Milliken era was a decidedly different time and place than the one in which she found herself. I acknowledged that she must be frustrated by her inability to get the GOP legislature to play bipartisan ball with her. I truly believed that in her heart of hearts, she wanted that in the worse way. But she confessed that Lansing was all about gaining a political advantage.

"It must have been different years ago?" she asked.

It was, I confirmed. In that climate, you could have partisan disagreements, but at the end of the day, it seemed everyone tried to do the right thing for the state. I also recalled that in those days, before term limits, when a lawmaker gave his or her word to a colleague or a governor, the word was not broken. And if it had to be broken, everyone was given a heads up in advance with an explanation. "The citizens really do want you guys to cooperate," I suggested. "And in the end, if you do, everyone wins, not only politically but from a public policy standpoint as well." She agreed.

DeWitt stepped in and announced it was time to go. "That's it?" I incredulously responded. "No media avail?"

The governor said she did all those interviews with the local TV stations along the parade route. Great. The dry hole I had dug was now getting deeper. I was getting squat out of this exchange. Just as I am figuratively kicking myself in the behind for screwing up this whole event, who walks up but Secretary of State Terri Lynn Land. Fresh off the parade route herself, she had this observation for two of her aides as she walked up to say hi to the governor: "Looks like one of the governor's constituents is working her over." Then Land realized it was me. She extended her condolences to the governor for having to put up my cross-examination. Land had found herself in similar situations over her three years in office and had some empathy with her democratic counterpart. We all laughed.

"You know, three years ago at this event, Skubick actually helped me out," the governor told a startled Land. "We were all set to get into the parade, and Skubick came up and asked for a response to the fact that they had a VW convertible for me to ride in." A democratic governor riding in a foreign-made car in a Big Three state would have been a great story.

"Yeah," I jumped in to finish the story. "She immediately went over to Candice Miller's Corvette convertible [Miller preceded Land as the SOS], took the Miller sign off the car, and put the Granholm sign on it. More laughter.

There are probably some Granholm backers who will conclude that was the first and last time I did anything nice for the governor. At any rate, as the governor's security detail was headed for the SUV, the governor and I shook hands. She was headed for a pig roast in some berg down the road.

"Have a safe trip," I offered.

"Peace," she responded as she dashed for the front seat and rode shotgun out of town.

I chatted with Ms. Land for a few moments, wished her well, and started back up the parade route hoping to get some face time with Dick DeVos. He was not allowed to march in the parade and was relegated to working the sidelines. The Cherry Festival folks don't allow politicians who are running for office to hijack the event.

There was no way I was going to find him, so as I slowly walked back to my car, having blown this assignment to smithereens, I did ponder one thought. In my mind's eye, I recalled seeing the governor standing on the curb at the end of the parade route. She looked lonely as she played spectator to the floats before I interrupted the scene. I don't know what I expected to see, but maybe something that looked like a vigorous campaign with lots of balloons, banners, hats, and horns with tons of bowing and fawning supporters surrounding her. But instead, she stood alone.

I was told later that DeVos had his whole family enthusiastically working the crowd, and Traverse City GOP Senator Jason Allan informed me the next morning that the crowd was "lukewarm" to the governor. What did I expect him to say?

Hours before the T.C. event, the news media was dominated by another story that had the candidates talking, and the insiders trying to figure the angles on the so-called Hitler ad. You read that right. Former Nazi leader Adolph Hitler had amazingly found his way into the 2006 race for governor. What next? And the whole shebang had caused quite the stir.

The *Michigan Chronicle* is a very influential Detroit newspaper, and it recently ran an ad that broadly suggested that African American voters should not vote for Granholm. The premise of the ad was nothing new. It confronted black voters with the notion that, "For over 50 years, the democratic leadership's condescending attitudes toward the black community has helped put African-Americans in dubious positions that have resulted in dependency on welfare...disproportional amount of black men in prison, and the highest unemployment rate in the country."

Blacks being taken for granted was hardly a new theme, but the way it was presented was certainly new, "repugnant" and "despicable," as the Granholm and DeVos campaigns described it. The ad featured a picture of Hitler and former Gold Medal Winner and African American runner Jesse Owens, who was snubbed by Hitler at the 1936 Munich Olympics. No surprise there, but Democratic President Franklin D. Roosevelt refused to shake Owens's hand, too.

The full-page advertisement also painted into that same picture former presidents Carter, Johnson, and Clinton. It concluded with this direct line, "And now, during this crucial election year, the democrats expect African American voters to stay in their place. African American voters should not only demand respect...but say NO to Governor Granholm in November." Other than that, it was a noncontroversial piece that blew this town wide open.

Everyone wanted to know, who was behind this thing? The MIRS folks did a Google and discovered a group known as Voice the Vote run by Nataki Harbin. No light bulb there, but one went off when it was learned that she worked with Mongo and Associates owned by Adolph Mongo, who was a well known and controversial Detroit political consultant. He had been beating up the governor for months, but none of it was resonating. The ad changed all that. He was a one-person wrecking crew trying to dismantle whatever black vote Granholm was trying to piece together in Detroit, and the ad was the most controversial move yet. Democrats immediately wondered if DeVos was behind all this. After all, the word on the street was pretty loud: republicans were on their own mission to depress the voter turnout in Detroit, thus diminishing the Granholm bounce out of that city.

Quicker than you can say, "Our hands are clean," the DeVos campaign denounced the ad saying, "There is no place in Michigan politics for this ad. It is appalling, and this approach is despicable and wrong." And, in case you didn't get the message, DeVos added, "Use of imagery and text that trivialize the worse tragedy of the 20th Century is disgraceful and vile."

MIRS quoted Democratic Party Vice Chair Tina Abbott saying, "I am shocked and outraged...this is not politics, it is fear mongering and race-biting of the worst kind. Who is behind the Voice the Vote PAC? They are cowards who do not have the courage to engage in civil debate." Mongo told the *Detroit Free Press* that the group had no connection to and received no funding from DeVos.

Detroit political consultant Sam Riddle, who cut his teeth during the anti-Vietnam-war movement at Michigan State University, waded right in telling reporter Dawson Bell that Mongo's group was getting support from allies of DeVos.

As huge as the story was, it might have remained a one-day wonder if it was not for the Democratic Party, which staged a telephone conference call in an attempt to give the story legs. Representative Mike Murphy (D-Lansing) and the chair of the Legislative Black Caucus told reporters that it was his understanding that "Mongo is a hired consultant for Dick DeVos. I believe he was hired to be part of the campaign," the MIRS newsletter reported.

Of course, everyone wanted some proof of the headline-making story—if it was true—but Murphy seemed to back off a bit. He indicated the Mongo and DeVos "were together recently at a Pancakes and Politics gathering. I think it's something that certainly should be checked out." That wasn't a smoking gun by any means, and the DeVos folks quickly rebuffed Murphy.

"Absolutely not. If Representative Murphy is saying that, it's 1,000 percent a lie, and an elected official should be held to a higher standard. We've had nothing at all to do with that crap that's been going on down there," protested John Truscott. And then he turned the tables pointing the guilty finger at the dems, "What we're really seeing here is that the democratic hit squad is running full speed."

But what about that pancake event. Spokesperson Truscott acknowledged that DeVos had attended such an event but noted there were 200 persons there and "If Mongo was there, it had nothing to do with us....If he was there, he wasn't part of our table."

Murphy was asked if he believed the GOP was behind the Hitler ad and he sheepishly suggested, "You can come to your own conclusions."

Representative Mary Waters (D-Detroit) was not so oblique. "In my opinion, they are," she opined. She told reporters that she had been told by members of Mongo's family that they'd received money from republican sources. Yes, but that did not mean GOP money had gone into that ad.

Everyone in town was trying to figure the angles on this story and who got a bounce out of it, if anyone. One resident of the Granholm inner circle thought it was a plus for her. The story gave her a chance to renounce racist attitudes. For DeVos to be linked in any way to this thing would make mincemeat of his methodical strategy of working Detroit to squeeze out as many votes as possible, no matter how puny. Which is why on the Monday after the ad appeared, Devos released a "Dear Governor Jennifer Granholm" letter to the Capitol Press Corps. It was not a "Hi, how ya doin?" piece of prose.

"The attempts by your campaign to smear me are very offensive," he writes in paragraph two. Without saying that democrats were attempting to link him to the Hitler ad, he calls on her to "take the appropriate action to correct this matter....Only you can stop the negative campaigning." He signed off, "Thank you, Dick."

Not to be outdone, the state Democratic Party fired off it's own missive, calling on the state GOP to "condemn last week's Voice the Vote ad" and demanded that the party and Dick DeVos disclose any Republican supporters of the PAC. Party Chair Brewer noted that "The Michigan Republican Party had refused to denounce the ad in any way...The MIGOP's silence on this issue is deafening."

But the war of words did not end there, as the State GOP did issue a statement later that same afternoon as the two sides played a round of "Can you top this?" Chairperson Anuzis did not blast the ad but the governor instead. He noted that the governor said to "follow the money" for the ad, but "apparently public disclosure is only relevant when it benefits Team Granholm." And then he rehashes an old GOP charge that she is raising money from a "super secret slush fund" and refused to give an accounting on that front.

On the Capitol steps the next day, I asked him if he opposed the commercial, and he was straightforward. "It's wrong. It was in poor taste. It was not very politically bright at all. It was bad," he said and refuted Brewer's claim that the GOP was not reacting to the ad. Nonetheless, I asked Anuzis why he didn't issue that same statement a week ago when everyone in town was falling all over themselves to hack away at the Hitler ad. He paused for a moment and offered, "You didn't call." What? I noted that the phone lines ran in both directions, indicating that he could have called me. "You're the reporter," he jostled with me. I continued. So you or the party had no role in this directly or indirectly. "We had nothing to do with it," he ended the give and take.

With all this contradictory spin, it seemed the only way to get to the bottom of it was to go to the source. My e-mail to Mr.

Mongo was short and sweet: we would like to have you do our OTR program this Friday at 8 a.m. in East Lansing. Let me know if that will work. He let me know.

That Friday at 8 a.m. I greeted one Adolph Mongo at the WKAR-TV back door. He and his wife arrived about 15 minutes before the reporters, who are seldom on time. I escorted them toward the studio and explained that I was happy to see them. That morning, there was a huge traffic jam on I-96 near Novi, where three weeks earlier I had traveled six miles in 90 minutes due to a massive construction project. I had visions of them phoning in the show from there, but they avoided the mess. It was the first time I had met this man. I asked him what his nickname was in high school. Without missing a beat he said with Adolph for a first name, he had often been called "Hitler" by his classmates. He also revealed that he also attended a Jewish school for a time. The irony of it all, given the flap over the Hitler ad, did not escape me.

Things poked along as first Peter Luke, then Bill Ballenger and then Dawson Bell, arrived to round out the panel. They chatted with Mr. Mongo until it was time to get what we affectionately term, the "mug shot." That is the still pic of the guest that we use at the top of the program to identify who the guest is on that broadcast.

The floor director moved him over to the seat and I watched from the control room. Once he was in place, the guest is always asked to smile. "Give us a nice big 'Off the Record' smile because you are so happy to be with Skubick," the F.D. often jokes with the guest. Mongo did not laugh. Mongo did not smile. Mongo just glared into the camera lens. I knew we were in for a great show. "He's obviously not going to smile," I concluded as I told director Dick Best to use that shot of him glaring into the camera.

We would find out in 15 minutes why he refused to smile. Turns out Mr. Mongo was "pissed off." In 34 years of doing this show, no one has ever said he or she was "pissed off." Mongo said it five times in 17 minutes.

Correspondent Bell got things rolling by asking the author of the Hilter ad what his "excuse" was for using that picture to denounce Granhholm and other democrats. Mongo explained that in order to tell the Jesse Owen story, you had to include Hitler, because the German leader was the guy who refused to shake the runner's hand.

"To leave Hitler out is like talking about the civil rights march in Selma with Dr. King and not mentioning Bull Connor," Mongo gave as his "excuse." (Connor was the cop who water hosed Dr. King et al. during one of their confrontations.)

Mongo confessed that if he had to do it over again, he would have expunged the swastika from the ad, but Hitler would remain. He conceded, however, that his message that democrats were taking Blacks for granted got lost in all the hu-la-ba-loo over Hilter, but "The message got out to the people of the City of Detroit," he went on. "Sure, not everyone agreed on Hitler, but the people that I talk to everyday say it's about time somebody stands up to Mark Brewer and the governor. They take us for granted."

Then we got to the P.O.ed stuff. Mongo was "pissed off" because he was not getting any consulting contracts from the democrats. "It is personal," he said as he finally revealed his motives for coming after the governor and others. "I've been in this business for 20 years. I've never worked for the democrats. They've never given me a contract but yet I'm supposed to be in lock step with them all the time. That's ridiculous."

Come to find out, the Mongo vendetta for the governor went back to when she ran for attorney general. He contends he got her elected by helping her in Detroit and got nada in return.

"So this is all about getting even?" I inquired.

"Absolutely," came back the candid response.

"I'm pissed off that black political consulting firms can't get any work with the democrats. I'm pissed off that we don't run their campaigns, and then they come to us as an afterthought...we get no respect."

At the heart of the political firestorm was the alleged role DeVos and/or the republicans played in the ad. Mongo denied any connection.

"I'm not working for DeVos or [am I] on anybody's payroll that supports DeVos," he asserted during the post interview free for all.

"Who paid for the ad?" I pressed on during the show.

"Who paid for the ad? Well, you know, I had a credit."

"It's a simple question. Who paid for the ad?"

"Me...I work for a living. I had a credit with the *Michigan Chronicle*."

Near the end, I closed the show out with a question that provoked an answer that must have sent the governor up the wall. It was innocent enough, "If the governor was sitting here today, what would you tell her?" The response was anything but innocent.

"Be real and don't be phony, because the governor is phony when it comes to African Americans." And then he mocks her in a high-pitched voice as if she was talking to a black audience, "Oh, Oh. I love you. Oh. Oh." And he is still not finished.

"She has a phony attitude, and she knows it."

And there's more. He references the debate with DeVos and the governor at the NAACP event in Detroit, noting that she did go into the audience to introduce the black members of her administration. Mongo reflects, "I wouldn't have stood up." He concludes that during that event, she treated her appointees like "black field hands" in reference to plantation workers. Man, that is the toughest rhetoric I'd ever heard aimed at the governor.

Days after the event, the governor told WWJ radio that his remarks were "incredible. I'm a person who has totally embraced Detroit." She bemoaned the campaign that was "descending into the gutter," as she labeled Mongo a "hired gun" working "on the other side." The Hitler stuff was "repulsive and repugnant," she argued.

Brewer's squad fired off a press release in which he accused Mongo of flip-flopping on whether he conferred with DeVos. Prior to the OTR appearance, I quizzed Brewer, and he sighted what he termed, "more and more evidence of a connection between Adolph Mongo and the republicans on behalf of DeVos." Let's have it, I asked. Brewer says he attended the Detroit political event and saw Mongo at the DeVos table and "Mongo worked the room on behalf of DeVos."

"How do you know? Did you walk along with him and listen in?" I asked.

Brewer says he talked with folks who had talked with Mongo, and that's what they reported. I asked for a list of those folks, so I could verify the story. The list never materialized.

"I don't think it is enough for DeVos to say this was a bad ad. Dick DeVos needs to acknowledge that Mongo is working on his behalf, and he needs to fire him."

Always the devil's advocate, I asked Brewer if maybe the dems were really behind all this in order to make DeVos look bad. Brewer laughed it off, "Tim, you've been reading too many political conspiracy books."

The dem chair and the governor were hanging their accusatory hat on the fact that Mongo did collect 20,000 petition signatures of support for DeVos. Mongo says he was collecting the names to send the democrats a message that if they didn't stop taking blacks for granted, there would be support for DeVos in Detroit.

The day after the show, I asked the GOP chair to check in on all this. He concluded that Mongo had a "very powerful message that could cause the democrats a lot of grief." But Saul Anuzis reaffirmed, "He's not our guy. He's not necessarily for DeVos...he's against Granholm and Brewer. So my enemy's enemy becomes my friend or beneficiary." But then Anuzis offered the questions that everyone in this town was trying to figure out as it related to the contest in Detroit. "The key is, how will Detroit react? Are activists pissed off? Will they sit on their hands? Do the minimum?"

The GOP was obviously hoping Mongo was plowing some fertile ground that would reduce Granholm's margin in Motown. Interestingly, the weekend after the Mongo appearance, DeVos led a group of 50 volunteers as they did door-to-door groundwork in Detroit. He got a mixed review, but it underscored the steps he was willing to take to slice into the governor's Detroit support, too.

I came away from the Mongo appearance with the sense that this guy was clearly angry for being ignored and was acting accordingly and not necessarily in concert with the GOP.

"If DeVos called you and offered you a job, would you take it?"

Mongo said no. I was not so sure.

All this back and forth and jockeying for position on the race issue just underscores how volatile the race card is in Michigan politics, and if this was how it was in the middle of summer, what would it be like in the fall?

But there were other things to ponder about the fall. I felt the Detroit Tigers could have a prominent role in the final outcome of this heated race for governor. I got the idea after watching the Tigs pull off a come-from-behind win over the St. Louis Cards two weeks ago when it dawned on me that the team was for real.

As I write this chapter on the eve of the All Star Game and the mid-season break, the once lowly Tigers sit on top of the standings with the most wins, 59, in all of Major League Baseball. And as I pondered their winning ways, I realized the team could actually be in the hunt for a playoff spot and might even have a shot at the World Series. That gave me an idea for the column. It was the only original thought I had during 2006.

Normally, citizens don't really tune into the race for governor until late September and early October, and in most years, that is the dominant news story until Election Day. But what if there was another "more important" story that would shift attention from the race for governor to the race for the pennant? I was convinced that if the Tigers were contenders, it would push the political story off the front page, and anybody who wanted information on that would have to launch a scavenger hunt to find it. That would hurt both campaigns, as they moved toward the wire—with nobody paying attention.

The media would be a co-conspirator in all this—a willing co-conspirator. Newspapers, everybody knows, are in trouble, with only about 10% of the population buying papers. Which is why you see more sports headlines on the front page these days.

You want proof? Last week, former Red Wing captain Steve Yzerman retired. Banner headlines all over the place. Then the guy who couldn't make a free-throw if his life depended on it, Ben Wallace, took a fatter paycheck and headed across the pond to Chicago in the National Basketball Association, leaving the Pistons to ponder life after Big Ben. The papers and broadcast folks were all over that, too. Even today, another Red Wing, Brendan Shanahan, left for the Rangers in New York. It got front page coverage, even though the Vice President of the United States was also in town the same day.

The point here is clear. Papers need to sell more papers, and given a choice between the Tigers in a pennant drive and Granholm and DeVos in a drive for the statehouse, the sports stuff will get top billing thus relegating this major political story to who-knows-what section of the paper or the newscasts? TV news would not be any better. It has pushed political news off most newscasts, although it did cover the Hitler ad.

I could see one more impact. It is my deep sense that this down-in-the-dumps state is starving for a good news story—something to lift our collective spirits—and we crave anything to take our minds off the fact that our jobs may be shipped off to the Far East. The Tigers could provide that boost, and the governor could benefit as a result. With the team on the right track to a championship, the political right track/wrong track numbers could improve and with it, her chances to win.

I ran these theories past the OTR panel one week and got a few heads to nod. Hoffman from the AP admitted that at first, she thought it was a stupid idea, but she conceded there might be something to it. Ditto from Ballenger and Christoff.

Days after the column ran, I got a call from Rusty Hills, who was currently doing media for Attorney General Mike Cox. Hills was an original Engler-ite and had seen many a war for governor. "You know, I never thought about that before. There is something to it," he patted me on the head. I thanked him for the call, and now as you read this with the outcome being known, I either look like a champ or a chump to have even raised the Tiger angle.

Footnote: As I proof this chapter for the publisher on September 20, the team has a razor-thin lead of one lousy game over the Minnesota Twins. Maybe I should just press the delete button and be done with it?

14

Going Ga-Ga
over Google

For the last three years, there's been a running joke between the governor and me regarding an alleged hidden microphone in the governor's inner sanctum, because I occasionally find out stuff that I'm not supposed to know. Such was the case on July 10, 2006.

Nobody really knows a big story is brewing unless there are some clues. Getting the word from the governor that I really needed to be at a news conference the next day was clue enough for me. And within an hour or so, I had the story. Ann Arbor was going to get 1,000 new jobs.

I let the governor know that I knew, and she admitted that she had forgotten about the hidden microphone. But that did not bother her in the least. The magnitude of the announcement was impressive, and getting scooped meant she got more exposure for her good news story she badly needed for her own political health.

By the time I woke up the next day, the Granholm team had

leaked the story to the two Detroit newspapers, which rewarded the leakers by giving the story top billing. "Google coming to Ann Arbor" was the headline on the Tom Walsh story in the *Free Press*. "Google to hire 1,000 in Mich," trumpeted the *Detroit News*. When I read the stories, I just knew the governor would be bouncing off the walls over this biggie, and sure enough, when we showed up in the Romney building news auditorium, there was a sense of excitement and anticipation.

Across the hall from the room were a bunch of college kids wearing Google t-shirts. Inside the packed press conference room, the local legislators from Ann Arbor were ushered in, while the staff from the Michigan Economic Development Corporation was beaming all over the place. Then the props, err, students were brought in to provide the backdrop for the governor to make the announcement as the anticipation level rose. It reminded me of when the audience anxiously waited for late night comedian Johnny Carson to come out for the opening of the "Tonight Show." Only on this day somebody could have said, "Heeeeere's Jenny!" She confidently entered to thunderous applause—25 seconds worth.

As the ovation died down, she began her monologue, "I am here with friends to make an important announcement...Michigan has been Googled!" The roof came off for a second time. She smiled. Her MEDC guy smiled. The two guys from Google smiled. The students smiled, and the disinterested Capitol Press Corps sat there and waited for the smiling to end.

This was a huge story. The California-based Internet search engine had rejected Boston, Phoenix, and Boulder, Colorado. It picked Michigan for the new headquarters for its AdWords service, a pay-per-click site that put ads on the Googled web sites.

The governor unfolded some of the details. Besides the thousand jobs over the next five years, the state would get a spin-off benefit of another 1,200 or so related jobs. It was not the jobs so much as the type of jobs that sent the governor into orbit. The employees had to be educated, talented, and computer savvy, and would earn about $47,000 if they were. They were also the exact target group the governor had been talking about for months, as she boasted about her 21st Century jobs blueprint.

Here was living proof that, in her mind, her plan was working. Here was living proof that she was doing something to stop the brain drain to other states. Here was living proof that kids had a reason to get educated here and stay here. She also confessed that the Googlization of Michigan also provided a badly needed psychological boost for the weary state, much like the Tigers were doing on the ball field.

The state did shell out a hefty $38-million tax break for the next 20 years to nail down the deal, but MEDC director Jim Epilito quickly added that despite that, the state would still realize a $165-million gain for the economy.

Epilito, who had been under fire from some republicans in the legislature for making partisan remarks he should not have made, was elated but muffed his baseball analogy. For months, Epilito had observed that he and his crew were creating jobs, but most of them were drowned out by all the bad economic news. "We've been hitting singles and hitting some doubles," he started his pitch but looked at the press corps and blamed us for not covering the hits. Before he finished his last line, however, the governor said, "What about the homerun?" And then, Epilito, realizing that he did not complete the analogy, blurted out, "A homerun, obviously." More cheering.

But there was no cheering from the DeVos camp. It issued a terse two-paragraph statement. "Congratulations to the University of Michigan and welcome Google," it began. What, no pat on the head for the governor? "The promise of more high-tech, high-paying jobs are a reaffirmation that one of Michigan's strongest assets remains full of promise for a complete state "Turn Around," DeVos went on. Note that "Turn Around" was the name of his recovery plan.

Frankly, the statement, I thought, was a missed opportunity. It was a rare chance for DeVos to take the high road. Everywhere he went, he professed to be a non-politician offering the voters something different. However, by ignoring the governor and not even tossing her a "way to go," he was acting like the very politician he suggested he wasn't.

How much nerve would it have taken to say something such as, "We welcome Google to Michigan, and we are pleased that the governor found a way to get them here. This is good news for Michigan, and if I'm elected, you'll be hearing more good news down the road." GOP Party chair Anuzis wasn't much better. He wondered what role the governor actually played in the Google get. He also welcomed the company but added that the 1,000 jobs "were a drop in the bucket compared to the 90,000 jobs the governor lost on her watch."

I got that quote from Anuzis before going into the Granholm celebration news conference, so it was only fair that I quiz her about the negative reaction from the other side. Granholm refused to take the bait but hit a nice line drive to centerfield with a steely glare in her eyes. "I'm not going to respond to the criticism of naysayers on a day when we have a phenomenal story about Michigan. Those who are not jumping up and down [and here she could have added, 'And you know who you are'] perhaps have another motivation. Republicans and democrats can be united, and be proud of our state." And the peanut gallery behind here erupted again.

After the newser, the governor hung around for even more questions, which was not her normal routine. After most press conferences she makes a mad dash for the back door to avoid more questions from all of us. But you could tell she was geeked and wanted to drain every last bit of positive news out of this event so she hung around and hung around. It was the first positive event she had anchored in quite some time.

"Were you surprised you won?" I asked. There was another smile. She basically implied that since they had worked hard on it, she was not that surprised.

Larry Page, who launched the company, of course, had strong Michigan ties and that was a deciding factor in the decision to go to Ann Arbor. Page graduated from East Lansing High School and earned an engineering degree from the U of M. He offered this in a statement; "We hope to establish as wonderful a home in Michigan for Google as I enjoyed while growing up. Our goal is to have many Michiganians call themselves Googlers."

"So, did you wine and dine him?" I continued.

Yet another smile. "We wooed and wooed him," she revealed.

When you just read that last sentence, did you make the same conclusion that I did at the time? To "woo" anybody implies a concerted effort to show him your best side—to do things to get him to like you with the hopes of getting something in return. Sort of like dating in high school. But the impression the governor left with that statement turned out to be real long on the hype and real short on the "woo." All she really did was have one conversation with Mr. Page and a few other folks who knew him. She left everything else to the MEDC crew.

I stumbled into that revelation by chance. I was in Traverse City and happened to get in a conversation with somebody who knew one of the Google guys in Ann Arbor. This source told me, "The guys were laughing at how Granholm was acting at the news conference when she did not do that much to land those jobs." That prompted me to ask media secretary Liz Boyd to give me the details on what the governor really did do. Maybe she wasn't the wooer she pretended to be? In a subsequent e-mail and phone chat, Liz could only confirm that there was one conversation with Page and other ancillary calls. She added that a year before the decision was made; the governor had ordered the MEDC to get those jobs. And that was it.

"This is not the kind of company you can wine and dine," Boyd said as she tried to take the edge off the story I was working on. She knew where I was going with this, so she added, "It's a very quiet company."

"So there were no roses, no e-mails, etc?" I asked.

"They don't operate that way," she went on.

"They did stand there with the governor" at the news conference, Boyd tried to win me over to her side. At that point, I revealed what I had learned about the "chuckling" behind the scenes over the governor's relatively minor role in all this. Boyd had no rejoinder to that.

To be fair here, there isn't a governor that I have covered who did all the legwork to land this company or that. That is not their job. But when a governor tells me there was some wooing going on, I think most folks would infer that means more than a couple of phone calls. The wooing stuff aside, as this whole event was unfolding, it struck me that this might be a critical fork in the road for the governor. You never know, but it did have that feel.

After being down in the polls, after not having the moola to compete with DeVos in the ad war, and after beating back those democrats who thought she was blowing this campaign, at last here was something she and they could get their arms around and feel good about. It was a badly needed kick in the pants, a jumpstart, and a chance to build some momentum that was sorely lacking in her effort to date.

This one day encapsulated the very message that she wanted to spread across the land. Even though she would not be re-elected on this one victory alone, it was still worth asking her, "Do you think this is a turning point in the campaign?"

"This is a turning point for Michigan," she suggested, as she again tried to keep politics out of the story while heading for the exit with, what else? Another smile.

Her husband was a little more forthcoming on that issue, but not much more. I had not seen him for months, so when Dan Mulhern was done working the front of the room after watching his wife go ga-ga over Google, I took the chance to get his feel on the race.

"How's the book coming?" he started our chat before I could launch into my first question.

"Got 13 chapters done."

He had some empathy for the project, having just completed his own book on leadership. However, he was sitting on the publication because he did not want it to interfere with the election story.

"How many more chapters?" he wanted to know. I guessed another 12 or so, but this was getting me nowhere, so I started asking the questions.

"Is this Google announcement a shot in the political arm for her?"

"It's a shot in the arm for Michigan [sound familiar?], you know, and to the degree the governor embodies the state, sure it's a great thing for her. She's working at this 24-7. I know, because I sleep with her, and she's thinking about it when she's sleeping."

I neglected to ask how he knew that but forged onto other

questions, such as, how he was feeling about the campaign?"

He and she are like two peas in a pod. She's not visibly worried about the race, and neither is he.

"I think it's fine."

Fine!? She has lost a 20-point lead, her opponent is outspending her 10 to one on advertising, DeVos has slick ads, her's are slick-less, and the hubby says everything's fine. It is vintage Mulhern.

"We knew we were going to be running against a billionaire, and that it was going to be close. Nobody has ever seen anything like this in terms of spending. So, we're where we need to be."

"Are you the underdog?" I tried to keep him on camera as long as I could.

"In terms of money, absolutely," he suggests. Then he launches into an analysis on the intelligence of voters and delivers a theory I felt was a contradictory.

"Unfortunately, so many people decide based on 30-second ads that get to their gut and do not get to the depth of the issues. I think we are an 'underdog' on that front," he concludes. We agreed on that. That was something I have been saying throughout, but then he seemed to do a 180-degree turn in the other direction.

"But in the long run, people who are thinking will see that we have a better standpoint—a better plan for Michigan—and that will weigh out in the end."

Holy cow. This guy is depending on thinking people to figure all this out and then vote for her? That's exactly what he was suggesting. "Voters are a lot smarter than people think. I've seen that many, many times, and I'm confident in the end that will pay off."

I could not resist the follow-up, which was, "If the voters were so smart, how come DeVos erased the governor's 20-point lead with commercials that had no substance, only image?"

"It's kinda like asking people in November, 'Are you gonna want steak or salmon?' They say steak sounds good."

I didn't get it, so I asked, "Did you just call DeVos a piece of salmon?"

Mulhern, who has a subdued kind of laugh, suggested,

"You'll have to decide who is the steak and who is the salmon."
But the upshot of our exchange reflected the inner-circle thinking:
it's a long time until November; people will get more focused and
talk to one another. "They'll read some papers. They'll hear some
news stories, watch a little bit of the debate and talk to each other.
That's what is going to make the difference in the end," the First
Gentleman said as he finished his curbside analysis for me.

I thought it was an overly optimistic expression of confidence in the I.Q. of voters. Maybe he knew something I didn't
know. And apparently, his wife knew it too, as she stayed on exactly
the same message when we chatted for a moment outside her SUV
after a successful rally in Lansing a week later.

"We've got four months to go," she said as she looked me
in the eye. "He [DeVos] is out of step with Michigan. I know; I've
been around the state," she said as she sought to reassure me that
she can win this thing. And before she jumps in the car, she empha-
sized a theme that came through loud and clear at the rally, "He is
extreme."

At the rally itself, it was a beautiful, 85-degree day with the
sun beating down on a crowd of mostly woman, who were there
to cheer the governor on and hear the words of wisdom from the
founder of Emily's List, Ellen Malcolm. Her group title means
"Early Money Is Like Yeast" and for years Malcolm et al. had been
spreading lots of "yeast" including a few bucks here and there for
Granholm. I could tell the "yeast" would be rising this day because
it was hot on two counts. The unprotected bald spot on the top of
my head was heating up, and the governor took off her blue blazer
and rolled up her sleeves when she got rolling with the audience.
But the crowd first heard from Ms. Malcolm, who had obviously
been briefed on what to say about opponent Dick DeVos, whom she
didn't know from Adam.

"He's selling himself like soap," she advised the cheering crowd. There is no way she could have known about DeVos,
Amway, and selling soap. The governor's guys got to Malcolm
first, so she could do all the dirty political work, while the governor
remained perched on the high road. That way, with a straight face,
the governor could say she never attacked her opponent. Ah, the

games they do play. Meanwhile the governor played the "innocent bystander" role perfectly as she sat in her chair, legs crossed, sort of nodding in approval while delightfully soaking in the soaking Ms. Malcolm was giving Mr. D.

"DeVos wants to turn Michigan into an incubator for extreme right-wing policies," Malcolm said and brought delight to the crowd. The anti-abortion demonstrators who were protesting the event were not smiling.

More on that in a moment.

She lumped DeVos in with "Bush and Engler," and said he wanted to turn Michigan to the right. Malcolm said the governor would take the state "into the future."

During all this, a subplot quietly unfolded involving those aforementioned anti-abortion folks, who started out near the street and a half a block or so from the podium. But slowly, one by one they infiltrated the Granholm rally with their "Stop Abortion Now" signs on one side and "Thank You, President Bush" on the other. Two of them were so bold as to take two vacant seats in the front row within spitting distance of Malcolm and Granholm.

I told my camera guy Steve Coon to get a shot of the Lansing police officer who politely asked the pair to vacate those folding chairs. They did. There were about five of Lansing's finest assigned to this event—just in case.

Going on at the same time was a battle of the placards, which was actually rather comical. Other anti-abortion folks moved from the street curb to mingle with the governor's backers on the lawn of the Michigan Women's Historical Center and Hall of Fame. As they held up their anti-abortion signs, the Granholm folks moved in front of them and held up their signs to block them out. This went on all over the place and obviously for the benefit of our cameras.

But the topper was the exchange with one college student, who had an extra-tall sign that she proudly hoisted just to the left of the governor. Tim Hughes, who lobbies for Granholm, was shadowing the protestor wherever she went. He had to stretch to do it, but with his tiny Granholm sign, he tried to upstage the college kid. She moved her sign one way for the audience to see. He moved there, too, to block it out. She moved another, and he countered that as well. And on and on it went until she bailed out. I asked Hughes afterwards, "Don't you wish you were 6 feet 8?" He laughed. There was no pushing or shoving during this jockeying, but one officer called me off to the side.

My cameraman had recorded an up-close conversation between the officer and one of the infiltrators he was trying to relocate peacefully.

"Was that your camera guy, Tim?" he asked.

"Yeah."

"No problem," he went on. "He was just sort of in my face, and I wanted to know."

I asked him on what grounds he was asking these folks to leave, since this was a public place. Shrugging his shoulders he conceded he and his pals were on shaky legal ground, but since nobody was arrested, no foul, no harm. But back to the main event.

Now it was the governor's turn to get the troops engaged, and it didn't take her long to launch into what she and her hubby had been talking about in private, i.e., once the voters find out who DeVos really is, the election would turn.

"The republicans like big government in your bedroom, in your doctor's office, and in the confessional, but no government when it comes to a safety net for those who are most vulnerable. That's the agenda of the far right," she shouted out as the crowd got hotter in the warm summer sun. While blasting those conservative GOPers, Granholm worked in a nifty pitch to "You Milliken moderates out there, welcome here," she waved her hands as if to motion them into her corner. "You're party has left you."

I thought back to the Milliken interview the governor and I had talked about at the Cherry Festival. The Millikens said they would not leave their party, but Granholm would not take no for an answer. She not only wanted the former First Family on her side, she wanted everyone of their ilk there, too.

Finally, some 45 minutes into the rally, it was over, and now it was time for the "availability" as they call it. It was a chance for reporters to interview the guests on what we wanted to talk about.

I was doing a story for TV-10 that night on the polling data suggesting Granholm was in trouble with segments of the female voting public. "Watch this one," the governor said as she nodded toward me and warned Malcolm before I could speak.

"Isn't it true that some women don't believe other women should be governors?" I started the exchange.

Pollster Ed Sarpolus had told me that about an hour earlier for my TV story, but Malcolm would have no part of that. She called it an antiquated idea. I thought she was wrong but didn't say so.

She did, however, make a good point about the time frame for women to make their political decisions, which might account for why some were not on the Granholm bandwagon. "Women are very busy, and they decide late in the game. And right now, most people—men and woman—are not paying any attention—and the final people that decide will be women," and she felt they would come home to the governor.

I quizzed the governor about the under 40 and independent females who were voting for DeVos.

"Voters, Tim, do not know my opponent. All they know is that he is a businessman. They do not know he is a republican." She made it clear that by the time November rolled around, they would know who he was, because she and her troops would paint the picture, and I was pretty sure it would not be a glowing personality sketch. She obviously wanted to downplay this "female" problem and therefore did not tell me that 16% of her advertising dollars were reportedly going into commercials during the afternoon soaps, where the gender makeup is decidedly one sided.

DeVos, by comparison, was shelling out only 9% of his ad dollars for viewers who were hopelessly trying to figure out how in the heck the world really did turn.

Malcolm jumped in to underscore her theme that DeVos was extreme. "He opposes abortion for rape and incest victims. He is very much out of the mainstream." I was getting the message. Here was the touchstone of the Granholm anti-DeVos theme: paint him as "not one of us." I was curious to see what paints they would use.

One little sidebar to this event: July 19, some six months into the campaign, I finally saw, in the flesh, one Howard Eldleson, the governor's campaign manager. I invited him to do the show. I knew the answer before I asked the question. He declined. But the next day, the head of the DeVos campaign said yes to what turned out to be a revealing on-camera interview, as I sought his reaction to the Granholm rally.

During a campaign, all sides are super hyper about the "fairness" thing in media coverage, and Greg McNeilly was firing off protest letters to news directors when he felt his guy was not getting equal time.

I knew this, because one such letter sat on the desk of TV-10 news director Kevin Ragan when I made a rare appearance to chat with him. The correspondence was direct and left no doubt that McNeilly was watching—apparently with a stopwatch at his side. He was complaining that one of my recent stories gave more time to the governor.

Anyway, when I finished my story on Granholm, I knew I would not have enough time to include the other side in the story that night. I thought about giving McNeilly a heads up that I would cover his side the next day but decided against that. I wanted to see if he would fire off another letter. He did not, but I was on the e-mail at about 7 a.m. asking if I could come over to get his reaction.

At about 9:30, cameraman Rob Gingrich and I rolled into DeVos headquarters on the west side of Lansing. I strolled in with this, "If you don't want me to read it, cover it up," I jokingly announced. The crew of clean-cut, college-aged DeVos groupies laughed—and then covered everything up. Not quite.

McNeilly came out of his cubbyhole office, which I asked to see. You never know where you'll get a story. Soon as we walked in, my eye caught the wall, where a big newspaper section was hanging down. It had pictures of DeVos at the Pancakes and Politics breakfast in Detroit. Remember the infamous story involving Mr. Mango?

"Hey, you got a picture of THE picture?" I joked. Remember, the democrats said DeVos and Mango were buddy-buddy at the event. It would have been a great story for me if there had been a shot of the two together. But on the other side of the picture was the infamous Hilter ad.

"Do you think that story is over?" I asked.

McNeilly said he did. Ironically, just the day before, someone in the Granholm campaign whispered in my ear that based on what Mongo had said on OTR, they were considering some sort of legal action to prove once and for all who paid for the advertisement. I did not share that with McNeilly. He did joyfully tell me that the weekend before, he and a bunch of volunteers had knocked on the doors of 400 homes in Detroit. "Only two closed the doors on us," he happily reported.

We next moved out to the front of the building to set up for the interview. McNeilly had seen my story the night before and did not need a briefing on the rally. He had seen the event without being there. One of those smiling volunteers did attend, recorded everything, and gave it to Mc to review overnight.

Both sides were involved in this camcorder gorilla warfare.

So what about the bar of soap charge that Ms. Malcolm had used on DeVos? I began as the camera rolled. McNeilly begged off, saying this race was all about jobs, but he did concede that the other side was a bunch of "negative campaigners, and they're not interested in jobs."

"So you deny that your guy is a bar of soap?"

"Absolutely," he laughed at the end of the quickie sound bite.

Next, we got into the Granholm/Malcolm charge that DeVos was an extremist.

"Dick's position on those social issues is the same as Frank Kelley, the same as Scott Bowens. It's right in the mainstream."

Stop the tape for a second. Former Attorney General Kelley and wanna-be A.G. Bowens were both pro-life, and both are democrats. Roll tape.

"So in terms of who is extreme, I think you have to look at our opposition, who is radically out of step with the majority of Michigan voters on those issues."

It was a good bite but did not jell with reality. On the abortion issue in Michigan, a majority is pro-choice. However, on partial-birth abortion, that number flips. So McNeilly was half right.

To understand this next segment, we have to stop tape again. On the ride over to the interview, I got a cell phone call from Chris DeWitt on the Granholm side. He was trying to line me up a guest for OTR, and in the course of the chat, he said, "Did you see the A.P. story on the rally?" I had not, but I figured I was going to hear about it right now. He proceeds to tell me that John Truscott, speaking for DeVos, was adamant about not speaking about the rape and incest issue. The wire service wanted to know if DeVos opposed abortions under those circumstances.

"We're not going to get into parsing on this a thousand different ways," he told correspondent Kathy Barks Hoffman,who then quoted him as concluding, "Those [issues] have not been discussed. End of story."

It was a curious answer and one that deserved further exploration, which I did with Mr. McNeilly.

"Does he [the candidate] favor abortion in the case of rape and incest?" was the pointed question.

Equally pointed and evasive was the response.

"Dick is pro-life and is endorsed by Right to Life of Michigan."

"But that doesn't answer my question."

"Dick is pro-life and is endorsed by Right to Life of Michigan." Hum, didn't I just hear that, which led me to inquire, "Apparently, you're not going to answer that?" Now the answer was down to one word, "Correct," which was met with my one word response, "Why?"

"Because we think that answer suffices. Dick wants to bring jobs back to Michigan. That's what this campaign is about, and no matter what the governor or her special interests do, we're not going to allow Michigan voters to lose focus that this campaign is about the issue of jobs and jobs lost."

That's why Truscott refused to answer Hoffman's questions, and McNeilly was doing the same thing. But I was not through.

"Can I infer that he would not favor abortion in those [rape and incest] cases?"

"Dick does not favor abortion in those cases."

Bingo—but I really didn't get the full impact of what he had just said. He actually answered my question but since I missed that, I followed up, "Can I make an inference from that?"

He said, "Yes."

Before wrapping up, McNeilly wanted to say something concerning the Granholm barb about Milliken republicans. He thought it was "disingenuous and insulting" for her to invoke the former governor's name. He said one of the many Milliken virtues was his civility, and he felt it was anything but civil for Granholm to bring that up at a rally where there was "fist pounding" and shouting. "It was a cheap political ploy," he concluded, and with that I thanked him and moved on.

Before the afternoon was over, DeWitt was on the horn. "So?" he wanted to know. How did the McNeilly thing go? I explained that I didn't want to be a go between for these two camps but indicated he would be interested in what the MIRS newsletter would report the next day. I hinted that it might be different than the A.P. story on rape and incest.

And just to be fair, I also chatted with Truscott a short time after that to give him a heads up that he was out of step with McNeilly on that issue.

"Thanks. I appreciate that," he said.

I finished this chapter just after the Tigers won a matinee game and took two of three games from the White Sox. I thought my "Tiger's impact on the governor's race" theory was looking better all the time.

15

You Can't Use My Name

A lot has happened since we put Chapter 14 to bed.

1. To no one's shock, the dems put up a Google ad for the governor.
2. The governor got a little buzz going with new jobs on top of the Google stuff and by doling out some road pork.
3. DeVos launched new ads that had the Granholm folks and the newspapers up in arms.
4. A new poll was released with the same old same old, but the Amway thing raises its ugly head for the first time.

As noted, the Google ad was not unexpected. The governor is still not talking to the camera, but you saw all those polished college kids standing behind her and the announcer explains that "Granholm put her team to work" to land all these neat hi-tech jobs. There was no mention of the fact that she did very little to help the team, but then, why mess up a perfectly good ad with some unpleasant facts.

In the last chapter, we did talk about the need for her to par-lay the Google story into more of the same, and there were signs she was doing that. "This is great news for our state," the governor gushed at a news conference in Pleasant Ridge were she trekked to announce 450 jobs at ePrize, an Internet promotion company. "And it's great news for all of the young people who have been looking outside of Michigan," she gushed some more.

DeVos was talking about young kids as well. He was run-ning an ad showing them packing their boxes and moving off to any-where but Michigan. A giant moving company drove home the point by announcing that during the first six months of 2006, it handled 2,912 moves out of the state, while only 1,570 moved in. That fig-ure was good enough to rank Michigan as first in nation in outward migration. The last time it was that bad was in 1983.

The governor also masterfully played the pork barrel game by announcing the accelerated state spending to pave new roads. It was about the third or forth time that she milked this story, and each time it got good play in the media. "Granholm finds a way to create jobs: Fix more roads," read the *Detroit News* headline.

And I'll be darned, part of the $44 million found its way into Oakland County, Macomb County, and Wayne County. Golly gee, just the areas she needs to win in the fall. But then, who is keeping score. Granholm was no different than any other governor who took control of the purse strings and used them for her own political gain. DeVos could not do that, but then if he wanted to, he could have seen her $44 million and raised her another $44 mil.

While she was getting her post-Google mojo working, DeVos stayed the course by staying on the air with another batch of ads. First, there was the ad where he explains that some people are blaming Washington, Lansing, the unions, foreign countries and the like for Michigan's mess. DeVos suggests "Let's not get down in the mud, let's create new jobs." He never mentions his opponent's name, but if you are halfway literate, you know he's really talking about "her." In the next ad, he left nothing to the imagination, as the spot began with a mug shot of the governor and some newspaper clips that criticized her, but the ad itself produced some criticism from the newspapers themselves. Next to the governor's pic, there are several newspaper quotes: "The press says it's all negative, all the time." "Granholm is on a mission to get re-elected...perhaps at any cost."

When I saw the spots and read the quotes, I thought to myself, "Those quotes look kind of familiar." That's because they were mine. The DeVos camp had swiped the quotes from a column I wrote for 22 newspapers around the state. The ad, however, credited only one of them: the *Lansing State Journal*. Even though my name was not in the commercial, which would have been even worse, I felt uncomfortable anyway. No reporter likes to be "used" in any way for political gain by either side in a dogfight, which is why *Lansing State Journal* executive editor Mickey Hirtin was on the phone complaining to me that the ad was misleading.

"That was from your column," he stated the obvious, "and not from our editorial pages." I agreed. "I'm going to ask them to pull them," which meant he wanted them off the air.

That was the same sentiment expressed by Ron Dzwonkowski at the *Free Press*, who was also quoted in the ad. Word has it that somebody in the Granholm camp stoked this story by bringing the ad to the attention of both papers in the first place. "The central issue for us was they were taking comments from a *Free Press* columnist and attributing it to the *Free Press*," Ronnie D. told the MIRS guys.

The DeVos folks took the criticism to heart since it made no sense to make an enemy. Hence the new ad attributed the anti-Granholm quote to a "*Detroit Free Press* columnist," and lucky for Brian Dickerson, his name was not included. It cost DeVos $3,000 to make the change.

But then the sky fell in on yours truly as my worse fear came true. I knew I was in trouble when my sister Jill in Grand Haven called. "So you're supporting DeVos, hey?" she began with a laugh. She was referring, of course, to the revised ad that had come out after Mr. Hirtin at the *LSJ* did his number on the DeVos folks. He read the riot act to John Truscott in what J.T. described as a "very heated exchange." Truscott agreed to make another correction for that paper, too. But in the Sunday paper, the *LSJ* opinion writers blasted DeVos anyway. "Campaign hurts itself with disingenuous attack ad," the headline on the op-ed page began. The piece opined that, "It illustrates DeVos's unwillingness to play straight with voters." And on and on it went as it explained the ad had left out the fact that I had written the piece. The editorial folks were kind enough to point out my criticism of DeVos was in there, too. The editorial concluded by urging the DeVos campaign to stop trying to fool the voters. The DeVos side was not amused and felt it was bad form to run the editorial after it had agreed to change the copy. Oh, they changed the copy all right and put my name in it.

But back to sis. I thanked her for being so attentive. Her call dashed any hopes that I harbored that my name was so small that nobody would notice it. A day later, my cousin Nancy in Fraser wrote to say she had seen it, too. I reflected that at least this was a good way to know that all my relatives were not horizontal.

At first, I was very unhappy that the DeVos folks would do this to me. I never expected any favors from them, but they knew full well it might take a chunk out of my nonpartisan credibility with readers. Rather than gripe about it and try to influence their campaign in any way, I decided to suck it in and hope the ad will not stay up for very long. I also thought it would be interesting to see on the rubber chicken circuit if anybody else caught it. Besides, I did say those things, and I did believe them at the time, but it still left an empty feeling inside to be drawn into the fray. But, as it often happens, a new twist emerged.

In the course of grilling J.T. on who they were going to pick for lt. governor, the ad came up, and he disclosed that it was Mr. Hirtin's demand and not the DeVos campaign to put my name in the commercial. Truscott told me they were content with just saying a "*Lansing State Journal* columnist," but Hirtin would have none of that. I debated whether to call him but decided to let it ride. The damage, if any, had already been done, and talking to him was not going to change one thing. And while on the subject of newspapers, during all this, the *USA-Today* folks finally discovered this national story unfolding in Michigan.

Right there on the front page, writer Susan Page told everyone across the nation that when Gov. Granholm was elected, "the buzz…was that she'd be president one day if only she hadn't been born in Canada." Then Page lowers the boom, "That was then," and notes that Granholm is now tied with a "political neophyte." "The issue is jobs, jobs, jobs," Granholm tells Page. Hey, that's former Governor Blanchard's line. Page has fun describing the governor thusly. She was "sipping a Diet Coke and absentmindedly running a hand through her cropped blond hair." Oh, pleeazee. DeVos took a hit, too. "DeVos, 50, is tall and rail thin." There was no hand running through his hair, because he had "a balding pate and an unblinking intensity." I figured this would be the first of many national accounts of this historic race.

Back to the ad. Apart from the moaning and groaning from the abused newspapers, the Granholm folks called it an attack ad. The DeVos team denied it, but it was clearly sensitive to the charge that it had started this fight. To underscore that, I came home the other day to find a manila envelope sitting in the chair on our front porch. In it, was "proof" that the dems had drawn first blood. Campaign manager McNeilly protested that her "re-election effort continues to be focused on negative attacks and misinformation.... The attacks come from the same people who said, 'Let's elevate this dialogue instead of really descending into the mud.'" He was quoting the governor from "Flashpoint," a WDIV-TV show in Detroit way back in February.

On the campaign trail, the candidate himself was quizzed about the ad. It was a scorcher of a morning on July 31 at the Zeeb farm just outside of Lansing. DeVos bounced out of his Lincoln SUV with shirtsleeves rolled up, as he prepared to unveil his agriculture blueprint. He worked the crowd of local farmers who were there, and eventually, he walked up to me.

"How do you like this heat?" I began on a nonconfrontational note.

"Actually I like it," he reflected while adding, "however, my body doesn't." I noted I liked the heat, too, and that was that.

After pumping a bunch of paws, he moved to the podium that sat on several bails of hay. Behind him, the Zeeb family had parked a giant tractor and what looked to me like a combine, but what did I know being from Okemos and all. DeVos launched into his farming speech. He read it, and far as I could tell, didn't make much news

with it. I had been handed a copy earlier and found lots of generalities but very few specifics. "I will work with the legislature and
agricultural industry leaders to devise a plan to reduce Michigan's
farmland property taxes," he read to the assembled farmers. The
stuff about how much the cut would be, how it would be funded,
and who would get it were left out. This was nothing new. Earlier
that morning, I had told my TV-10 assignment desk that we should
cover this event, but I would come back with a different story than
the one DeVos et al. offered.

I got my chance after the speech when DeVos kindly made
himself available to the media as we all roasted in the sun-baked
barnyard looking for some morsel of news out of this staged event.
His advance team had set up a blue backdrop with "DeVos for
Governor" or something on it for the interviews, but the candidate
wanted to stand in front of the tractor instead. I joked with him
about getting on the tractor and maybe wearing a helmet ala former
presidential contender Mike Dukakis, who self-destructed one day
by wearing a helmet on a tank in Warren. DeVos confessed that he
had driven a tractor but fluffed off the notion of playing the fool.
The other reporters started off with farming questions, which was
the logical place to begin. I waited until I thought everyone else was
done on that subject, and I waded in.

"What's your position on capital punishment?" I said as I
looked him in the eye. Each candidate has an inner voice, and I
figured his was saying at that very moment, "Stay on message. Talk
about farming. Talk about cows. But stay away from the wedge issue."

"We're here to talk about farming," he stated and tried to get
off the hook as he listened to his inner voice.

"Let's see if we can move the agenda down the road," I offered as I tried to keep him on it.

He relented, saying, "I've said I have no opposition to it, but
I'm perfectly comfortable with Michigan's existing prohibition."

"So you would not try to change that if elected?"

He said he would not. It seemed like he wanted it both ways.
Yeah, he believed in the death penalty but apparently not enough to
do anything about it.

Then in rapid-fire succession, I asked two more social issue questions. What about embryonic stem-cell research? Remember he danced around his original answer on "Off the Record" six months earlier. He had one now. "I think we should not proceed in that direction at this time." At this point, he pulled a Granholm on me. He turned his head away from me and looked for another question from somebody, anybody, else. But I ignored his attempt to wiggle away, as I continued, "How will you vote on the dove hunting issue?"

Michigan voters would decide this hotly contested issue in November, and DeVos revealed that he would be a "yes" vote on continuing the experimental hunting season on the birds of peace, as the Humane Society liked to call them. On that, he and the governor agreed, as she would be an affirmative vote on killing the little birdies, too.

I had shot my best shots, and the Q and A returned to the farming stuff. Not that I don't like farmers, but I could not sell that story to my decidedly urban audience. As it looked like DeVos was ready to ride off into the noonday sun, I tried one more.

"How many debates do you want?" I've found that even when a candidate wants to end a press conference, if you hit the right nerve, they will stay put, and his nerve was hit.

"As many as the governor wants," he answered. But then he launches into this monologue about how he is disappointed in her response to his debate letter. He says his letter was businesslike. What he got in return was another attack, he explained. "The governor doesn't appear to want to debate...and is more interested in throwing around negative invectives....It's just disappointing."

He laments that he has been under attack from the day he announced on the Island over a year ago and confesses, "We're tired of it." That's why they were running the anti-Granholm ad with the newspaper quotes mentioned above. These are "cynical and personal attacks," he warms to the subject in the driving heat with sweat now forming on his exposed forehead. "These are negative and bitter comments...which are misleading the voters."

I asked him to list two of the personal attacks. He suggests that in the debate letter, the Granholm people "insinuate" that he doesn't know what he is talking about. And he says it is a personal attack to say he favors spending more money in China than he does in Michigan, which he adds is not true. I think a personal attack is like calling the kid on the playground a "big fat scaredy cat" or accusing his mother of wearing open-toed combat boots. I thought afterwards, if he thinks this stuff is bad, wait until they really get personal.

Anyway, the news avail ended, but I decided to hang around to walk to the car with him. Another 20 minutes went by, as he continued to work the crowd while drinking some bottled water. His handlers wanted to know why I was hanging around. I explained I wanted to chat with the candidate without the camera. You most always get good stuff from a politician when you dump the camera and microphone, and this time would not be any different. DeVos walked across the driveway, and we hooked up as he moved toward the SUV.

"I'm writing the book chapter on Detroit," I advised him.

Before he spoke any further, he inquired, "Are these the same ground rules as the e-mails?"

I confirmed that it was, that is, what he was about to say would not get into print until this book was published. He also asked if the e-mails were helping. I told him they were. With that confirmed, we began.

I wanted him to confirm that his Detroit strategy was to neutralize the black ministers there. He drew back on his business background to give me the answer.

"People always say in a business deal there are only two options: either you get the deal or you don't. There is a third," he went on, "if you neutralize someone, there's a chance down the road you can eventually get them." So the answer was yes. "It is a win" to keep them neutral, he revealed. He would be more than happy to accept that and had been working for more than a year to build that fence so they could sit on it.

He said he understood that an attitude change in Detroit regarding black support for a GOP governor would not happen overnight, but he told them, "If I am elected, I want to work with you." Then he sort of smiled and added that over time if he was elected, they might eventually move from neutrality to buying what he had to sell. Then I asked him what he was thinking during the Detroit NAACP debate, when Granholm called on her black appointees to stand up at the end. Now he pauses, just for a moment, because he knew his answer would be newsworthy if it got out before the election, but he answers anyway. Basically, he felt it was "pandering," and he suggested it didn't work, and that others in the audience had told him the same thing.

Out of the corner of my eye, I could see his aide moving to open the backdoor to the SUV, so it was time to end this exchange. He parted company by saying he appreciated the fact that I was trustworthy. I thanked him for that and told him to say hi to his wife Betsy.

He got in and drove off. I dashed to the news van to write down what I had just heard. It had been a fun and productive morning. I got the candidate to address something other than jobs; I had some face time to plow some fertile ground with DeVos to share with you; and to top it off, a little 10-year-old young lady confessed that she watched our TV show. I was more than happy to give Nicole an autograph. Maybe our efforts to drive down our demographics into a younger age bracket were working.

The new DeVos ad was fodder for the OTR crew that week, as was the new poll conducted by EPIC-MRA for the *Detroit News*, Channel 7 TV, WILX, WOOD, and WJRT-TV. Frankly, the polling was starting to get a little monotonous, because the race was still tied, but the governor had managed to flip her numbers. In June, she was down, with 44 points, and he was at 46. Now she was at 47, and he was at 44. In other words, she gained three points. Ed Sarpolus credited the Google jobs and the Granhom TV ads for giving her some badly need momentum. But Eddie also stuck in a question that captured everyone's attention. He had given me a heads up that he was going to test the "Amway" attitude in the electorate, and the results made for interesting reading.

Recall that for months during my speeches, I had detected this wealth of negativity over Amway. The formal poll confirmed what my informal polling had shown. A hefty 41% of voters had an "unfavorable" impression of the company, while only 17% had a favorable one. But that was only the tip of this potential dangerous iceberg. Respondents were read the DeVos bio, which included this line, "he served as president of Alticor, formerly known as the Amway Corporation," and as vice president, he helped to "expand Amway throughout the world." After that was shared, respondents were asked if they were less likely or more likely to vote for him. Twenty-one percent said less likely, and 14% said more likely. The DeVos camp spun the results by correctly noting that everybody else, about 62%, didn't give a hoot.

Sarpolus, however, suggested on camera that in a close election, the Amway factor could be a deciding factor. And then he told me privately that Amway was an even bigger factor with the 9% of the undecided voters. And to underscore the potential pop of all this, when voters were asked why they would not support DeVos, the most popular reason, at 11%, was Amway.

For months, like an underground spring, the Amway issue bubbled beneath the surface. But now, it burst into the open, as the *Detroit News* played the angle in its lead paragraph and WOOD radio in Grand Rapids had fun with it during its morning drive time. And like everything else in this campaign, both camps went to work doing their best to take advantage. I made sure I got to everyone for my story for TV-10.

"We're more than happy to talk about what Dick DeVos did as a leader of Alticor." That was from John Truscott, being careful not to use Amway in his sound bite.

"He took a company that was going downhill, reorganized it, reshaped it and turned it around to be a very strong, very profitable company that's had six years of record growth." But I wanted to know if it was an Achilles heel for his candidate. Truscott felt the dems would "try to make it one, but in the end, once people have all the information, I don't think it will be." Oh my. Here was another person, like the First Gentleman, pinning his hopes on an informed electorate to save the day.

While J.T. was, in effect, saying, "Bring it on," Chris DeWitt was a bit more cautious, not wanting to overplay his hand.

"Is DeVos vulnerable on the Amway issue?" I wanted to know.

"Maybe he is. Maybe he isn't," he said as he cautiously

avoided a yes or no response even though he knew the answer. He suggested his side would not use Amway, per se, but the DeVos record while running the company was fair game. And then for the one-millionth time, he repeats that DeVos laid off 1,400 workers in Michigan while creating 1,000 jobs in China. His answer did represent some progress. He did not say DeVos shipped the Michigan jobs to China, which was the original song and dance at the outset of the campaign.

Truscott, of course, rebutted the China stuff. "They will tell you that he invested $200 million in China, but at the same time, he invested $700 million in Michigan."

And on and on it went. The OTR crew of Hoffman, Ballenger, Cain, and a newcomer, Ivy Hughes from MIRS, jumped into it on OTR that week. Ballenger promptly dismissed the Amway angle as pure hokum. He suggested that people don't like any corporations. The rest of the panel gave it a little more credence than the man from Princeton.

We then discussed the newspaper quote ad that had created such a fuss in newsrooms all over the state. Hoffman thought it was an attack ad. Hughes did not. Cain chimed in and told everyone that two of the newspaper quotes were from me, for which I thanked him profusely. And then the two females opened a whole new can of worms. Hughes said that she thought women were put off by DeVos's speaking style, and Hoffman agreed. I had never heard that analysis before, but after chewing on that, we got down to the real nitty-gritty by discussing the governor's glasses. I must confess that sometimes the program gets sidetracked over issues that don't amount to much, and this was a borderline example of that. Hoffman noted that the governor was wearing her reading glasses, along with the industrial protection glasses, in all of her commercials. Somebody had suggested that she was doing it to appeal to female voters. Hughes said glasses made the governor look more like a governor. Ballenger tossed in the fact that, "Maybe she is just near-sighted." Leave it to Billy to state the obvious. I argued that somebody must have thought the glasses would help it in some way, "because nobody ever does anything without a reason."

Well, the governor had a real hoot watching all this on her

laptop computer on the way home from an event. And the word filtered out that these were prescription glasses that she needed to read
despite laser surgery years earlier. And there was no hidden agenda.
I didn't buy that for a second. She obviously needed her cheaters to
read all the campaign checks that had flowed into her coffers. At the
end of the month, both campaigns had to file their financial reports.

A record $21 million had been spent to date, with DeVos
taking $17.5 million of that total, including a whopping $12.8 mil of
his own money. The governor raked in $11.2 million but spent just
over $4 million. She was sitting on her powder, just as she said she
would.

One of the questions we are going to answer in this election
is, can somebody spend an unlimited amount and win? The *Detroit
News* reported that the track record of that happening was not very
good. A California businessman, Al Checchi, shelled out $40 mil-
lion and lost. In the same state, Michael Huffington saw $27.5 mil
go down the drain in his failed 1994 senate bid. But the New York
Mayor Mike Bloomberg won office, writing $70 million from his
own checking account. Would Mr. DeVos be a Bloomberg or a
Checchi? Everyone in this town wanted to know the answer, and
foremost among them was Dan Mulhern and Jennifer Granholm.

16

You Want to Do
a Debate?

It was about 7:15, and I was about 25 minutes into my daily two-mile jaunt on the treadmill when the phone rang. Gayle, for years, has pleaded with me to take the portable phone so I could give her some relief from playing personal secretary, an unpaid position, when "news" calls come in. After I heard who was on the other end, I was thankful I had listened; otherwise, I might have missed this news-making call — a news-making call that I had to agree to sit on and not report.

"I don't want to see this in the paper or on TV," the caller warned in his best warning voice. "You can maybe use this in the book, but it can't get out now," he said as he drove home the point once more. Normally, I would think twice about making such a deal, because after all, I get paid to report the news and not put my posterior on it, but this one was easy. I agreed two minutes into the conversation. I did it, because I trusted the guy on the phone, and I knew that he trusted me.

Mark Fox wanted to know, "What are you doing?" as he heard the methodical strange noise in the background.

"I'm on the treadmill," I revealed. "Maybe I should call you back?" I asked

"You'll want to talk to me," the democratic lawyer said as he dished out some free advice.

Fox, as I explained earlier, is one of the original Granholm kitchen-cabinet residents. We went back a ton of years, and what he was about to tell me was music to my ears: if everything fell into place, I was going to anchor the first TV debate between the governor and DeVos.

I have not written much about debates so far in this book because there really wasn't much to discuss. Months ago, the DeVos guys took a stab at making some news and smoking out the other side. They issued a press release announcing that THEY had agreed to a series of televised debates, including one "hosted by Tim Skubick on Michigan Public TV" in early September. Other stations got one, too.

While it was certainly nice to read, the news release was meaningless with a capital M. Within hours of the release, TV-10 news director Kevin Ragan was on the horn. "Did you see that Channel 6 got a debate?" he frantically quizzed me. TV-6 is the other news shop in Lansing, and Ragan was ready to blow a gasket if they got a debate and he didn't. I explained the debate facts of life. "Kev, settle down. That announcement doesn't mean anything. Look: the DeVos folks have no control over debates. This is all up to the governor. She has total authority, and she will use it." I was not shucking and jiving. The incumbent always holds all the debate cards. The challenger can pretend to have some say by publishing useless press releases, but the incumbent will determine the end game. End of story. Ragan got it. I assured him he would get a debate.

A couple of weeks later, I got the idea to sweeten the original public TV offer to the two campaigns. I asked the WKAR-TV folks for permission to create a multi-media coalition to help co-sponsor the event. I got the green light, and within two weeks, I had added virtually all of the newspapers I work for, the Michigan Radio

Network, the MIRS newsletter, TV-10, Michigan Public Radio and all the public TV outlets. I joked that I was putting together an offer the governor could not refuse. The letter went to both camps, and on June 15, 2006, the DeVos camp responded. "We accept this invitation to debate...I have been in contact with the Granholm camp [and] they continue to dodge the issue," wrote campaign manager Greg McNeilly. You gotta love these guys. They never miss a chance to get in a dig or two at the other side. "We stand ready to begin discussions, even if the Granholm campaign does not respond as Michigan struggles with a single-state recession...." Yeah, yeah, yeah, etc., etc., etc. Cordially, Greg McNeilly.

He was right. There was no response from Granholm's side. But I was not disappointed, because based on earlier informal chats with the guy who was now on my phone, I knew they would remain silent until after the August 8 primary or maybe even later than that. Having said that, however, I was concerned that I might be frozen out of the high-stakes debate sweepstakes. I never really shared that with anyone except my wife. "Don't they have to give you a debate?" my lovely spouse blurted out, noting that I had been doing debates since 1970, and after all, I was the senior capitol correspondent in town. Oh, if it was only thus. I told her there were some folks who were not happy with my coverage of the governor over the last three years. Heck, for all I knew, the governor was one of those. In fact, I'm darn sure she was.

She was not unique. Every governor I have been honored to cover had taken "exception" to some of my reportage. I was totally comfortable that, over time, I had been fair with the current chief executive. But that aside, somebody might try to even the score by dishing out debates to everyone but me.

I was sort of preparing Gayle, and frankly myself, for that possibility. I didn't want to think about it but couldn't erase it either. That is, until tonight, July 26, 2006.

"The boss has signed off on doing your debate," Fox informed me in our phone conversation. He disclosed that there were "some" in the inner circle who were not in agreement, fearing that I might ask a question that might make the governor look bad. "What if he asks a sinking funds question?" someone in the room at this "high-level meeting" wondered, as the Skubick debate was kicked around.

During the primary debate four years ago between then candidate Granholm, former Governor Blanchard, and Congressman David Bonior, I had asked one questions that no one had anticipated. "Do you favor expanding the definition of sinking funds?" I innocently asked the trio. None of them knew what it was, and right there on statewide public TV, they had to reluctantly admit it. To be honest, three weeks earlier, I had not known what it was, either. But I found out by attending a news conference. The Michigan Chamber of Commerce told us it opposed a little-known school fund-raising mechanism—sinking funds—to pump more tax dollars into the classroom.

I will plead guilty to trying to hone questions to secure what I term "first-impression answers." Candidates at this level, by the time the debates roll around, have heard every question imaginable, and during debate prep, they get even more. They could regurgitate their answers in their sleep, and come to think of it, they probably do just that.

Anyway, I like to see if they can think on their feet. I want to judge how they handle a question they have not rehearsed. Often times, it is revealing. I justify these kinds of questions, because as governor, sometimes snap decisions are required. There is no time to focus group an answer or ask your aides to develop the correct response.

The apprehension in the Granholm inner circle over that type of question was debated and then dismissed—thank goodness. Somebody pointed out that, after all, she was the governor and was capable of handling any stuff I tossed her way. She had been doing it for over three years.

Fox continued with the purpose of his call as I was now off the treadmill and sitting on the bedroom floor. "We think the first debate is the most important one." I always felt the last one had the most cache, but I was willing to listen to his line of thought.

Team Granholm was anxious to see if DeVos, who was lookin' real good on his TV spots, could "perform" live without a teleprompter in a no-holds-barred format. "We don't know if he can?" wondered Fox. But it was clear they wanted to find out, and they figured allowing me to anchor the thing might prove the point one way or the other. Ah, but, there is always a "but." Fox was not content with doing this debate on public TV as I had suggested. If it was going to be a high-risk, let-it-all-hang-out gig, he wanted a larger audience. To my delight, he was also forceful in not wanting any of the local TV anchors to join me.

"We want you," he repeated. That made at least two of us. "Would you be willing to do the no-rules debate on a commercial TV network?" he said as he waded into water neither of us had been in before. Fox went on, "We sort of said, Skubick will do this thing on Mars if he had to." And of course, they were right. He excluded doing it on the NBC affiliates, because it was likely that my pal Rick Albin would get a debate on WOOD TV in Grand Rapids that could be fed to all the NBC outlets. ABC was excluded, because Channel 7 in Detroit would never allow me to anchor a debate on their airwaves when their guy Chuck Stokes was the obvious choice to do it.

"What about doing it on FOX?" Fox inquired.

At this point in our candid exchange, I decided to reveal something that nobody really knew. I was already working for FOX 2 . About two months ago, I got a call from my news director at WWJ NewsRadio 950 in Detroit. Rob Davidek had just gotten off the phone with somebody at FOX 2 in Detroit. They had been listening to my radio reports and wondered if I would be willing to do some stuff for them. I was more than willing, but I did have one reservation. More on that in a moment. The station had the top ratings in the morning. If everything worked out, it would be an ironic homecoming of sorts. I had worked there many moons ago when it was known as TV-2, WJBK-TV. That was before they fired me when it became clear they were done covering the capitol and politics. Scrapping such coverage was the trend at the time at all TV stations in the state.

Rob and I concluded the talk, and I tried to figure out how to proceed. He gave me the name of the news director, whom I did not know, and I took it from there after thanking him for the lead.

After playing phone tag for a couple of days, Dana Hahn and

I finally hooked up. She said she wanted me to do a "phoner" every Friday morning at about 6:30 a.m. during their morning show. In other words, talk with their anchors on the phone about what was politically "hot" that day. I could do that. I said I was interested, and we agreed to meet the next week after I gave a speech in Troy, which was next door to the station in Southfield. I did some checking around first, because my one fear concerned the public image of this FOX station. On the national level, everyone knew that Roger Ailes's network had a reputation for being a tad on the conservative side. The last thing I needed was to wreck my credibility by hooking up with any news outlet that had that perception. I got back on the horn with Rob and asked him about the FOX 2 image. He reassured me that there was no conservative agenda that he was aware of. That was good enough for me.

Long story short, I found myself back in the newsroom I had worked in years ago and in the office of Ms. Hahn. As I walked in and shook hands, she immediately called me the "Legendary Mr. Skubick," (Legendary, all right. What did she know that I didn't?) The whole thing lasted about 10 minutes and concluded with, "I'll talk to the general manager and let you know what I can afford."

We agreed that at their pre-election news meeting later that day she could announce that "in principle" I had agreed to work with them through the election. About a week later, she made the offer by e-mail, and two hours later, I accepted.

When I shared this with Mark Fox on the phone, he was shocked. "Honest? We didn't know that." I knew he must have been smiling. Here he was suggesting I anchor a debate on all the FOX stations in Michigan, and I tell him I'm already on the payroll. Talk about fate stepping in. However, I had a problem. Yeah, I wanted to do the debate, but I did not want to leave my public TV folks on the outside, angrily looking in.

"How about if I ask the public TV stations to broadcast it along with FOX?" I fished for a compromise.

"Not a problem," he reassured me. He wanted a larger audience, and if he got the FOX stations and the public TV gang too, so much the better. I pointed out that McNeilly had already signed off on my revised offer. But Fox, foxily advised, "Yeah, but that was when it was only on public TV." He wasn't sure they would agree to a broadcast with a broader audience. We would have to wait until September 6 to find out. That was when both sides would sit down to debate the debates. Little did I know it would take almost a full month to resolve their differences nor did I know I would become part of the delay.

We left it this way. I would consult, in general terms, with the public TV leaders. I would not reveal the nature of our conversation, which is revealed here for the first time. I would feel them out by saying, "How do you feel if we have to partner with a commercial network in order to nail down the debate for Public TV?" To me, it was a simple choice. Deal or no deal? I wanted the deal. We could land the coveted first debate for our loyal public TV audience and let the rest of the world in on it, too.

I was eager to make the pitch the next day to WKAR-TV executive producer Tim Zeko and our program director Kent Wieland. But before I got to them, I had to deal with a mini panic attack of my own. Moments after I hung up the phone, it hit me, as I went into the kitchen to clean out the refrigerator. You see, my wife was up North, and I had promised to remove all the dead food and penicillin mold before she returned home. But as I scrubbed away, I wondered if I had done something wrong? I asked myself, should I have talked with Fox in the first place? Was I aiding and abetting his side at the possible expense of the other? Honest, a sort of sudden chill came over me, and it was not from sticking my head in the refrig. Protecting one's credibility is Job One in this biz, and if I had put that at risk by conversing with Fox—well, it was not a pleasant thought. In these cases, I usually do two things. I ask myself, what if the public knew I was doing this, how would it react? Second, I always ask my wife for her take, but she was not home. So I scraped off the last bit of cheese that was stuck to the shelf and decided to put this on hold until I talked with her.

Friday rolled around, and after the taping of OTR, I sat down on the set with the WKAR guys to feel them out on the partnering concept. "Here's the deal," I cautiously began. "How would you guys feel if we had to share our debate with a commercial TV network?" I explained this was not a done deal, but I was trying to gauge their reaction and the reaction from the other public TV outlets. Zeko and Wieland quickly grasped the gravity of what I was saying. Either we do this, or there was a good chance we would be watching a debate on somebody else's channel.

"Would we like to have exclusivity?" Wieland asked out loud as he answered his own question with a quick, "Sure, but we would have no problem sharing it."

"But what about the rest of the public TV folks?" I wondered. It was decided not to share any of this with them on two counts. First, the chance of a leak went up exponentially with more persons in the loop. Second, it really didn't matter what they said. If one station or all of them didn't want to share, it was their call, and if there was any public backlash, they would have to deal with it. WKAR-TV was committed, and that is what I wanted to hear.

I got on the horn to Fox to square it with him and explained that my station wanted full control of the broadcast in our studios with my crew whom I have worked with for 30 years. He had no problem with that. But I was still grappling with my "ethical" question, as I headed up North to see Gayle.

"It doesn't sound right to me," was her first reaction after I told her what Fox and I had originally discussed. It was not the calming response I was looking for, but I appreciated her honesty. For the next hour we proceeded to bat it around every which way from Sunday. Was it wrong? Should I have told Fox to go ahead and do what he wanted to do and then get back to me after the fact? We both thought maybe I should explain all this to Zeko, but I reminded her I had promised Fox not to share the details with anyone else. Although to his credit, he did tell me I could confirm the conversation if the other side called me. Gayle and I decided I would sleep on it. The discussion had been great, but I was still not at peace, and I did not like that a bit.

By the next afternoon, I had reached my decision. I would let it ride. I concluded that when I talked with Fox that night, I was acting as a producer and not a reporter. It was exactly what I had done in previous campaigns when discussing debates, and no one criticized that process. I was merely providing information, and he was free to do with it as he saw fit. In my head, I reassured myself that if the DeVos team had called with the same request, I would have treated them the same way. Ultimately, if the public found out, I would explain that I was only sharing information that had been requested as a representative of Michigan Public TV. There was nothing unethical about that. Peace at last.

Prior to the phone chat with Fox, the two campaigns exchanged public letters on debate negotiations. The one from the Granholm camp was a little snarly. Of course the DeVos camp took exception, as it did with just about everything she said.

Her campaign manager, Howard Edelson, who had been rumored to be on his way out, by the way, noted that the governor looked forward to "a healthy exchange of ideas unfiltered from the unprecedented $10 million of packaged and scripted television ads" from Mr. DeVos. That was zinger number one. Her side never missed a chance to do that, either. Zinger two suggested when it was time for the debates, he hoped DeVos "will have finally decided what his positions are on the issues and will be willing to share them with the voters." There was a real tone of cooperation—not. That tone was duly noted by the other side, which suggested it was not going to wait for a September meeting to iron all this out. Media guy John Truscott said they would unilaterally start accepting debates with our without the governor's input. So there!

DeVos campaign hancho McNeilly offered his own glib shot, "It appears Granholm's confidence in her Harvard debating skills has fallen with Michigan's employment rate." Now children, go to your rooms and come back with a better attitude.

Fox, who did not like the "unilateral" attitude, drafted his own private letter to the DeVos debate guys, whom he had known for years. He suggested to Dan Pero, the former chief of staff for Governor John Engler and long-time Lansing insider and GOP confidant Richard McLellan, that everyone knock off the rhetoric and get down to business in September to get this debate thing resolved. Fox suggested September 6. McLellan had a conflict. He was scheduled for a delicate outpatient exam, so he jokingly asked himself: delicate procedure or meet with Mark Fox on debates? He chose the exam, so everyone huddled on September 5 instead.

I would have to wait to complete this chapter on debates until after that. But, at this read, I am as confident as anyone could be that one of the coveted debates will land in my lap. I am so confident that right here in the desk drawer is my list of potential debate questions—I've already got two, and sinking funds is not one of them.

17

Working Hard for the Blessing

Glory be, the governor rediscovered her voice. No, she didn't have laryngitis, although this week she does have a slight cold. The reference is to her first campaign commercial, which started last week. In it her lips moved and words came out. Up to now, we have only seen the governor but not heard from her. In this one, she sits in front of a black drape and talks to the voters. About what? If you guessed the economy and jobs, you'd be wrong. It was about gasoline prices. As July segued into August, folks around here were shelling out $3.19 a gallon. That's the highest price ever, and the governor tried to tap into that consumer unrest, which was rapidly reaching epic proportions.

"When some gas stations tried to gouge their customers, I stopped them; I took them to court and made them pay customers back," her first "talky" spot begins. She goes on to tell viewers that she ordered the pump police, my term not hers, to inspect gas stations, and then she takes an indirect whack at DeVos. "While others [she means him] would protect oil companies, I've told the President [ah, yet another swipe at "W"] to cap their outrageous profits." And then, with all the sincerity she can muster—and she musters real well—she reassures everyone that she will stand up and fight back "against anyone who threatens your paycheck, and I'll put you first."

Anyone? Does that mean the governor will come to your defense if someone tries to rob you, or she'll take your side if your boss cuts your salary or fires you? To me, it was a good line, but what did it really mean to the typical viewer? What she should have said is something such as, "While my opponent cuddles up to Big Oil, as governor, I will stay on your side and fight them." And in an oversight that I think was a huge mistake, she neglected to include one of her most glorious accomplishments in the gas price war. Last Labor Day in 2005, the governor amazingly jawboned the head of Marathon Oil and actually got him to slice pump prices by a whopping 30 cents a gallon just as thousands of motorists were heading up North for the final fling of the summer. No governor has even tried that before, let alone succeeded. But that was not in the spot.

I wondered, "What the heck are these folks doing when they write these commercials?" Compare the line that she "sent new inspectors across the state to end price gouging," (yawn, yawn) to what she could have said, "On Labor Day weekend, I saved you and your fellow motorists thousands of dollars at the pump." But that type of line was either not considered or ended up on the cutting room floor, although it did appear on her campaign web site. It was not an earth-shattering goof but part of a pattern of tiny goofs that seem to be dotting the landscape of the Granholm re-election bid so far.

The other aspect of the commercial that some viewers picked up on is that the accomplishments she bragged about were when she was attorney general and not governor. Does she have such a lousy record as governor that she has to go back four years to find something to boast about? Several viewers asked me.

The governor did pick up a significant "get" in the City of

Detroit but she had to work hard to nail down. We spoke in the last chapter about the DeVos full court press to neutralize the Council of Baptist Pastors in Detroit. Last week, I got a call from the legal advisor for the group. He was giving me a scoop. Bertram Marks told me that the next day, the council would endorse Granholm. I thought that was a major development and shared the story with FOX 2. They wanted me to drive to Southfield to do the story Live at Five. When I got there, the first guy I bumped into was anchorman Huel Perkins. He remembered me from my last stint at WJBK, and when I told him about my story, he blurted out, "But she was going to get that anyway." Then I explained that it was not a gimme, and that DeVos had been working the ministers very hard to keep them on the fence, but he had lost the battle. Now Huel's head nodded in agreement. This was a good story, and at 5:20 p.m. that night, we broke it.

The next day, the council staged a news conference. The governor was there with all the men of the cloth, as were several TV cameras, but the announcement got no play in the two Detroit papers. Several days later, it did appear in the *Free Press,* but the paper reported the endorsement was no surprise.

The DeVos camp agreed with that analysis. Manager McNeilly fired off an e-mail after hearing about my report. With "all due respect," this was no more a breaking story than the Chamber of Commerce blessing DeVos. "History isn't going to give you credibility on this one," he ended his two-sentence analysis of my report. I wrote back, "On this one, we will agree to disagree." But you have to give him credit for manipulating the story with the rest of the media. He created so much fog, nobody saw the fact that DeVos worked hard for, but did not land, the endorsement. McNeilly knew that, but never admitted that to the newspapers. Instead, he told them it was no big deal, and they bought it. Granholm's guys, on the other hand, played it up as a "major endorsement."

Just to make sure I had not screwed up this story, I called one of my GOP sources in Oakland County. This person agreed that the pastors' endorsement was "in play," and it was "not a gimme" for the governor as the DeVos folks wanted viewers to believe. But then this source added another good point, "Skubick, another part of the story is how hard she had to work to get it." That was correct, too. Because some folks in the city were not happy with her, she had to overcome that with the ministers to get their blessing. I also doubled back to Mr. Marks to reconfirm my story, and he reported, "There was never an assumption that either candidate would have the endorsement predetermined."

But there was more to the story from the DeVos camp. For weeks, as the pastors contemplated what to do in the governor's race, unconfirmed reports reached this listening post and others in town that the subject of money had come up in relationship to the endorsement. The unsubstantiated word on the street was that DeVos was offering $250,000 to keep the ministers on the sidelines. I asked Marks about that. He denied it, and said it would be offensive to the ministers if that were the case.

John Truscott revealed a different angle. He says he sent word "through an intermediary" to the council that DeVos did not play the game that way, and then Truscott sort of hinted that maybe some Granholm supporter did play that game. Her side would obviously deny it, and minus any "proof" about "street money," it was just a rumor, but lots of folks had heard it.

Now back to the subject of debates. Mr. Fox was back on the phone with some juicy stuff for this book. On August 6, the Granholm inner circle held a 90-minute meeting on debates. In the room, besides the Boss, were Fox, Rick Wiener, Chris DeWitt, David Lewis Baker, who did debate work for Detroit Mayor Kilpatrick, and campaign manager Edleson stuck his head in and out. First Man Dan Mulhern was not there.

"The Skubick" debate was on the agenda for part of the time. The question was again raised about the advisability of doing this risky no-rules format with me. Again, there were concerns. Turns out some folks, not necessarily in the room at the time, had this notion that I was a "gotcha" kind of reporter.

I had defenders, however, in the meeting who understood my style, and the governor repeated that she had no problem with that. "Tim will be fair," she reassured everyone. She concluded that she had been governor for three and a half years and could handle this type of format. They also discussed broadcasting the thing on

FOX 2 in Detroit to get a bigger audience. Both DeWitt and Fox knew I was working for that station, and the governor found out for the first time that night.

The next day just before a news conference, she mouthed to me, "You are working for Fox." I waited until afterwards to confirm it, saying this was good for everyone, because for the first time in the campaign, a major Detroit station had actually expressed more than a cursory interest in covering it. "We'll see," she told me, as apparently she was not so sure it was a good thing.

But back to the skull session with her kitchen cabinet, as things were wrapping up, Granholm did tell everyone, "I know I'll get a sinking fund question." And everyone had a good laugh. I must admit I got a good chuckle when I heard that, too. That meant I had to craft a similar-type question if this debate thing fell into place.

Fox was now calling, asking me to make the overture to the FOX 2 guys to see if they would join in the fun. Two days later, I talked with news director Dana Hahn, and to put it mildly, she was ecstatic about plucking this plum. She did not flinch when I told her I would be the only moderator. Normally, a station would want to showcase their anchors by allowing them to moderate. "What about the public TV folks, what will they say?" she inquired. I reassured her that would not be a problem.

In the fiercely competitive TV news game in Motown, channels 7 and 4 were pushing hard for their own debate. I told Ms. Hahn that she might be the only Detroit station with one. She liked the sound of that and agreed to discretely contact the other FOX stations in Michigan to see if they would carry the show, too. I asked her to get back to me as quickly as possible on that.

As I juggled all that, I still had my regular job and had decided to do a column on the governor's first ad, in which I took her to task for leaving out the Labor Day pump price cut angle. Meanwhile, the Granholm camp was wondering why DeVos had such high negatives in the last poll. Thirty-two percent of the voters had an unfavorable opinion, and 25% had no opinion.

Stop to think about that for a moment. This guy has spent over $12 million, and 57% of the electorate either doesn't like him or know him. "Were the ads a waste of money?" was the question I put to McNeilly. He had a good response.

The 32% with the negative attitude about this guy correlated to the number of democrats in the state who had no reason to like him in the first place. McNeilly also pointed out that the governor's unfavorables were at 42%, which meant she was no better off than he was, and in fact she was a little worse. And then he focuses on the 25% who had no opinion about his man. He noted that 6% had no opinion about her, which meant everyone had pretty much made up their minds about the governor. With 25% not knowing much about DeVos, McNeilly concluded, "We still have room to grow. She has none. I'll take that dynamic any day." Next, he shares with me the notion that the TV ads, per se, can only do so much for a candidate. "People ultimately get most of their political news from news coverage, not TV ads."

You gotta know that McNeilly lives and breathes this campaign from sunrise to sunset every day of the week. Somebody observed that the Granholm campaign guy was seen on the golf course the other day with a bunch of lobbyists. It was rather a cheap shot, since no one knows if he was "doing his business" on the links. Regardless, McNeilly never hit a single golf ball during the campaign. He was too busy studying presidential race research that showed, "ads flavor perceptions, but they don't tell or inform voters." That was certainly the case with the DeVos ads, which I had criticized for months for being long on the image and miserably weak on content. Ditto for the governor's ads.

That said, the commercials had done their job having moved him from "Dick who?" to "Oh, Yeah. You're Dick DeVos, the guy I've seen on TV."

And then Mc shares a significant insight that could well determine the outcome of this hot little race. It's the inoculation thing. "One of the most unreported stories by the professional political media" in 2005 was DDV's schedule. "He worked his butt off getting to every nook and cranny," the campaign manager reports. The goal was to have "an interactive experience" with citizens, which McNeilly claims is a "vital component of modern campaigns."

DeVos would go into city halls, court houses, businesses, you name it. He would focus on what they call the "influencers among us: the 10% that informally make decisions and recommendations with broad impact and influence on others." We used to call them the opinion leaders. And that is important, Mc goes on, because "DDV was able to build a foundation upon which people will, in the next 13 weeks, defend him and go to bat for him in the face of false advertising." In other words, all that statewide travel—those 89,000 miles they boasted about—had two objectives: boost his name ID, but more importantly, inoculate himself from the negative ads that would eventually hit the airwaves. Once again, an example of how candidates try to control their own destiny.

But on the subject of my own debate destiny, all the confidence I so joyfully exuded in an earlier chapter flew out the window, and I had myself to blame. Stay tuned for more on that. But first, the catchy phrase "Who's your Tiger?" has worked its way into the daily water cooler chatter around the state, as the pennant race looks better and better for the Bengals. Even DeVos got into the game—and struck out!

18

Tigers to Determine Next Governor?

You won't believe this, but we begin this chapter with yet another angle on the race for governor involving the aforementioned Detroit Tigers. I figure that if I make four more references to them, we can officially call this a sports book.

The story that follows is one of those poignant examples of how something seemingly so harmless can turn into a potential political nightmare, and this time the victim was Dick DeVos.

I was working on something on primary election night, August 8, 2006, when I got an e-mail from the DeVos camp. It advised that a "mystery" guest was going to be interviewed in the late innings of the Tiger baseball game that night. It was obvious that DeVos was going to be on, and since I was going to watch the game anyway, I figured this was a two-fer: I would see the Tigs win and see DeVos in a completely different venue, the broadcast booth with the Tiger announcers Rod Allan and Mario Impemba. They were definitely not members of the State Capitol Press Corps, but Allan could have been.

It was somewhere between the fifth and sixth innings when, sure enough, there's DDV sitting between the sportscasters. DeVos is there because his friend Chris Illitch, a member of the Mike Illitch family who owned the team, invited the candidate to stop by. This would be nothing new for viewers, since they had seen a lot of Dick DeVos on all his TV commercials that ran between innings night after night. The advantage of those ads is that they are tightly scripted, and the candidate can't slip and fall. Ah, but live TV was a different can of worms. The guy who came to scarf up some free exposure and impress all the angry white males out there in TV land got something else instead.

The bit began innocently enough with Alan reporting that DeVos was a "huge Tiger fan." DeVos, with his omnipresent smile, gladly nodded his approval. DeVos noted that he was "stunned and elated" that the home team was doing so well. Just then, the umpire got "drilled" in the shoulder, as Impemba continued his play by play. It was the second time that night that the guy calling the balls and strikes had gotten whacked. DeVos was next.

Given that DeVos had been all over the state, Mario wanted to know what the "vibe was about the team out there?"

"This is helping to unify Michigan," DeVos said as he lapsed into his political speak. "It's not been a great few years in Michigan in so many ways." Here I expect him to launch into his plan to turn things around, but he smartly does not. Instead he says, "And what a bright spot. We've been looking for a bright spot. The Tigers are providing us some excitement…and a great bright spot for Michigan."

Thank the Lord the Tigers were providing excitement on the field, cause this interview was going nowhere. DeVos looked totally uncomfortable and out of his element, and it got worse. Innocently, Allen asked "Of all the Tigers you've watched this year, and I'm sure you are fond of all of them, has any one or two that kinda stand out in your mind as a couple of guys who are having a stellar year?"

There's a homerun ball waiting to be slammed over the

fence. Instead, it turned into a bean ball. During the asking of the question, you can see DeVos looking into left field, as he knows, he can't answer this simple inquiry.

"Oh my goodness," he begins as he fumbles for an answer. "That's a hard question," he deadpans to Allen, who doesn't miss a beat. In the best traditional of political interrogators, he tosses it back to DeVos, "You're used to hard questions?" Now the trio is laughing, but DeVos can't laugh forever and tentatively continues, "This has been…it's been a good year. That's so hard to say. The thing that's impressed me is how well they have played together; how well this team has come together…."

Ouch. This is painful to watch. On statewide TV, the GOP candidate for governor, the man who has traveled over 100,000 miles meeting with common folks everywhere, can not name two players in the Tiger's lineup. DeVos is the proverbial deer in the headlights, and the interview mercifully ends without him naming one Tiger.

Wonder what Joe Six-Pack thought about that? Better yet, wonder what the DeVos handlers were thinking as they saw a total melt down? I decided to sit on what I had just seen to see what would happen next. Sure enough. The next morning the phone rang. It was a democratic operative. "Did you see the Tiger's game last night?"

"Yep," I replied.

"DeVos couldn't name any Detroit Tigers," he said and you could hear the glee in his voice.

"No kidding," I deadpanned.

"My wife and I were watching. She was complaining about Granholm getting equal time, and I told her to shut up and watch DeVos."

Later that day, Chris DeWitt checked in wanting to know if I had seen the game. "Did you know DeVos was on?" Yes, I knew and wondered if he had seen it. He had not.

A couple of days went by, and nobody in the media picked up on the story. I had a speaking gig in Gaylord where we were doing what we call "Off the Record-On the Road." Three regulars on the panel and I re-enact our show in front of a live audience, and the

Tiger thing did come up there.

The A.P.'s Kathy Barks Hoffman reported that she was watching the game with about six other people, and they were all amazed at how poorly DeVos had done. There were about 100 people in the room, and I asked for a show of hands, "How many of you saw DeVos?" This was good news for the candidate—only one hand went up from a Lansing lobbyist. I put the mike in his face, "How was it?" "It was uncomfortable to watch," he suggested. Since nobody else had seen it, I filled everyone in on what had happened. But in the back of my mind, to be fair, I also pointed out that candidates live in what we call the bubble, where they lose track of the day, the town they are in, or the name of the host ushering them around. But this was something different. The Tigers were in the pennant hunt, and the whole state was watching—except for the guy who wanted to lead the state.

I asked the audience if it made any difference to them that he didn't know. As I recall, a majority of hands went up. Maybe that suggested they felt DeVos was out of touch, as the democrats had suggested.

I came back to town and still nothing in the mainstream press about the story. Finally, the *Free Press* reports that DeVos had achieved a "political coups" by scoring the interview during the game. Obviously, nobody at the *Freep* had seen the game. A spokesperson for the Fox Sports Network said, "Rod and Mario stuck to baseball-related questions for the most part [because] we have no interest in politicizing the conversation." Next came a news release from the democratic state chair. Tongue in cheek, Mark Brewer lamented that after the DeVos appearance, the Tigers lost five games in a row, and it was obvious DeVos was to blame, he concluded. All this time, the DeVos folks must be thinking they are safe, because other than the playful Brewer statement, nobody had written anything negative about it.

One week and a day after the fateful interview, I was on the campaign trail for the day with DeVos, and in the course of one of our exchanges, I decided to get to the nub of the story. "You couldn't name two Tigers in that interview," I bluntly observed. DeVos chuckles. "You know, I'm a basketball fan, fundamentally...." He goes on to explain that his schedule prevents him from being on top of everything, and he finally confesses, "I went brain dead." I suggested on camera that the democrats might use this little "brain dead" confession to tell voters that DeVos is not "one of us." He quickly dismisses it and notes that on his web site, he had mentioned one of the Tiger aces, Justin Verlander, whose first name I just forgot for a second. The upshot of it all is DeVos does not think this is a big deal, and if someone tries to make it such, "That's sad for Michigan."

The next day, I am thinking it may be time to do this story but I can't unless the democrats make something out of it. So why not ask the governor? Why not? She was attending a news conference where she got the endorsement of a statewide police officers group, and she was in rare form. At the end of her acceptance of the blessing, she says, "Any questions?" There are three of us in the room to ask questions: Larry Lee from Gongwer, Rick Pluta, my public radio buddy, and me. We remain dead silent. The governor advises us that she will only take questions "on this," referring to the endorsement. The silence continues. To reinforce her point about only taking questions on what she wanted to talk about, one of the officers tells us, "We all have guns."

The governor says, "They all have guns."

I asked, jokingly, if that was a threat? She says she was merely repeating what the cop had said, and the whole thing ends right there with some laughter.

Next, they take the appropriate "grin-and-grope" pictures of the governor smiling and shaking hands with the police, and then she moves over to answer the questions we want to ask.

For weeks now, the most popular word in the democratic lexicon has been China, which they use to blame DeVos for creating jobs there while laying off workers in Michigan. But in recent days, a new word is gaining on China. I wanted to know why the governor thought DeVos was so "extreme."

Remember that she has remained on the political high road during all this DeVos bashing, and she is intent on staying right there, despite the directness of my question. She deflects it by not buying the premise of what I was asking, "Well, first of all, I'm not sure I've used that word." Oh she has used the word all right, just never on camera—so far. I tried to nudge her off the high road. So, I try again.

"Will you use the word to describe him?"

And ever so cutely she uses the word—without using the word. "That word is not an inappropriate description of where they are coming from."

As this thing begins to wrap up, I ask her, "Can you name two Tigers?"

"Pudge" she shouts out loud. Then Brandon Inge gets a mention, the Tiger third baseman whose wife has done campaign work for the Granholm campaign, and then for good measure, perhaps showing off just a tad, she also reports she likes outfielder and home-run slugger Craig Monroe. I have a follow up, of course.

"What does it say about a politician if he or she can't name any Tigers?"

With this shocked look on her face, she wonders how that could be possible. She concedes if that politician could not name anyone on the team, "They must be out of touch."

Finally the Q and A is over, and I walk out of the room with her.

"You know where the Tiger questions come from?" I ask as I try to squeeze more out of the story. Oh yeah, she knows but admits she has not seen the now infamous DeVos interview, but she has been told about it. As we get outside, she seems to express a little sympathy for her archrival. That's a first.

"Do you ever go blank on a name?" she asks me as I call her Linda. (No, not really.) I answer in the affirmative and suggest that maybe on this one, she is going to cut DeVos some slack. "I'm not gonna cut any," the always competitive sports fan/governor laughs. She got in the car and that was that.

But later that same day, somebody from her office calls telling me there is a sports show in Detroit, and they have "reportedly" named DeVos the "Monday Afternoon Moron" for not knowing any Tigers. None of this gets into print. DeVos should feel mighty lucky. Weeks after that, who showed up between innings? Yep, the governor. I didn't see it, but was told she was grand, but she was not asked, "Who is your Tiger?" Knowing her, I'm amazed she didn't request the question just so she could show up you-know-who.

Back to more important stuff. Knowing that the use of the word "extreme" or "extremist" would be coming up over and over again, I asked DeVos on my day with him what he thought of the term. I suggest to him leaning against his SUV that it looks as though the dems have focus grouped the word, and it resonates with voters. He agrees.

In one of my interviews with him that day, he says, "Name calling doesn't move us forward. Name calling doesn't create any jobs in Michigan, and while the opposition [notice he does not mention her by name, either] wants to make this personal...it can't be personal. It's got to be about Michigan."

Meanwhile, the newest survey is out and the two are still deadlocked.

Monday, August 14: the long-awaited announcement on the DeVos running mate was going to be made at 10:45 a.m. We were told that in a 7 a.m. e-mail, which meant I had just over three hours to find out who it was. I assumed I was not the only one in town hoping to scoop the DeVos guys.

Actually, I had started working on this running mate story several weeks ago but ran into a brick wall. I was told in no uncertain terms that only three people knew who it was, and they were sworn to secrecy. To confirm that, I called my usual list of GOP suspects to see if they knew, and sure enough, none of them did. I concluded this was going to be a tough assignment. Consequently, I did not waste any more time on it until that early morning e-mail. I tried all sorts of sources and drilled one dry hole after another until....

I ran into one source who graciously told me that at 10:15 a.m. there would be a conference call with key GOP big wigs, and they would be given the name. All I had to do was get to one of them, get down on my knees to beg, and I could get the story before it was announced. You must be saying to yourself, "Come on Skubick. At best, you might get a half-hour jump on the story, so why not let them make the announcement and be done with it?"

Agree, but all of the folks I work for wanted the story in advance, so it was my job to get it. Plus, it was now a game as well.

The DeVos folks were pretty smug—no, make that very smug, about keeping a lid on the announcement, and any reporter would love to remove the smugness.

The clock was ticking toward the 10:45 announcement, and reporters were starting to arrive. I made one phone call at l0:20 to a source who I was sure would help. "No call yet from the DeVos people" was the disappointing comment from this inside source. Now I am thinking this is not going to work, as I headed over to the news conference room. Just before going in, I called this source one more time.

"Have you heard?" I anxiously started the conversation.

"Yeah, but...."

Those are the two worst words in the world. "Yeah, but" means I'm not going to get what I want. The source goes on, "There were only six people on the call. I can't tell you." That meant the DeVos gang might be able to figure out who leaked the story. I pleaded but was getting nowhere fast when it finally hit me. "Look, you don't have to tell me. Just answer this, if I go with the name of Ruth Johnson, am I O.K.?"

"You'd be O.K.," came the reluctant, yet revealing, response. The source had his or her cover and could honestly say he/she did not tell me.

I gave out a big thank you and started to dial the phone. The MIRS newsletter folks were first. They could issue an immediate bulletin to the 2,000-plus subscribers who were all political insiders and would appreciate the scoop. The call to Kyle Melinn took all of about 15 seconds. "It's Ruth Johnson. Go with it," I advised him.

Next, I called the FOX 2 assignment desk in Detroit. They would not be on the air until 11 a.m., but I gave them the name and told them I would call back.

Then It was onto WWJ NewsRadio 950 in Detroit. Earlier in the morning, I told them I could only guess at who it was, but now I had the name and was eager to share. "Let's go live. It's Ruth Johnson," I told the guys on the desk. Within 30 seconds, I could hear the bulletin music in my ear as the morning anchors announced, "Breaking news out of Lansing where our Tim Skubick has the name of the DeVos running mate. Who is it, Tim?" "It's

Oakland County Clerk Ruth Johnson," I reported. Then I went into her background as a former state lawmaker, former Oakland County commissioner, and a now the county clerk. I noted that DeVos needed to win Oakland County, and while the selection of Johnson would not assure that, it certainly could help. The DeVos folks had reached the same conclusion. With the, "Tim Skubick reporting live from Lansing," sign off, I went into the building with a nice smile on my face. I had a 20-minute jump on the story. It wasn't much, but I would take it.

I walked off the elevator and took another call from yet another source who told me it was Johnson. I thanked him/her for the "old" news and turned around and ran into none other than Ruth Johnson coming down the hallway.

"Congratulations," I offered.

She gave me this look like, "What could you possibly mean?"

Johnson had a red, white and blue scarf around her neck and was headed for the room where other female politicians were awaiting the announcement. Outside the room, the rest of the Capitol Press Corps stood. She went in and the door quickly closed behind her. I got a peak at the room, but that was all.

All the scribes were left cooling their heels. Then, there was a huge round of applause and shouts of joy from inside. Obviously, DeVos had just told everyone Johnson was his pick. Finally, the media was let in. DeVos and wife Betsy were at the head of the room, but Johnson was not with them. It was obvious they were going to drag out the suspense a little bit longer. Seated around the table were former and current female legislators, all of whom were part of a regular group that had met over the months with Betsy DeVos. Seated inconspicuously among them was Ms. Johnson.

DeVos smiled that "now famous" Dick DeVos smile, and welcomed everyone to the show. He launched into the requirements he was seeking in a running mate. It was the usual stuff: somebody who could takeover if he was unable to govern, someone with the background and experience to make government work, blah, blah, blah.

While he is going through all this, I happened to catch the

eye of John Truscott, who was basking in the moment. I stared at him and mouthed the name "Ruth Johnson" just to show off a little bit. He smiled and gave me a noncommittal look. Weeks afterwards, J.T. said he immediately thought that Oakland County executive Brooks Patterson had given me the story, but at least he had waited until 20 minutes before the event to do it. "What would you say if I told you it wasn't Brooks?" I asked Truscott. "Really," he blurted out. And I confirmed that it wasn't. But I am sorry to say I cannot reveal the name or names here, because I will need them again somewhere down the road.

Back to DeVos, who moves closer to the announcement. He concludes, "And so I am proud to announce the next lt. governor of the State of Michigan [pause for dramatic effect] Ruth Johnson."

The joint erupts again as she gets up and heads to the front. First, there is a hug from Betsy and Dick, and there she stands waiting for the pep rally cheering to die down. She unfolds her script and begins by saying what a proud day this is for her and her family, who she introduces but she quickly adds, "This is not about me." It's about the state, of course, and how it is time for a change and how the DeVos administration will be that change agent and so on and so forth.

To the reporters in the room, the calculus on this one made sense. He needed Oakland County support, and he probably needed a female on the ticket as well. Both Johnson and DeVos would later deny that, but Johnson told a very female story during her acceptance speech. She recalled that when she was 14, her father died, and it was just her mother and three kids. Johnson said she wanted to get a job as a newspaper boy. She used that "boy" term on purpose, as she told the audience the local newspaper only hired boys and men and not girls or women. Johnson reveals she got the job anyway. On the application, she reveals she used the name of her next-door neighbor, Kevin.

The women in the room got it and responded accordingly while the media watched. She finished, and the Q and A began. Johnson seemed a little nervous, which was normal. Even though she had served in the legislative trenches for a number of years, she had rarely gotten this kind of attention.

I watched from the back of the room. Often times, before answering a question, she looked at DeVos to see if he wanted to handle it first. After about 15 minutes, I wanted to find out if she would take a shot at the governor. Many in the room thought Johnson would be the attack dog, while DeVos stayed on the high road. I wondered if that was the case.

"Having served in the legislature with her, how effective is the governor as a leader?" I innocently asked. Johnson ducked. She talked about how the state needed effective leadership, and how she and DeVos would provide that. I essentially repeated the question and got the same non-response. I figured they had told her not to blast the governor—at least not at this event.

The news conference broke up, and reporters moved in for more questions with the two candidates. DeVos told us the lt. governor nominee did not have to be a woman, and while the Oakland County vote was important, he figured "statistically" he could still win without it. Yeah, but it would be a long shot.

Johnson explained that she had not been told to lay off the governor, and then she left to do a radio interview. Not much more came out of the session, so I moved to the back of the room just to watch.

I put State Senator Nancy Cassis on camera. The Oakland County republican was on the list for lt. governor, but she expressed no regrets and said only nice things about Ms. Johnson. That never got on the air. As I was leaning against the door, Mr. DeVos and sidekick Greg McNeilly came up to shake hands and do a little gloating—right in front of me.

"Hey, we got ya," DeVos smiled even broader than before. They knew I wanted the story in advance and had run into one blind alley after another. I let them gloat a little more and then advised them, "I had it on the air at 10:38." Now we all laughed. I got no pat on the head, nor did I expect one. I conceded that they had done a great job at keeping it a secret for so long, but I did get it first and did pre-empt them—by a lousy 20 minutes. But a scoop is scoop, no matter how meager it is.

I had one more piece of business involving Ms. Johnson. A couple of days earlier, one of my really great inside contacts had told me that Secretary of State Terri Lynn Land had "shouted" at Johnson on the phone. Since last May, Clerk Johnson had been very vocal about the new optical scan voting machines that had been installed statewide. Johnson reported a 15% error rate when voters used them. Then on the eve of the August 8 primary, Johnson was back at it again, forecasting long lines, machine breakdowns and all sorts of voting chaos if the machines failed again. Land was concerned. Her political neck was on the line, and if there was a voting screw-up, her neck could be politically severed. I ran a story on this, and no sooner had it hit the MIRS newsletter, there was Kelly Chesney, who handles media relations for Land, on my line. "Your story is wrong," was her opening salutation. She wanted me to do a "make good" by talking to elections director Chris Thomas, who would put a more positive spin on the negative story on behalf of his boss the secretary. I did and wrote another story putting his two-cents worth into the mix. My source said that Land had called Johnson, and the two had an animated discussion. Now with the lt. governor candidate in my sights, I wanted to see if I could get her to admit it.

I started out innocently enough, asking Johnson to recount the problems at the most recent election. She is very forthcoming, reporting that some of her local clerks had to call in their husbands to use duck tape, what else, to make sure the machines worked. When I covered her in the legislature, I found her to be accessible and always direct, and as one observer put it, "Once she latches onto something, she won't let go." The voting machine issue was exhibit A. "It's taxpayer's money. We should have gotten a product that was 100%. We're working on it," she advised me.

With the TV camera grinding, we got to the good stuff. "Terri Lynn Land was not happy with you on your comments about this stuff?"

Johnson stands her ground but ignores the thrust of my question. "I spoke with her. I'm hoping she comes up with the action plan so we can get all of this fixed." Notice, no reference to the "happy" part of my question. One of DeVos's handlers, Phil Novack, has been standing next to Johnson during the interview, and sensing that this was slowly getting out of hand, he moves in and gently moves Johnson to the door and away from me. They walk. I walk.

"Did she tell you she was unhappy? She hollered at you, didn't she?"

They continue to walk. I wait for an answer—that never came. "Thank you madam clerk," I said as we got a shot of her moving off camera.

I wrote a column on the Land vs. Johnson thing in which the Land folks completely denied the "shouting" match. They called it a "gross misrepresentation." But I had two sources who confirmed it. The column ran, and I ran into McNeilly, who reported that my sources had left out one important part of the story. Land had sent a dozen roses to Johnson to congratulate her on getting the second spot on the ticket, but he denied that it had anything to do with the "shouting." And, he informed me that Land was going to give the nominating speech for Johnson at the party convention that very weekend. That only confirmed one thing: the story was true. And weeks after that, Johnson told me, with a smile on her face, she would have to watch out for me on the campaign trail. The feeling was mutual.

Until the bitter end, the DeVos camp kept that lid on the list of other potential running mates. But the other names were reported to be L. Brooks Patterson, who was given the customary first right of refusal, which he exercised. Next, came Congresswoman Candice Miller, who reportedly expressed more than a passing interest in the post. But the talks never got to first base because Karl Rove killed it from the White House. He feared losing her seat in the Congress. Other unconfirmed names included Kathy Wilbur, lobbyist for Central Michigan University; Nancy McKeague, from the Michigan Health and Hospital Association; Beth Chapel, a Detroit businesswoman; Gail Torreano, who runs the Michigan branch of ATT; another Detroit businesswoman Cynthia Pasky; Paul Hillegonds, of DTE Energy; and current Ann Arbor police chief Barnett Jones.

19

Earth Moves
for Granholm

On this August 24, 2006, we are at the 75-days-to-go mark in this hotly contested race, and we have plenty of new and significant dots to connect in this chapter. (A) For the first time since she sat on a 20-point lead way back when, the governor now has a seven-point edge in the latest survey. Talk about your flip-flops. And the DeVos folks are attacking the pollster who released the numbers. No surprise there. (B) For the first time, Dick DeVos has broken with the White House on an issue near and dear to the State of Michigan. And (C) the TV debate has taken a turn. For better or for worse? Read on.

Let's begin with my own personal perception: I can begin to feel the earth move in Granholm's direction, and the proof comes from the DeVos camp. She was finally showing some strength on the weight of her new ads and some post-Google job gains, even though the state's jobless rate staggered at a not so glorious 7%. This notion of movement was confirmed for me as the DeVos campaign launched the "Honda" ad. It was really the first TV spot that singled the governor out for failing to land the Honda plant that went to Indiana. Recall that she was in Japan at the time the Honda decision was being made, and she did not meet with the Honda officials at the time. She did send her team and told us that she had met with Honda earlier, but none of that stuff was in the GOP ad. No surprise there either.

Some segments of the media described it as the first "attack" ad of the season, but that was an overstatement. This ad was on her leadership abilities, which was certainly fair game. Nonetheless, based on what I had seen from the DeVos boys over the last months, it was clear that she was making some inroads in the race, which is why the negative ad came out. They were trying to bring her down, and what better way to do it than by telling viewers she blew it when it came to creating new auto industry jobs.

My suspicion was confirmed by the DeVos insiders, who revealed that every time she started to move in the polls, they would move on the air to beat her back.

On the Granholm side, when the Honda spot hit the airwaves, the first response was sort of, "Whoa, what's this?" They were taken aback for a moment, but then it sunk in for them as it did for me. If DeVos was running negative spots, she must be gaining ground. The surprise morphed into a satisfying smile on the governor's side, I am told.

Another DeVos event documented they were even more concerned that she was making headway. The DeVos campaign took on President Geroge Bush, who was taking hits from other republicans all over the nation.

First, some context. The president's popularity numbers were right down there with journalists, used-car salespersons and murderers. A meager 37% of the citizens gave him good marks, and even though he was not on the ballot in November, lots of republicans were. So rather than go down with the ship, they were, like rats, jumping the *S.S. Bush*. DeVos showed every sign of joining the exodus when he staged a rare and hastily arranged news conference in the middle of the afternoon on August 23. To my recollection, it was the first full-blown news conference that he had called since he announced over a year ago. In that regard, he was acting like the guy he was about to blast.

All the Capitol Press Corps regulars were there when DeVos walked in his signature blue sport coat, no tie, and no signature smile. However, he tried to kick it off with a funny. His "podium" was a series of boxes stacked on top of one another with a DeVos sign at the apex. He made note of how cheap the whole thing looked, but nobody laughed. Greg McNeilly spoke first, advising us that the candidate was on a tight schedule, which meant he would not be hanging around for a ton of questions. Maybe he had a tight schedule, maybe not. I got the impression that the "sked" excuse was to allow him to get out of Dodge when the questioning got tough.

DeVos launched into his spiel. He was calling on the White House to "get it done" and meet with the Big Three automakers asap. This story had been percolating on and off since last May when the Big Three car guys announced they wanted to huddle with the president to discuss foreign trade and health care. This was now August, they were still cooling their heels and DeVos wanted that to stop.

"It is not about politics. It's about jobs…let's make this meeting happen," he told us. Asked what kind of "politics" the president was playing, DeVos had no idea, but he sure knew that the governor was playing politics, and it was time for her to stop, too.

John Lindstrom from the Gongwer news service noted that this had been a long-running story, so why was "Dick," as he referred to him, getting into this now? Well, turns out in the morning, *Detroit News* columnist Daniel Howes had lambasted the president for stiffing the auto industry moguls. Howes basically said Bush was telling the Big Three to "drop dead." Having read that, DeVos decided it was time for him to move the situation off dead center. I was not alone in theorizing he had a hidden agenda, too. But I never got a chance to ask my pointed question, because after seven minutes, DeVos left Dodge, leaving McNeilly at the front of the O.K. Corral.

"Will you take some questions?" I asked him. He nodded yes, and we were off for another round.

For months, the Granholm campaign had been linking DeVos to Bush and blaming the president for Michigan's economic case of pneumonia, so I wanted to know if this news conference was in any way designed to put some distance between DeVos and the prez in order to blunt the Granholm attacks. "No," was the crisp response from McNeilly. He went on, "This is about doing the right thing." He told us DeVos made the attack "after seeing a continued lack of respect shown by the White House to the largest employers in this state."

I wasn't buying it as the only reason, and I was pretty sure the transparency of the news event was not lost on the rest of the crowd in that room either. When we got done, everyone was handed a press release, which was even stronger than the candidate's news conference remarks. "It is wrong, and the behavior is inexcusable. The president needs to meet with the Big Three and it must happen soon. Jobs are at stake," DeVos was quoted by his own campaign. And for good measure he adds, "When I am governor, things will be different. I won't ask for a meeting, I will 'tell' them we are having a meeting. It is sad that our governor cannot make a meeting happen. This is just incompetence all around."

Hold the phone. Last time I checked, governors did not "tell" the White House what meetings to hold, and to accuse this governor of not being able to pull it off was a bit disingenuous. After all, she was a democrat with little or no influence on Pennsylvania Ave., and I was not so sure that even republican DeVos, as governor, could throw his weight around to get it done either, but it made for a nice quote.

As you can imagine the Granholm machine went into high gear to put its spin on all this. No sooner did the press corps leave the DeVos newser, than we got this message from Chris DeWitt from her side. He fired off press releases showing the governor had been calling for the meeting for months, and all the way back to November 2003, she had called on the president to change federal trade policies to help the auto sector. Then, DeWitt blames DeVos for causing this problem in the first place. Geez, there was a sorts of stretching going on around this story. "Dick DeVos was the largest contributor to Bush-Cheney 2004, but in front of the cameras, he's happy to sing a different tune. This time he's not lying about the governor's record, he's lying about his own."

Then he points to a 1993 *Grand Rapids Press* article in which DeVos says the auto industry should "stop crabbing" about foreign competition adding, "I'm not very sympathetic with the auto industry, because some of their problems are self-inflicted....The problem is not with Japan, it's with the American auto industry," DeVos is quoted in the article.

Even Liz Boyd got into the action, and she seldom ventured into the political fray. The governor's media secretary fired off "proof" that Granholm had been involved dating back to July of 2005, when she called on Bush to meet with domestic automotive leaders. There were no less than 18 citations to document the fact that Granholm was in there battling for the car guys. Boyd and I chatted about it late that afternoon, and she raised an interesting point that I had not thought about. Maybe the news conference was a set up? Perhaps DeVos had word from the White House that it was going to meet with the Big Three after DeVos demanded the meeting.

Couldn't you see it? A picture of "W" standing with the car leaders, and DeVos could take credit for making it happen. Take that, Jennifer Granholm. As it turned out, the White House did issue a statement some time after that saying the meeting would be staged after the November balloting. And the president made a much-publicized call from Air Force One to Bill Ford, Jr., who ran the company with the same last name. He was hanging on to his own job by a thread.

In a true irony, the DeVos comments came on the very day that White House operative Karl Rove was at a Grosse Pointe fundraiser and national GOP party chair Ken Mehlman was crisscrossing the state, too. Mehlman had no choice but to take both sides of the controversy. He said he appreciated "where Dick DeVos was coming from on this." But maintaining his loyalty to the president, he added that the charges that the W.H. was indifferent to the Detroit-based carmakers was "inaccurate and unfortunate." In fact, he said, without saying it, DeVos was wrong. The Bush administration was not 'sending that message."

Whatever the motivation was, DeVos had hit a nerve, and I was wondering how the rest of the media played this thing the day after. Dawson Bell of the *Detroit Free Press* got it right when he wrote, "Wednesday's announcement was clearly an attempt by DeVos to create some daylight between himself and the president." At the Booth Newspapers, Peter Luke reported the remarks of Chris Dewitt: "Calling President Bush incompetent is one of DeVos's biggest steps to distance himself from a president he has supported both financially and on policy issues." To me, DeVos had tossed a high hard one at the president because he had to do it. He was slipping in the polls. Granholm was gaining ground. A seven-point lead was nothing to sneeze at. And while there was no outward sign of panic, I knew Team DeVos would try to reverse the trend before it got away from them.

The DeVos campaign had hoped that the aforementioned Honda ad would help, but pollster Ed Sarpolus reported it was not meeting expectations. Many union workers did not give a hoot that a non-union carmaker had chosen another state. Sarpolus, who released the new poll on the same day as the White House attack, has his own take on why the governor had this lead. "After 16 million dollars, people still don't know who DeVos is," Sarpolus opined with the cross-tabs to back it up.

Heretofore, DeVos had battled Granholm for that all-important independent vote. Granholm, in the new EPIC-MRA survey for the *Detroit News*, WXYZ-TV, WILX-TV, WJRT-TV, and WOOD-TV, had a six-point lead with independent men and a very respectable 24-point lead with independent women. That was a first for her. Another first for her: she beat him 50% to 42% for the over-40 female vote, but more importantly, she erased his former lead with the under-40 female crowd by another respectable 23 points. The earth was shifting. She remained behind with women with no college education but had 33% of the women who called themselves pro-life. That was the rock-bed of the DeVos political base, and the Right to Life folks would not be happy with that, and neither would he.

This new poll offered up some categories to look at, which confirmed that the DeVos "businessman" message was resonating but with only one group—those without jobs. He clobbered her 70% to 23%. But those who had full- and part-time jobs, those who were self-employed and the retired were all going for Granholm. DeVos was within striking distance, but those groups were apparently not buying what he was selling.

Sarpolus hit again on democratic themes that were working against DeVos: China and Amway. So far, DeVos had not answered those issues in his paid advertising. It was only a matter of time before he had to, because the democrats had an ad on China to blame him for the umpteenth time for ignoring Michigan while helping out a Communist country. Interestingly, in the DeVos shop, they were totally discounting any of the data from the Sarpolus poll, as they were getting very close to basically ignoring him in the future by refusing to comment to the media on the results he was getting.

Apart from all that activity on the campaign trail, the phone was ringing at my desk today with some unexpected good news regarding a debate. When we last left this saga, everything was sort of up in the air, because we could not find a date and time to do the thing. In subsequent conversations with Mark Fox and then with the FOX 2 folks, it was painfully clear the baseball playoffs were screwing up the works, even if the Tigers were not in them.

The playoffs were set to start on October 3 with one game at 4 p.m. and another at 8 p.m. So why not do the debate at 7 p.m.? What if the first game went into extra innings? Then you had the unsavory prospect of the two candidates and yours truly sitting there ready to go, waiting for some pitcher to get a third out, and who knows how long that could take? Under the worse-case scenario, there would be no debate or one that lasted less than a hour. The "solution" was to stage the event on Monday night before the playoffs kicked off. But attorney Fox nixed that "easy" solution. At the proposed starting time of 7 p.m., Yom Kippur was still going on, and there was no way the governor was going to intrude on the sacred Jewish holiday. I figured DeVos would think the same thing. I felt this whole shebang slipping away, but days later Mr. Fox called back. He had checked and discovered that the holiday would end at 7:46 p.m. on that Monday night, which meant the debate could start at 8 p.m. in prime time. The only question was would all the public stations and FOX 2 agree to the shift from 7 to 8 p.m.?

It was back to the phones to get the answers. Kent Wieland at WKAR-TV e-mailed all the Michigan public stations, and they signed off. The word was not nearly as encouraging at the commercial station. The new fall season was beginning on October 2, and the blockbuster show "Prison Escape" was slated for 8 p.m. Fox 2 news director Dana Hahn and I bemoaned the fact. I was pretty sure the higher ups would never sacrifice an evening of revenue to perform a public service. She was just as eager as I was to carve out a compromise somehow, so she suggested the station could run the show at 11 p.m. the same night it aired live on public TV. I was pretty sure that would not ring the bell in the Granholm camp. I told her I would check on that alternative, and she promised to get back to me after the suits had discussed the 8 p.m. airtime.

The drama continued when Mr. Fox called me trying to gently nudge me to get a final answer so he could tell the governor. She apparently was getting antsy, and he wanted to please his boss. Working on the assumption that we would never get the FOX folks to pop for the coveted 8 p.m. slot, I suggested doing it on Thursday, September 28, and Fox said maybe we could do it on Sunday, October 8. I went back to WKAR-TV and asked for a third time to poll the other stations on those alternative dates. After I put that into motion, I called Ms. Hahn to check on those times, as I desperately tried to salvage this thing.

"You're going to be sorry you ever hired me," I began as I realized this debate thing was getting to be a pain. Then I started out, "Could we do this on September 28 or October 8?" and she interrupted me.

"Hold on," she joyfully stopped me in my tracks, "They will do it at 8 p.m. on October 2!"

"I can't [expletive deleted] believe it," I shouted back.

"Neither can I," she echoed.

"I'll get back to you with the details," I told her, and with that I called the other Fox in this triad.

"Are you sitting down?" I began in a low-key and rather solemn voice. Fox picked up on it, and in a dejected tone asked, "Now what?" He must have been thinking here was one more hurdle I was going to toss at him.

Instead I said, "They'll do it at 8 p.m." He was astonished, too.

I said I would write a letter to both camps and make a new offer, hoping that the other side would jump at this chance. I hand delivered the revised debate proposal the next day right after we taped OTR. Kent Wieland had the letters ready for me when I walked out of Studio C. I made a quick phone call to McNeilly.

"Are you gonna be there for a while?" I asked, not wanting to drive to the other side of town and find him out.

"Yeah, but what do you want?" he cautiously asked.

"I need to talk to you about something...about the debates." He said he would be there.

Even though I had resolved the "ethical" issue weeks ago, still very much on my mind was the glaring fact that for several weeks, I had been engaged in a series of secretive discussions with Fox about this debate. I wanted to share that with McNeilly, knowing that there was a possibility he might be hacked. I didn't think that would be the case, but with everything starting to heat up, one can never be sure if your instincts are correct. To resolve this thing one way or the other was part of the reason I wanted to hand deliver the debate letter rather than wait four days for him to reply. I frankly did not want to ruin my weekend by worrying about his reaction. I strolled into the office, and the first guy I encountered was Phil Novack, one of the DeVos handlers.

"I owe you a C," I blurted out. In that day's MIRS newsletter, I did a story in which I misspelled his name twice. I wrote Novak when it is really Novack. He let me off the hook, and up walks McNeilly. We moved to his office, and I announced that I was now appearing as a TV producer and not a reporter. I handed him the letter. It said we were revising our original proposal and offering October 2 at 8 p.m. on the public TV and FOX 2 stations.

I studied his face for any visible reaction one-way or the other. There were no signs. He finished reading it, and said it sounded interesting. He checked his computer and then smiled. He had already written in October 2 as a possible debate night. I was afraid DeVos had another prom gig with his daughter.

"What does a no-rules debate mean?" he asked. It meant no opening statements. One minute for closing statements to be determined by a flip of the coin, and the rest of it would just happen. No time restraints on answers and the opportunity for the two candidates to actually talk to one another. How novel. He seemed cool with that but for one point.

"What if one candidate gets more time than the other?"

I explained that over the years, I used my internal clock to judge the time as the debate was rolling along. And if one or the other started to go on too long, I knew how to cut them off. This time fairness issue had been a constant thing with McNeilly. He wrote letters, as I mentioned before, to news directors complaining about his guy getting 10 seconds less than Granholm. I tried to address his concerns by quickly suggesting that I would appoint someone to sit in the control room and keep a stopwatch on each answer. If there was an imbalance, they could relay that to me through my earpiece on the set, and I could make the mid-course corrections. I was more than willing to do that because I also wanted to be fair to both sides, and this was one way to assure that.

"8 p.m.—prime time," he said. He liked that. Fox was concerned that having it at 8 on a commercial Detroit TV station might scare McNeilly away. After all, somebody might actually see the debate, and DeVos was not a champ at that. However, as I studied McNeilly, he was not shaking in his boots. I thought to myself, this is going well.

"What does Fox [the lawyer] think about this?" McNeilly wondered. If we were going to have a problem over my back channel discussions with the other side, I thought it could happen right here and right now. "I have every reason to believe this will be acceptable to him," I advised him.

I knew he would want to know how I could say that, so I just up and told him, "I have talked to Fox about this."

McNeilly did not balk nor did he say, "You SOB. Why were you talking to him and not me?"

Being the pro that he was, just like Fox, McNeilly understood.

"I know that Fox holds all the cards here," he let me off easily.

I agreed, adding, "I could have talked with you first, but what good would that have done?"

I could see the wheels turning and McNeilly, now knowing that I had been in conversation with the other side, did what anyone would do: he tried to pump me for more information. He wanted to know how many debates Fox was going to offer, because he said doing our debate would be tied into that. "We accept your debate but with an asterisk," he suggested. "If they are going to give us only one debate and this is it, we will want to offer it to more TV stations." I knew they were going to get more than one but did not let on. "If ours is the only debate, we would be open to allowing other stations to carry it," I said as I tried to address his second major concern. He pressed for more information, but I told him I could not play the game. I had made a commitment to the other side not to play the go-between. Had I been working with McNeilly, I would have honored the same pledge to him. He understood that, too. It does help to have a long-term relationship with the folks you are dealing with, because it takes time to develop a mutual trust.

I told him I was on my way to drop off the same letter to Fox and asked McNeilly if it was O.K. to tell Fox that the DeVos folks were signing off on this debate with that caveat. McNeilly had no problem with that. At this point, I shared with him that I had been concerned about the appearance that I was cooperating with the other side and not with him. Again, he reiterated that in order to get the job done, he knew I had to start with Fox. "It was my job to get this debate," I repeated. He nodded in agreement. We shook hands, and I was off to see Fox.

I was relieved to get that ethical monkey off my back. Now I could shift my worries to other stuff, but Fox was not one of them. I got on the cell. "Mark? Skubick. How long you gonna be there? I just hand delivered the letter to McNeilly and want to give you a copy."

"How did it go?" he obviously wanted to know. I told him I would tell him when I saw him. He would have none of that, so I revealed, "It went well. See ya in five minutes."

I had been in Fox's office numerous times over the years. He was actually lucky to be sitting in his big leather chair when I rolled in. On January 17, 2006, he had been spread eagle on the floor, suffering from a sudden cardiac death. It's only because somebody in the office knew how to use a defibrillator that he was alive. He tells the story that moments after he got to the hospital, the governor showed up, too. "Mark, you're causing a lot of trouble," she told him. He responded from the gurney in the E.R., "Don't you have anything better to do?" He was touched by her arrival in his hour of need. Fortunately, there was no damage to his heart. We get back to the matter at hand of working out the delicate debate details. I foolishly believed everything was finally set in stone. Silly me.

Fox reveals that the governor has signed off on the WKAR debate and three others. I could see that my calendar for early October would be wall-to-wall debate coverage. There was our debate on the 2nd, WOOD-TV was getting one on the 10th, WXYZ Channel 7 was doing a town hall session, which was the governor's idea, on the 12th. Then it would end with the Detroit Economic joint appearance on the 16th.

With the debate "back and forth" finally out of the way, Fox settles back in his chair. Now we are just shooting the breeze. He confesses that he is a "debate freak," as he shows me a scrapbook filled with debate memorabilia from his previous debate negotiations. He also takes the opportunity to once more remind me that he wants podiums for the October 2 meeting. "Yeah, yeah, yeah, Mark, I concede the podiums to you," even though I wanted the candidates to sit in chairs. McNeilly had raised the podium issue too. Now that we had an agreement in principle, there was plenty of time to hammer out the particulars.

Fox predicts that Granholm is going to do well against DeVos and seems a tad surprised that the DeVos gang did not balk at the proposal. "Look for a letter from the governor to confirm all this," he tells me, and then look for some sort of public announcement about the four debates.

Fox was fixing to head up north to spend a week with his wife at some camp run by the University of Michigan. I was headed home to remove a pretty-good-sized tree that had fallen over our driveway during a thunderstorm the night before. From one form of debate heavy lifting to another. It had been a great day, but my euphoria was short lived.

20

Amway, Conventions, and a Day with

Labor Day weekend. Ugh, the end of summer. That means the campaign only gets more intense as the push to November goes up another notch. Double ugh.

Back in chapter something-or-other, we talked about the Amway card being played. I think I reported it was only a matter of time. It's time. And none other than Jennifer Granholm played it. Up until recently, other democratic minions would mention the name Amway, but the governor always shied away. Last weekend at the state democratic convention, she was anything but shy. "My opponent was the CEO of Amway," she bellowed at Cobo Hall to three thousand shouting democrats. "Amway used to stand for the American Way. Is it the American Way," she asked "to ship American jobs overseas?" Never mind that DeVos says he is not guilty.

A couple of days after the speech, an e-mail arrived inviting me to take a gander at a new elongated video that democrats had on the web. It was called "See Dick Run." It was a little cartoon lampooning DeVos for sending jobs to China. They even had a head shot of him in a boat headed overseas. They used a little kid's voice, and she told us, "See Dick get a business from his Daddy. It's called Amway....See Amway sales go down. Down and down. Dick has to do something. See Dick downsize. See Dick layoff workers. See jobs go bye bye Michigan."

The quick response team at DeVos headquarters refuted virtually every line in the democratic script, saying it was "Dick who provided leadership to cut the fat out of management and protect factory jobs." It quotes the *Detroit News* and *Free Press,* saying the "shipping Michigan jobs to China" charge was "phony, demagoguery [and] the allegation does not check out."

Party Chair Mark Brewer turned a deaf hear to that and followed up with a news release getting into something a little more serious. He brought up stuff that I stumbled across last January when I ran a Google check on Amway. Turns out the company had some legal problems. Brewer was more direct. "Amway is not the good corporate citizen it claims to be...Amway has been found guilty in numerous lawsuits around the world."

And then he lists some of them, as he accuses DeVos of "trying to hide the fact that they have pleaded guilty to fraud and was forced to pay a $25-million fine to the Canadian government." He reports the Canadian trade office slapped the firm with a suit, blaming Amway for "undervaluing its merchandise to avoid paying full custom duties." The company reportedly shelled out $38 million to settle the suit in 1989. In a little play on words, the comical Brewer ends his release with, "These lawsuits are just the tip of the pyramid." Boom. Ching. (Amway officials were accused of running an illegal pyramid scheme but were not found guilty of the charge.) So now the Amway-run-in-with-the-law cat is out of the bag. So what?

Two weeks before all this information broke, I spent the day with DeVos and asked him on camera about Amway's run in with the law. At first he joked about me giving him "inside" information about stories that were not in the news as of yet. I knew it was only a matter of time and recorded his answer for use at a later date. He says none of the legal woes occurred on his watch, as he dismissed it as ancient history.

Don't kid yourself. The Amway/Alticore folks knew this was coming, which is why current company president Doug DeVos started months ago to visit editorial boards around the state. The effort was to inoculate the company from these broadsides. In recent weeks, Doug DeVos has been back on that circuit doing the same thing again. He spent an hour or more in the living room of political analyst Bill Ballenger, who gave DeVos my name to call. I'm still waiting for the phone to ring.

Seeing the need to do more than that, the company just started running TV commercials for the first time in over a decade. Oh joy for the TV stations in Flint, Grand Rapids and Detroit—more money from the DeVos pocketbooks. These spots feature company workers talking about how great Alticor is to them. Doug DeVos told Kathy Barks Hoffman at the AP that "If people are going to define our company, we'd rather our employees be heard. They are the experts. We are running these ads because, in the hallways and on the factory floor, our employees feel like our company is under attack." They ain't seen nothing yet.

Of course, the two camps had to check in on the Amway spots. Democrats, rather predictably, saw it as just another way to promote Dick DeVos, while his defenders said there was no coordination. John Truscott told Hoffman he didn't think it would benefit DeVos.

Trying to top the comical Mr. Brewer, Chris DeWitt suggested, "If anyone believes that Amway [ah, it's Alticor] isn't doing this to help Dick DeVos and his run for governor, I want to talk to them about buying some soap from me." Boom. Boom. Rim shot.

So maybe you are asking, what in the heck does this have to do with the contest for governor? Pollster Ed Sarpolus, who first raised the Amway thing in his polls weeks ago, was on the horn suggesting that the company ad might backfire. Remember that DeVos has studiously avoided associating himself with Amway in his commercials, and I bet you most voters don't even know he worked there. By running commercials about Amway, it gives the media a chance to write about the spots and then report that Dick DeVos was the CEO. To the degree that anybody still reads the newspapers, the public awareness on the Amway and DeVos connection could go up. At least that's how Eddie sees it. DeVos himself tried to take the edge off the Amway thing in his own convention speech in Novi last weekend. "There is only one candidate in this race who has developed a business selling Michigan products in more than 70 countries across the globe, and there is only one candidate in this race who knows what it takes."

So voters, take your pick. Is Dick DeVos the unethical business guy who would try to cheat his way to fatter profits, or he is the business visionary who can lead Michigan to the economic Promised Land?

While the Amway angle moved into the limelight, behind the scenes, even though it looked as though the debate puppy was doing just fine, my psyche took a hit earlier this week when I caught up with the DeVos campaign bus in Lansing. After my chats with McNeilly from the DeVos camp and Mark Fox from the Granholm side on the public TV/FOX debate, that afternoon, Fox issued a press release revealing that the governor had agreed to those four debates. I read it around 3 p.m. that Friday and waited for a response from the DeVos guys. And I waited. Saturday. Nothing. Sunday. Nothing. Monday. Finally something, but not what I wanted to hear.

The whole session that morning began on a humorous note as DeVos took another shot at me. I'm losing count here, but I think he is ahead. Just after he got off the bus, DeVos and I huddled, as he ragged on me about a recent column. I strongly suggest that he needs to explain how he would replace the money when the single business tax was buried. He tried to deflect my comments about him by reminding me the governor had not done that, either. I said I knew that and had written that as well. Just then, McNeilly joins the confab, and I bring up the issue of debates and can immediately feel there is a problem. They won't agree to any of them. "Well" I blurted out, "I guess I don't need to buy a new suit for the debate." DeVos zinged me as he strolled away, "You could use one." Funny line. What he didn't know is the new suit had been purchased a week ago.

Sensing there was a story here, I got my cameraman and put

McNeilly on. His comments on the governor's debate suggestions were: "It was a political stunt. It was unprofessional. It was not businesslike."

"Ah, come on you guys," I lamented. Just when it appeared everything was set, here comes these complaints about the unilateral announcement of the debates by Granholm.

They were especially hacked that the Granholm release suggested that DeVos was negligent for not scheduling a TV debate in the Detroit market. When I first read that, I thought it was rather childish to take a shot at DeVos. DeVos thought it was wrong, but it was left to McNeilly to let it all hang out. "They put out a false press release...they are trying to bully the campaign into a series of three debates that they chose...it's inappropriate, and this may, in fact, impede the process." Not exactly music to my ears. I slowly slipped into a momentary funk as I see the debate headed down the crapper. But then I reviewed some of the additional comments they were also making. DeVos said, "We will get debates." McNeilly added, "We want debates, and that may very well be the debates."

Ah, that felt better. It finally dawned on me. What was going on here was the DeVos gang was staking out their turf for the September 5 meeting in which all this would be ironed out. Days later, I got John Truscott on the phone.

"You know those four debates are just about what we wanted," he advised me. Now I was feeling much better and called my news director at FOX 2 in Detroit. I had been keeping Dana Hahn advised, along with my public TV folks, and now I could tell her I was very sure this would happen. She wanted me to do a story on it and assigned the FOX 2 chopper to pick me up at the Capitol City Airport to fly me in for a live shot at 5 and 6 p.m. in Southfield. I kissed Gayle good-bye, told her the life insurance was paid up, said I loved her a whole bunch and dashed off to the airport. Three hours later, I was back home, having broken the news that FOX 2 and Public TV had nailed down the one-on-one meeting with Granholm and DeVos. But still, in the back of my head, I said to myself, until I'm sitting across from them in Studio A and waiting for the cue to start, there was still a chance the whole thing could blow up. Without knowing it, I was right. I continued to draft debate questions, however, just to keep my thinking on a positive keel.

There was not much positive stuff in the governor's acceptance speech at the State Democratic Convention that I mentioned earlier. You could use the term "brass knuckles" as one way to describe her comments. Twenty-eight words into the address, she starts using the word "fight," which she then went on to use in one form or another 20 more times.

"I have gotten up every day to fight for you."

"I'm fighting for you every day."

"I tell you today that we will win this election, because we know who we are fighting for and what we are fighting against." Wow, two "fighting's" in one sentence.

I suggested in a column that with all that fighting going on, it looked like she was really running for Heavyweight Champion of the World. Remember, earlier we talked about the Joe Klein book on politics and how finding the right word to use was a critical thing. It was clear to me that the word "fighter" had been tested, and audiences obviously liked it, otherwise it would not have shown up 21 times in one speech.

Granholm had taken some punches herself from the other side for not being a leader, and she hoped to overcome that with the voters by promoting the fighter persona.

"People like to hear that," she told me post speech, as she justified the use of the fighter term.

There were other words, too. By now you can guess them: China, President Bush, Governor Engler. All the usual suspects were peppered here and there throughout her remarks. There was another theme that was woven throughout the address, but the term was never mentioned, per se: class warfare. That was another issue that I identified months ago, and while the democrats nibbled around the edges most of the time, it was out in full bloom in the governor's message. Adding it all up, it came down to this: she wants to portray herself as on the side of the little guy.

Here's the best example. "We don't side with the wealthiest 1% when they lobby for their inheritance tax cut; we side with the 99% who think the wealthiest sliver ought to pay their share for schools and our homeland security." The only thing missing from that attack was a reference to the DeVos yacht, but that was coming, too. However, the section that got the biggest "hurray" from the dems in the room was when the governor launched into an A-to-Z list of companies she had brought to Michigan. "American Axle, Bosch, Cleveland Cliffs" and with each name, the crowd got more into it. The crescendo rose through "Raymond James, Second Chance, Toyota" and crested at "X-Rite, Yazaki and ZuSyn." It was brilliant stuff, and the joint was a rockin' when she finished it. But as reporters pointed out on OTR that week, it would not be long before the GOP would issue its own A-to-Z list of all the companies that had moved out on her watch, and it would be much longer than the one she rattled off.

"I ask you to stay with me; let me finish the job, and give me some friends in the legislature," she said as she came to the end. "This election is not about two candidates; it's about the people whose hard work has made Michigan what it is today…their dreams are our dreams. And on November 7, our victory will be their victory. Thank you, and God Bless Michigan!"

Dick DeVos ended his convention speech with, "May God bless our great State of Michigan." At least these two agree on that.

He started his speech in a dramatic fashion. With all the lights out in the Novi Convention Center, he stood quietly on stage and delivered his first line in the dark. GOP Chair Saul Anuzis reported that the audience thought there was some technical difficulty because all the lights were off. And there were major difficulties, but nobody in the media caught it. DeVos goes to center stage to deliver his opening line. When he speaks, the spotlight is supposed to pop on him. He speaks, but the mike is dead. He speaks again. Same thing. Now a normal person might chuck it all right there and call it a day. DeVos, however, walks over and picks up the back-up microphone, and then out of nowhere comes his voice and his first sentence, "My friends, the time to turn Michigan around has arrived."

With that, the lights finally came on, the GOP faithful shouted and there stood Dick DeVos, sans podium, sans note cards and looking completely different from that first day I chronicled his speech at the chamber lunch in Oakland County well over a year ago. McNeilly and Truscott were nervously and helplessly watching all this and "marveled at his calm in-stride ability to handle the curveballs of technical missteps." They discovered after the fact the sound guy forgot to turn on the DeVos lapel mike. Wonder where he's now working?

Watching the speech on the internet, I concluded he had come a long way baby, but something struck me right off the top: his hands. Former Governor Jim Blanchard had some word/hand coordination problems that often drew attention to his hands and not his words. DeVos seemed to have a touch of the same disease —not nearly as pronounced—but your eye was drawn to his hands, nonetheless.

Using teleprompters, DeVos moved back and forth on the stage much like the governor. "It's time to stand up for Michigan and to fight [there is that word again] for the change Michigan needs today." He had only three "fights" in his speech, but a whole bunch of "change" language, as he laid out his agenda for winning in November. DeVos has avoided using the party label on his campaign spots, and in his speech, he mentioned the word "republican" only four times in 20 minutes. One line, in particular, jogged my memory. He was going on about staying on the high road while the other side would be slinging mud, but then he added, "If we stick to the facts, we win." Flash back to the day after the primary for governor four years ago. I was standing in a Novi shopping mall parking lot with Rusty Hills, who was state GOP chair. We were awaiting the arrival of Dick Posthumus, who had secured the right to take on Granholm by winning the GOP primary the day before. We talked about Granholm's charisma factor and Hills said, "If we run on the facts, we win." Posthumus tried in vain to do that, but the facts were few and far between. I was wondering if this was a bad omen for DeVos to use the same theory for beating her this time out?

I picked up a couple of tidbits from his message. He came down hard on waste in the school bureaucracy. I thought I should ask him in the debate if he wanted to wipe out or slash the size of the state's unique Intermediate School District (ISD) system. His running mate, Ruth Johnson, had done an extensive probe of huge spending irregularities in the ISD system, and I was betting DeVos would go after all those educators in order to "get more money into the classroom." His talk about overhauling state government also perked up my ears. I concluded he would take on the state bureaucracy, and who knows what the civil service system would look like when he was done. I could hear the voice of former Governor John Engler in my ear as I heard DeVos says "It's time to build state government from the ground up with a focus on results."

Unlike the governor's address, there was no "red meat" in his. He did not attack her. In fact, he repeated for the millionth time that he liked her, but as he always did, he quickly added in relatively mild terms, "You have to judge a governor not on what they say, but on what they do and on what they get done."

One other little thing. He mentioned Detroit once in his speech when he said it was sad that the city sends more students to prison than to college. The governor did not mention Detroit at all. Guess old habits are hard to break.

As acceptance speeches go, both candidates got the job done by rallying the troops, but neither one of the messages knocked my socks off, although the fact that DeVos had cleaned up his public speaking act was a plus for him. Seeing the candidates "perform" on stage is a lot different than sitting next to them in an SUV on the campaign trail. Of the two venues, I much prefer the latter, and both DeVos and Granholm were accommodating.

Michigan Public TV asked me to do a one-hour documentary on the race for governor. The goal was to present the viewer with enough information to make a choice in the race. The intent was to go behind the commercials and get some meat on the voter's table. Toward that end, I requested a day with each contender.

My day with DeVos came first. We caught up with him at a West Bloomfield Hill's country club. Our camera crew of six was late arriving, so we found him in mid-sentence when we walked in with cameras rolling. He was talking to some juvenile justice folks, and they had plenty of gripes about the Granholm administration. However, our cameras were not allowed to stay. About an hour later, DeVos and his trusted sidekick Nick emerged. It was a wonderfully sunny day, and while the gardener trimmed the flowers around the clubhouse, DeVos and I did the first interview of the day. We kicked around the China, Amway, and other themes, and it was here that he gave me the line about his brain going dead during that earlier Tiger's TV interview. We wrapped it up and headed for Chrysler Headquarters, where our cameras were again excluded. Something about the company not wanting to get involved in politics.

We hooked up again about two hours later in front of a nursing home in Oakland County. The woman standing there as we arrived was the public relations person, so I said hello. We chatted, and I found out she was a Detroit democrat and was worried about the Granholm candidacy. One of the things she pointed out was that DeVos had a better staff when it came to arranging visits such as this. She complained about untimely e-mails from the governor's helpers, and despite numerous overtures, she was still unable to secure any of the governor's time for a visit. In and of itself, it was not a big deal, but the gripes about the governor's sloppy staff work had reached significant proportions. You heard it from every nook and cranny, and a lot of it was from democrats.

DeVos arrived on time and was immediately greeted by a blind man playing the piano and the trumpet at the same time. Okay, it was not a brass band, but it was not an accordion and a monkey either. He shook every senior citizen's hand. Many had no idea who he was. In fact, a delightful woman, Marilyn, asked me who he was, and then made a point of saying hello to DeVos. Most of the seniors were eating at the noon hour, and I thought this was really dicey. A politician interrupting lunch.

He spent quality time with the folks. He was not a "Hi, how are ya?" candidate. He was engaged as he laughed, shook hands and was lobbied by the owners on how to improve the care for seniors. He finished, and we moved toward his vehicle. It was now my turn to ride with him to the next two stops. "Why don't you sit over there on the left," he advised me. "You're more comfortable over there," he zinged me again. We made small talk on the way to the next stop. I asked him if he enjoyed working a crowd, and he said he got a lot out of that. I continue to marvel at how these major officer seekers never seem to get tired of pressing the flesh. Would you want to do that for a living? Not me.

Instead of going directly to the next event, the driver pulled off on a side street in Pontiac. "We are parking up," DeVos advised me. I had never heard the term. It meant they were taking a time out, because he did not want to arrive early to the next event. He told me he had learned later on in life that being on time was all about "respect." He hinted he had not learned that lesson as a young kid.

We talked about his daughter. While he was 200 miles away, she was home packing her bags to head off to her freshman year in college. He would head home later this night to participate in a going-away party. The exchange took me back to two years ago when we dropped daughter Carly off at an out-of-state university. I advised him it was not going to be fun. He acknowledged he knew that, having gone through it twice before with his other children. We talked about his childhood and I asked if he had any musical talent in his genes. He laughed and told the story about his mom forcing him to take piano lessons, which ended when "I was old enough to make that decision," he laughed again.

That triggered my memory about having lunch with his wife Betsy when she was state GOP chair. In that talk, she revealed that she had been a drummer in her high school band, and just about then, DeVos's cell phone rang. It was Betsy, of all people. I motioned that I would get out of the SUV so he could have some privacy. He signaled me to stay put. She was wondering how his day was going.

"I'm here with Tim," he reported to her. I couldn't hear the other side of the conversation, and I expected another zinger but didn't get one. DeVos then mentioned to her that we had just been chatting about her being a drummer. She immediately corrects him and says she was a "percussionist."

You have to understand drummers to get that line. Most drummers are very sensitive about that label. They think it is condescending, because drummers can't read notes. She told hubby that she played tympani, xylophone and other instruments that require note reading. He later relayed that to me, and we had a good chuckle about her taking offense to the term drummer.

He also reported that his daughter was on again and off again with tears about leaving. I fully understood that. I wished him well in getting through this painful, yet necessary, transition.

The rest of our day together made no news. But in the car,

I did learn some valuable things about his leadership style, which formed the basis for some debate questions. We talked about the layoffs at Amway and how he agonized about the impact that would have on his employees. "Did you pray about that?" I asked as we rolled down Woodward Ave. toward Beaumont Hospital for the last stop of the day. He acknowledged that he did. "I asked for wisdom" to do the right thing. And he recounts that after he fashioned a buy-out package for each worker, not one of them threatened to take the company to court. He contrasted that with the upheaval at the one-time giant auto-supplier, the Delphi Corporation, which was in bankruptcy and had tons of labor woes over buy-outs and a cut in benefits. Then he launches into his 70% doctrine. This was all new to me.

He borrowed the concept from the Marines, where they do not wait for 100% of the information before they make a tactical move. They move with 70% of the data on the table. I asked for more explanation sensing this was the way he would run state government if elected. "If you are always waiting for all the information, you end up never making a move. And while you are waiting, the information you do have often changes." But I noted that that strategy had to be risky. He acknowledged that but added it was not as risky as not acting. And then, we got on the subject of being the smartest guy in the room. It was my opinion that any successful CEO wanted to be just that. Turns out CEO DeVos never did and added, "I never had any trouble with that, either." We both laughed.

Here's his theory: you surround yourself with folks who are more intelligent in their specialty and let them go to work while the CEO carefully sets the big picture and monitors the progress. And then he comes close to criticizing the Harvard Law school grad, the governor, but stops short. He notes that his model for management is different than that of an attorney.

Sensing I may be onto something, I ask for more on that, too. Without mentioning her by name — and he didn't have to since we both knew whom he was talking about — he says a lawyer has a different attitude that is more about themselves. He does not use the word ego, but I get the message. I knew this would make an interesting area to explore in the debate.

DeVos tours the hospital, and we get video of him manipulating a robot that makes stitches. He should not give up his day job. Finally, about 4:30, we meet at the SUV to say goodbye. The next fundraiser with some local developers is off limits, so I thank him for the day, wish him well on his daughter's impending departure and shake his hand. Off he goes. It had been a good day and frankly a fun day. But after the crew and I climbed back into the news van, one guy asked a question that was on my mind, too. "He never talked to any voters," cameraman Dick Best observed. He was right. It was not the kind of retail politics I was used to with lots of hand shaking, asking for votes and hitting as many folks as humanly possible.

One source who knew what was going on explained it. During the week, the candidate only meets with opinion leaders and not the general public. That is done on the weekends. The objective is to make a good impression on those leaders and let them spread the word to the rank and file. Remember, they started that stuff almost a year ago to inoculate DeVos from democratic attacks. I thought it was kind of weird, but we would find out if it worked on Election Day.

The day with the governor was equally as much fun, although not as revealing. There was not much new to learn about her since I had a pretty good handle on that, having covered her for almost eight years.

It was Governor's Day at the Michigan State Fair in Detroit, and we would tag along to see what we could see. For the TV documentary, I needed to ask her the same questions I asked him. I advised press secretary Liz Boyd I would need about 10 minutes at the fair to do that. She called back and advised me that once the governor hit the ground, she would not have a 10-minute window open for little ole me. So we did the interview near Liz's office before we left. The DeVos campaign, upon seeing the interview, thought it was wrong for her to politic on state property.

With that in the can, the governor, Chris DeWitt, the timekeeper Jessica McCall, along with the state police driver headed for the basement of the Romney Building with me in toe. Oh, the timekeeper? It's her job to keep the governor on schedule.

I got in the left side of the car, having learned my lesson from Mr. DeVos, but she did not have a wisecrack. This chunk of time with her was a first for me. Despite the longevity, I had never spent this much time with her at one swipe. It was always two minutes here and there during a run-and-gun interview and that would be it. I think she was prepared for me to grill her all the way down I-96 to Detroit. That was not on my agenda. I just wanted to talk to see where it would go.

Kids going to college came up again with her, too. The governor's eldest daughter was a senior and fixing to head off to college. Being an equal opportunity sharer of wisdom, I warned her, as I had DeVos, that it would be tough to let her daughter go. Being a good mom, I'm sure she knew that.

As we moved down the road, we moved easily from one topic to another. We joked about the upcoming debate. I asked her if she wanted the "sinking fund" question now or later? We talked about music and how she was not a very good singer. "How did you get into acting school then?" I inquired. A singing audition was not required, she explained. We did talk a little more about the debate format. She liked the no-rules format better than the ones where there were time limits on answers and the inability to interact with her opponent.

I explained that I had spent a day with DeVos, and she wanted to know how it went. I had to pause for a second. I explained to her I did not want to be unfair by revealing anything that might be privileged information, just as I would conceal anything from him that she told me. I did report that DeVos was easygoing, and we had a good day. Out of the blue, I suggested she ought to call him. She seemed taken back by the notion.

Pretty soon, I could see the fair grounds along Woodward Ave. I told her I wanted a shot of her on the Tilt-a-Whirl. She advised she is more of a roller-coaster type and does not like rides that turn her upside down. Regardless, she will not go near the midway. Just then, the driver turned left into the VIP parking lot and hit the curb like we were on the dodgem cars. "That was for you," the governor ribbed me with a laugh.

Inside the lot, my camera crew was scrambling to get the

arrival shot. I had warned the guys that she would not stand still for anyone. However, she did stand still long enough for us to attach a wireless mike to her lapel so we could record her every interaction. She did not flinch at that, and neither did DeVos. And as if someone shot off a gun, Granholm turned from the unassuming and easygoing passenger next to me in the SUV to someone driven to find every hand to shake with a smile tossed in for good measure.

We're off. There's the fair manager John Hertel. She hooks up with him and calls the head of the Michigan Farm Bureau over for a handshake. "Wayne. Good to see ya," she tells Wayne Wood, whose group at that very moment was deciding who to endorse in the race for governor. I cornered him but could not weasel out of him where his group was headed. It never hurts to ask.

Next, there was the chair of the fair, Mark Gaffney, who runs the State AFL-CIO. He and the governor embraced. Next some folks just entering the fair get the Granholm touch. She is drawn to them for a barrage of handshakes, pictures, more smiles and "good to see yas."

Down the back lot, with our cameras rolling, she now heads for a VIP reception. These are all the corporate underwriters who pour in thousands of dollars to keep the fair in the black. She moves into the receiving line mode. Everyone wants to meet her. More pictures. More handshakes. More smiles. She confides to me afterwards that some of the repartee was censored because of the mike on her lapel. Darn it.

I've witnessed this scene a thousand times, so I pull Gaffney over for an on-camera interview. Turns out the labor boss has never met the man from Ada named DeVos.

"If you did, what would you tell him?" I loaded up a loaded question.

"I would tell him that he was a nice man and that he had the 34th largest yacht in the world...." Good ole Marky. Always a good sound bite.

Enough with the grip and grin stuff—that's what they call the handshaking and picture taking drill. The governor now moves to the pavilion for the lunch and an auction of live animals. As she moves, the governor does a walk-along interview with the local media. Detroit schoolteachers are striking, and she expresses hopes the schools will open on time. She finishes with that, and I catch up with her. "How's it going?" I want to know. She says she is doing well and asks me if we are getting good video. I tell her we are, and then she advises that the next big event is the auction in which she plays a major role.

First they do the lunch. She gives a short speech and then they bring in this huge black steer. It's the governor's job to solicit bids from the folks in the audience. The auctioneer begins his rat-a-ta-ta machine-gun-like dialogue with the bidders, while the governor, decked out in a royal blue blazer, gets into the swing of things.

As I watch her move from this table to that, putting the pressure on bidders to raise their arm and the bid, I reflect that this is a perfect picture of Jennifer Granholm at work. Whether she is in the sawdust of an auction ring or the legislative arena, she is full speed ahead all the time. The video is great, as she works the guy from the Meijer store to kick up the bid to $20,000 on a black steer. She fails. Undaunted, she moves to another bidder from Kroger but, just like her dealings with GOP lawmakers, she comes back to the same guy who shot her down in the first place. She never gives up. The steer eventually goes for a cool 25 thou. The money goes to a college scholarship for young farm kids.

Next, a hog is up for grabs. The governor works as hard for the hog as she did for the steer. This one goes for something like $12,000. She poses in the ring with the kid who raised the animal and the man who bought it. No wisecracks about the governor standing next to a pig. And in a twinkle, it was over.

She heads for the SUV as we dash out the back entrance to avoid the crowds. "Hey, it was a great day. Thanks for letting me tag along," I say to her. She says, "You bet." Into the backseat she jumps, the door slams shut, and she's off to a "private meeting," in which we were not invited.

Since she wanted no part of the midway, I did. I love carnivals, and as a nine year old, thought about joining one. Bet there are some politicians who wish that had happened. Anyway, I could not leave without checking out the rides so I asked the crew to join me.

I wanted to open this segment of the documentary at the fair with a camera shot from the top of the huge Ferris Wheel. We got a guy in a golf cart to take us there, but alas, the ride was under repair. That was the only disappointment of the day. But little did I know, I was headed for another disappointment. I found out our big TV debate had turned into a merry-go-round, and when it stopped, I might be booted off.

21

The Good, the Bad, and the Ugly

The good news is the Tigers are in the playoffs. The bad news for DeVos is he's behind. And the ugly? The DeVos side is accusing Granholm of "race baiting."

There are two competing stories in the news marketplace these days, and on September 25, 2006, it was clear which one was getting the most attention.

"Roarin': Magical Tigers celebrate playoff spot," blasted the *Detroit News* headline that you had to be blind not to see. Not to be outdone, the *Detroit Free Press* headline simply read: "Party Time."

Just as yours truly predicted months ago, the Tiger story was front and center, and you had to dig deep to find the other story: quietly and without much fanfare, the incumbent governor had opened an 8-point lead over the challenger. It was no longer a dead heat. Jennifer Granholm had a legitimate lead and you could feel the anxiety on the other side, although they tried hard to mask it.

In the early September EPIC-MRA review of the contest, Granholm was winning in every media market except in DeVos's backyard of Grand Rapids and in Lansing. He was not completely out of it, as he had a slim edge with independent male voters, but she secured the independent female vote. Refining the numbers even more, she had opened up a significant lead with both younger and older college women. She had struggled with that subgroup in previous polls.

While the DeVos handlers were fed up with the Ed Sarpolus polling firm, they could not deny, that in this case, he was probably right. There was a different public poll and one private survey that confirmed the numbers. A Zogby International poll released in the *Wall Street Journal* had the race at 49.5% for her and 40.8% for him. The *Journal,* which was not a Granholm fan, ran a meager one-paragraph analysis saying, "In a one-on-one match up her lead is the widest it's been since January." The survey found DeVos losing ground with his GOP base due to the "growing strength of a democratic ad blitz." On top of that the Michigan-based Marketing Resource Group had asked the same horse race question and got the same results. DeVos was down by an eight- or nine-point margin. But the DeVos folks deliberately sat on the data. If it had not been for another un-named source, I would have missed it. And the fact that they did not release the findings, only proved in my mind they were not happy. The findings came out on the eve of the first debate.

So as they say in ole Mexico, "Que Pasa?" DeVos who had overcome a 20-point Granholm lead, and actually held the lead for a time, was now sucking wind.

Answer: DeVos contracted a bad case of the Asian flu. No, not the kind that lays you out flat in bed with a fever. This strain he caught from the TV--a series of hard-hitting ads that centered on China. It was enough to make him politically sick. "China easily symbolizes to many workers the new global economy and their fears of where they will fit into it," wrote the AP's Kathy Hoffman in a September 12 piece that got statewide exposure. The China ad the democrats were running left little to the imagination as it featured the sound of a Chinese gong and Chinese music in the background. The announcer suggested since DeVos was so good at creating jobs in China, "Do you suppose maybe there's a province in China that's looking for a governor?"

The longer the gong rang, the more DeVos faded or so goes the popular wisdom in town. The ad did play to the fears of those in the union ranks, some of whom had flirted with DeVos but were now apparently ending the short-lived romance. As he had done in the past, once the gong started banging, DeVos took to the airwaves to call the whole attack, "Bull." I suggested to the DeVos folks, that he had used only half the word. The use of "bull" was a clear attempt to appeal to angry white males who are not afraid to add the s-h-__.

Looking right into the camera, DeVos tried to mute the democratic frontal attack by explaining one more time that he did not ship Michigan jobs to China. How many times did he have to say it given that he'd been saying it for over a year?

His side also took another tact at counter-acting the spot. They pushed TV stations to stop running it and for a moment some did, until the dems revamped some of the "facts." They changed the language to reflect that jobs had been eliminated at Amway when DeVos was boss and there were no layoffs as the original ad suggested. It seems like a minor point, but when you are fighting for your political life, you do anything to survive. DeVos and company were doing just that, but the majority of stations continued to run the ad.

Party Chair Saul Anuzis got into the act as well reminding anybody who would listen that "Ford, General Motors, Delphi, and DaimlerChrysler among many others, have major operations in China but are not attacked, nor should they be." For good measure he also tossed into the fire the charge that the ad amounted to race baiting. A theme repeated by campaign manager McNeilly. "To use the sounds and the imagery [of China] is to draw upon Michigan's fears and Michigan's past racial tensions....The governor has really crossed the line here. It is demeaning to her and her office. Racism is wrong no matter what type of label you put on it and this type of race baiting doesn't have any place in Michigan politics and the governor should immediately disavow it." This was the heaviest quote I had ever gotten from McNeilly to date and it reflected one of two things or maybe both: it was a desperation move to change the subject from China jobs to race baiting, and/or an attempt to get back on the offensive and push the democrats back to defense.

Naturally after his remarks, I headed to democratic head-quarters where a quietly confident Mark Brewer appeared on camera rejecting every word McNeilly had just uttered. "If you can't argue the facts, you just yell," he began. Earlier he had told the AP, "It's not about China. It's not about the Chinese people. It's about the bad business practices of Dick DeVos." Brewer must have known that the China ad was working or he would have yanked it from the air, so he continued, "They are trying to stir-up racial passions by making this kind of charge which is a complete canard." (Rather a high-priced word for the fourth-grade level of TV news viewers, but that's another story.) Brewer ended our conversation by arguing that if anybody was playing the race card, it was the other side.

Others got into the act as the gong continued to reso-nate across the state. In a Sunday column my buddy Ronnie Dzwonkowski summed it up, "Anyone with a global view of the economy these days knows that you have to be in China, or you're soon going to be nowhere." He noted that even the Granholm ad-ministration had an office in Shanghai. He concluded with, "The Democrats can flog the China thing until November if they want, but I think it's a wash at best."

As all this unfolded, around the OTR table each week the correspondents felt the dems had been successful in moving DeVos off his economic message. No one could remember the last time he talked about his alleged "Turn Around" blue print. But just then, DeVos found somebody else to do it for him.

"A lot of people have given up on Michigan—thrown in the towel. I haven't. I know you haven't and neither has Dick DeVos," former auto baron Lee Iacocca began his 30 second spot. There was big Lee, decked in his blue suit with power red tie, slightly off cen-ter, telling the voters in Michigan that when things were tough, Dick DeVos "toughed it out, turned things around, made things happen. Now he makes products that Michigan sends all over the world." (There was no gong in this ad.) He concludes with "Dick DeVos makes Michigan jobs. If you ask me, that's what Michigan needs right now." The only line that was missing was, "If you can find a better governor, buy him."

Iacocca, who salvaged the Chrysler car company from a certain doom, was back trying to do the same for his pal DeVos. DeVos made a special trip to California during the summer to huddle with Lee. Originally DeVos wanted to share his vision for turning the state around, but it ended up with Iacocca offering to be a pitchman one more time. How could DeVos turn that down? The DeVos copywriters wrote the script and Iacocca rewrote it to fit his patented style, and for a moment, it did help to shift attention away from the negative China ad.

The governor, who was reportedly miffed, dismissed Iacocca, saying he resided in California. Is the best she could do? It was lamer than lame. John Truscott noted that Granholm once lived in California, too, so "maybe we should dismiss her, too."

Either way, while the ad was nice and provided some badly needed breathing room for DeVos, it probably did little to even the score although the DeVos campaign was smiling again. When I did a man-on-the-street piece for TV, lots of twenty-somethings were going, "Lee who?" However, older citizens, who do vote, knew who he was, but I was from the school that believed endorsements meant very little in modern day politics. Endorsements have all the punch of a wet dish rag. DeVos would need more than a car salesman to turn his campaign around.

As if things weren't bad enough, DeVos was not only battling the Asian-flu, he also had a bad case of foot in mouth disease...self-inflected to boot. Just as he did back in that barnyard months earlier, DeVos got into trouble because he didn't listen to his inner "stay on message" voice. This time the scene was a 40-minute interview on education issues, and again Ms. Hoffman was reporting. The front-page headlines said DeVos favored the teaching of intelligent design in the science classroom. Everyone came unglued with that revelation. Hoffman began her story, "Republican gubernatorial candidate Dick DeVos says he thinks Michigan's science curriculum should include a discussion about intelligent design." Pretty straightforward lead paragraph that within hours was roundly rejected by the DeVos handlers.

"In response to an inaccurate AP story, the following is the accurate position of Dick DeVos on intelligent design," the blunt news release began. And it goes on to explain that while DeVos believes "children should be provided with more knowledge, not less," he also believes "in our system of local control. Local school boards should have the opportunity to offer evolution and intelligent design in their curriculums." Say what?

Don't these guys ever learn? There was nothing wrong with her quotes, but team DeVos did not like the sound of it, so it not only called the story "inaccurate," it tried to undo what the candidate had done. Either he believed intelligent design should be in the science room or he didn't. He could have said the issue was too complicated, but that didn't work when he tried it on OTR six months earlier on the stem cell question. His second option was to tell the truth. But he didn't. I thought it was one more example of how this candidate was unsure on his feet when the subject shifted to anything other than the economy and jobs.

And everybody let him know he screwed-up. Conservative columnist Nolan Finley piled on. "Jobs. Jobs. Jobs. Whenever Dick DeVos hears himself talking about anything else for the duration [of the campaign] it should be a clue for him to just shut up." Warm personal letter to follow. Finley called it a "colossal political blunder" which "allowed the campaign to shift toward social issues, where he's most assailable."

Exactly. That's why DeVos has been repeatedly told to stay away from the wedgies. But what was the poor guy to do? He was asked a question. He could act as he did almost six months ago on OTR and confess that it was too complicated or he could tell the truth. I think he did that, but the "truth" was not what the handlers wanted him to say so they took the words right out of his mouth and inserted new ones.

Democratic chair Brewer thought DeVos did this on purpose to get off the China ad. Wrong. This was just a plain old example of not sticking to your beliefs or forgetting how to articulate your beliefs. Regardless, it was not a magic moment for the underdog in the race for governor. But if it was any solace, Granholm had done the same thing over the years, too.

As I stepped back to observe, it had been a bad three weeks for DeVos. He was behind for the first time, he was being pummeled by the China ad, he had been off message, he had stumbled on intelligent design and the momentum he once enjoyed was a mere memory. In a word Dick DeVos was in trouble. But even in the darkest hour, if you work hard enough and long enough, good things do happen and DeVos reaped a little good news on another front.

Political endorsements are not what they used to be. Many moons ago if a labor leader got up and told the troops to vote for this person or that, rest assured, the troops marched in lock step to the polls and did...or else.

The "or else" is gone and so is the impact of a blessing from this group or that. Having said that, however, there were three plums sitting out there that both candidates wanted to pick.

The struggle for the Michigan Manufacturers Association endorsement was a prime example and worth recounting here to give a rare glimpse into what happens when the doors are closed and the vote counting begins.

Going in, Granholm was the odds-on favorite to emerge the victor. Over a year ago, she carried buckets of water for major manufacturers in this state when she proposed a hefty tax cut package for them. She proposed to pay for it by increasing the taxes on banks and insurances companies who were not members of the MMA. The governor was sitting pretty as the Big Three automakers, who tossed around a lot of weight in the group, felt they owed her something, and the endorsement would pay off that debt.

DeVos got wind of all this long before the vote was taken and went to work to undo what Granholm was about to get. However, he had some problems. The GOP legislature blocked the governor's original SBT plan and some MMA members concluded republicans did it to deny the governor a victory. In other words, the GOP put politics above policy. That attitude fermented beneath the surface as DeVos went into action. He called everyone on the MMA board and adopted the same strategy he tried on the ministers in Detroit. "If you can't endorse me, are you willing to remain neutral?" Some, but not the Big Three, were open to that. Granholm at this same time was also doing her homework, and when the endorsement day arrived, she was still feeling confident she had it in the bag.

DeVos goes first in a closed-door meeting with 22 board members. "He looked very gubernatorial. Never saw him do any better," reveals one of those in the room. For many this is there first look-see even though DeVos is a businessman. But he's from West Michigan and a lot of the MMA folks are from Southeast Michigan. He sells himself for an hour and leaves. He has, however, three moles in the room who stay in contact with DeVos supporters as the day wears on.

The lunchtime speaker was Ed Sarpolus who was on the agenda to share the latest polling data with the group. However, Eddie had to buy his own lunch that day because the DeVos camp protested his being there. It felt Sarpolus was biased, and the MMA took him off the program. During the lunch hour the chitchat in the room focused on one interesting angle. One of the board members was with the Alticor Company, and some wondered if he should be allowed to vote. In fact, the question came up with DeVos, and he basically said, it was their call. It was decided the guy could vote. Chalk up at least one vote for DDV.

The governor came in after lunch. A source says, "I didn't think she was on top of her game." And she may have sealed her own fate when the issue of China came up. One person, who was establishing a beachhead over there, said his employees were asking him if "it was a problem going to China," given the governor's rhetoric on the issue.

"But you're not running for governor," she briskly brushed him off. Another board member with interest in China thought she did not understand the implications of the first question. So he asked it a different way, but got the exact same answer. Needless to say, that did not play very well. "That was her least impressive moment," this source concludes. Here she was with a bunch of business types who were struggling to survive. They knew that expanding to China might save their companies and while the governor acknowledged that, she explained she still had to respond to DeVos in her advertising.

And near the end of the Q and A, the guy from Alticor, who had been raising his hand during the entire process, finally got recognized as she tells him, "I didn't see you." A likely story. Once he got the floor, he was not volunteering to distribute her reelection packets. There is one source who reported it got a little testy and the governor "lost it and got very hot." However, another source says the guy defended his company, but was "very polite." Obviously, it could not be both. Two other sources who were there reported it was a civil and not a heated exchange.

The MMA leadership wanted to forge a consensus which means it wanted a unanimous decision. There was sentiment for DeVos because "it would be hard not to endorse a manufacturer. He's a member. What does it look like if we don't?" But there were others who recall all the work Granholm did for the group. An informal test vote was taken and Granholm had a slight edge. Emails were now flying back to the GOP side as the group considered a formal motion to sit this one out...not to endorse. And that's what they did. "We were ecstatic with neutrality," reports GOP chair Saul Anuzis. It would have been a huge "get" for her to beat DeVos in his own sandbox, but she was the one with sand in her eyes. Maybe she would do better at the Farm Bureau?

Once again the word on the street was that she was going to win despite the strong and traditional republican leanings of this long-standing organization. It was also looking good for her from an organizational standpoint. Earlier in the year, Wayne Wood, who runs the Farm Bureau, rearranged the endorsement process. Instead of a small group making the decision, he opened the door to include 150 farmers from all over the state. He moved the final decision closer to the election to make the endorsement more relevant. Some felt this was done to help the governor which resulted in this juicy rumor. Wood was being offered a seat on the agriculture commission or the directorship of the department. A Granholm source familiar with the process says the rumor was heard, but "The governor does not work that way."

Regardless, DeVos was not conceding this group either and went to work again as he tried to uproot the grassroots support the governor enjoyed. While he feverously worked the phones, a former GOP speaker was working them as well...on behalf of the governor.

Rick Johnson and the governor became good "buds" during a contentious campaign to pass the so-called Agriculture Enhancement Package (AEP). Johnson was the former GOP Speaker of the Michigan House, turned lobbyist, with strong ties to the farming community. You have to love these guys…the "title of the package" was as misleading as the day is long. It was really a scheme to bring slot machines to racetracks. At the time, the horse racing industry was on life support and backers of the AEP knew that slots could be the oxygen or the "enhancement" the industry needed to go on breathing. Dick DeVos opposed that statewide ballot proposal and Republican Johnson has a long memory. He not only made phone calls to Farm Bureau members, but he raised money for Granholm. But when all the votes were counted, the person who was in line to get the blessing did not. DeVos did. So now he is two for two, having neutralized Granholm at the MMA and having picked off the Farm Bureau right from under her nose.

Which brings us to the endorsement at the Detroit Regional Chamber of Commerce. The governor had a leg up going in because the chair of the panel making the decision was none other than Dennis Archer, the former Mayor of Detroit and the former chair of the Granholm reelection committee. In order to keep peace in the democratic family, Archer subsequently relinquished the title because the current Mayor Kilpatrick was not happy with Archer because he supported Kilpatrick's opponent.

First there was an informal discussion about the implications of making an endorsement. It appeared the group was evenly divided. In fact both candidates had told their board members they were afraid the other guy was going to win. There was also an "honest split" among the leaders and the rank-and-file membership. Then a vote to remain neutral was taken and 60% decided to do just that. Even though he did not win, DeVos was content to have neutralized the Detroit Chamber.

All of this is recounted here not because it turned the election around, but it underscores the lengths to which candidates will go to get something that may be meaningless, but might make the difference in the long run. In a close contest no one could predict what would help or not help. No contender wants to wake up on the day after the election mumbling, "If only I had gone after those business or farm endorsements, I might have won." So they battle it out for endorsements just in case it does matter, and on this front DeVos got two wins and a tie, which his side considered a victory. His score in the first debate, however, was not nearly as good. In fact it was downright awful.

22

The Debate That Almost Wasn't

Candidate Dick DeVos and the New York Yankees share two things in common. They both possess a ton of money; but when the chips were down that money meant nothing. The Yanks lost to Detroit in the playoffs and in debate one, DeVos went down in flames.

But that first debate was the debate that almost wasn't. Back in Chapter 20, I hinted that the "sure thing" debate that started way back in July, showed signs of coming unraveled, and I had myself to blame. With verbal assurances from both sides that they would do the event, I was relaxed when the formal debate negotiations commenced just after Labor Day. I knew there would be a lot of back and forth because anytime you place two lawyers and two P.R. guys in a room to hammer out debate rules, you know there will be a lot of hammering before the final document is nailed down. This time the talks were more contentious than usual, thanks to Mark Fox and Chris DeWitt working for the governor and Dan Pero and Dick McLellan representing DeVos.

Based on information that found its way to this desk, the DeVos team went into the talks with one key objective: Skubick was not going to get a debate where he was the lone moderator. "We were not going to let Skubick dominate. There was great concern about the WKAR-TV debate because it was the most dangerous debate," was the DeVos company line going in. They knew the no rules and single moderator format favored the governor. She had performed in that venue before. DeVos had not.

There was nothing personal in any of this, but I learned that the DeVos side wanted to "slow Skubick down so he would not be able to do his thing. The intent was to dampen your free-wheeling style." They wanted to build in some safeguards for their guy which included an initial demand for a three-person panel of reporters instead of only one. That was rejected, but then at a critical juncture in the talks, I inadvertently and unknowingly stuck my big nose into all this.

I was hunting around for a column topic for the week and thought it would be interesting to write about the upcoming debate and solicit some input from the readers on what to ask. Two heads are always better than one, and I was interested to see what somebody else might ask if given the chance. The article ran on Friday, and Gayle and I headed up north for the weekend. For some reason, and I don't know why, I took along the cell number for Mark Fox. It had been awhile since we talked and I was kind of curious as to what was going on. The four participants had agreed to a "news blackout" which meant nobody would update anybody from the media on the scope or the success or lack of same in the discussions. I knew better than to pump Fox on that. I knew he would not budge and besides I did not want to put him or anybody on the spot.

Late Friday, I placed a call and got an earful. My column had set off a firestorm inside the closed-door meetings. The DeVos folks read my column in which I basically announced that there would be a debate on October 2 barring any unforeseen circumstances. It was an innocent column, or so I thought, but now it was being used, I concluded, by the DeVos guys to either get out of the debate or modify it beyond recognition. Now I was worried…really worried.

The DeVos camp was prepared to "walk away from the WKAR debate," a source familiar with the delicate discussions shared with me after the fact. The attitude after my article hit the newsstands was this: I was using the article to "manipulate" both sides to get this debate finalized and/or I was fronting for Granholm to do the same thing. "Fronting for Granholm?" Egads. That's worse than having your name in a commercial. I was doing neither. It was a no-brainer article asking for viewer questions and that was it. Plus all the players knew how badly I wanted to do this debate, so why would I do anything to jeopardize it? Nonetheless, the debate was hanging by a thread. My source later confessed that he or she could find no evidence that I was working for Granholm on this.

In addition to wanting to wiggle out of the gig, it got back to me that the DeVos gang "had heard" that KAR was "selling" seats to the debate and promising "special access" to the candidates after the debate. It was a bunch of baloney, and I made sure everyone knew that. And on top of that, McLellan and Pero suggested that I never had an agreement with McNeilly to do our debate. I poured water on that, too.

The Granholm folks wanted, above all else, the no-rules format and hung tough on that, but with my article, I'm told by another source who got wind of all this, that the DeVos guys had the other side over the barrel. They quickly demanded that a second correspondent be added to the broadcast. There was little wiggle room on the other side so the Granholm side agreed. But who would that be?

Both sides submitted a list which made for interesting reading. The DeVos list was a Who's Who of right leaning writers: Nolan Finley from the *Detroit News*, Frank Beckman from WJR radio, and Daniel Howes from the *News*. There were other names not associated with the right. Those included Charlie Cain from the *News*, Rick Albin from WOOD-TV, Sherry Jones, anchor at TV-6 in Lansing, Dawson Bell from the *Feep*, and Sam Logan from the *Michigan Chronicle*. Another list of "not preferred but acceptable" names was also on the table. On that one were Ron Dzwonkowski from the *Free Press*, Chuck Stokes from TV-7 in Detroit, and some guy named Skubick.

Someone reported that when the Granholm side saw the list, someone burst out, "Why not add Sean Hannity's name, too?"

Sarcasm duly noted. Hannity, of course, is the right wing co-host of cable TV's Hannity and Colmes show. The long and short of it, both sides settled on Cain. An exploratory phone call was made to see if he was interested "if" such an offer materialized. He checked with the suits at the *News* and got the green light.

At this point, I was brought back into the talks to see what I thought about sharing the stage. While nobody told me what was going on, I quickly figured out why another reporter was being added. Instead of a full hour of me grilling the candidates, I would get a half hour. My first reaction was, of course, selfish but I could also read the handwriting on the debate wall. If I balked, no debate. If I agreed, we got the debate. The answer was simple as I gladly signed off on having a sidekick, and the longer I thought about it, the more comfortable I got.

"I'm really sorry," Charlie Cain opened our conversation when we finally touched based a week or so before the debate. He was apologizing because he knew the original format was a single moderator. He also wanted to make it clear that he had nothing to do with any of this. I knew that, so I quickly relieved him of any guilt. I was actually glad to have him on board and told him so. We alo agreed that we would not compare notes on what we were going to ask. I did not want to be accused of conspiring to "get" either candidate. We did agree that if one of us was on a roll with a good series of questions, the other would lay low so as not to interrupt the flow. Our goal was to get some new info out of these two candidates.

Piecing together the rest of the debate negotiation puzzle helps to explain why it took almost a month for both sides to get this seemingly simple assignment done. They haggled over lots of other stuff. For example, the DeVos folks wanted an audience for all of the debates. They gave in on that for the WKAR event, but held fast for the WOOD-TV debate. And as Mark Fox reads this for the first time, his buddy of 32 years, McLellan, reveals that he snookered Fox. All along the DeVos side wanted the Democratic Party chair Mark Brewer in the studio audience. My source explains that the DeVos handlers believed that would "energize DeVos" if the Darth Vader of democratic politics was seated right in front of the candidate. The crafty McLellan, of course, did not reveal this to the other side during their discussions. Instead, he innocently suggested that Saul Anuzis, the state GOP chair, be allowed in. And when Fox and DeWitt agreed to that, it was only natural to let Brewer in as well. McLellan got what he wanted. I ran into him at the debate that night and asked if he was now going to share all this with Fox? Dickie chuckled and whispered in my ear, "I want him to read about it in your book." Mission accomplished.

Finally all of the painstaking details were ironed out and Pero and McLellan signed off, believing they had the final authority to do that. Everyone left the room and shared the document with the respective campaign staffs. McLellan and Pero were shocked to find out that their side would not sign off.

"We were miffed," McLellan explains long after the fact. He had given his word and now, "my credibility was on the line." He concedes there was a miscommunication on how much power they had. "We signed off. The principals didn't," McLellan had to tell Fox. The GOP counsel basically admitted, "I screwed up." It was the honorable and honest thing to say, although he never intended it to be that way. So rather than muddy the waters any further, he and Pero stepped aside and let DeWitt and John Truscott try to finish the job. After a series of false starts, the final four-million-page document...not quite that long, was inked by the candidates and party chairs. There would be debates. Glory be! I still wanted to see the whites of their eyes in Studio A on October 2 before I would be a believer.

I continued to draft questions and one week before the event, I had about eight pages including some reader inquiries from that ill-fated column. Truth be known, the first question came from a reader. It was, "Should there be a law making it illegal for a candidate to lie or mislead in their commercials." I tagged on for good measure, "And if such a law existed tonight, would your opponent be in trouble with that law?" That was a self-censored version. The original one read," Would your opponent be in jail tonight?" Even for me that was over the top so I took "jail" out, although it did have a nice ring to it, don't you agree?

Both sides wanted to have a set check and the WKAR folks set that up so that the lighting, backdrops, microphones, podiums, etc., etc., could be reviewed. Greg McNeilly came over the Friday before, spent about ten minutes looking at the studio and signed off. Mr. Fox was not nearly as easy.

When the set was first designed, I made it clear I wanted the podiums as close together as possible. I remembered seeing one debate involving Debbie Stabenow and Spencer Abraham where he was on one side of the gym and she on the other with about 65 feet between them. In reality she could have been in Marquette and he in Monroe, and nobody would have noticed the difference. I wanted Granholm to be able to look right at DeVos and vice versa. I wanted intimacy and my crew gave it to me. The podiums were just over four feet apart.

I got a frantic call a couple of days later from Fox. "I couldn't sleep last night." Join the club. "Those podiums are too close. The rules say they have to be eight to ten feet apart." Those darn rules. We kicked it around and we compromised at 7 feet. So what was the big deal? DeVos is taller than Granholm and the feeling was if they were too close, he would tower over her and that could be intimidating. This was a woman who did not cotton to being intimidated, and the sleepless Mr. Fox was going to make sure that did not happen. I called the WKAR folks and told them about the change. They were not happy because that meant the lighting had to be revamped, and the guy who did that was on daddy-watch as his wife was expecting their first baby. Begrudgingly, the podiums were moved and shortly thereafter Fox showed up with tape measure in hand. He got his seven-foot spread.

Remember he and I have been working on this stuff for three decades. I knew him. He knew me. The WKAR crew, however, did not have the same rapport based on earlier encounters with Fox in previous debates. Hence they had it in for him before he walked in the door and their attitude was apparent. Immediately he wanted to change…what else?...the lighting. That went over like the proverbial lead balloon. Remember, the goal here is to produce the first debate on behalf of the citizens of Michigan. But now we have a turf battle that endangers everything.

At a TV-7 debate years ago, Fox made some last-minute demands on the producers ten minutes before airtime and if they did not deliver, he threatened to keep Granholm in the Green Room. Needless to say, he got what he wanted. Faced with a possible repeat of history, I morphed into my best imitation of shuttle diplomat Henry Kissinger in an attempt to mediate this mess. We finally agreed that no final decision could be made on the lighting until the governor was actually on the set. Maybe no changes would be needed, my guys were hoping. The Sunday afternoon before the debate, with the Tigers battling the Yanks, everyone took a time out to stroll through the studio. The governor was in a good mood as she moved to her podium. Earlier that week both sides did a series of five coin tosses to determine who stood where and who did closing statements first. John Truscott told me, "I want this in the book. I won all five coin tosses." He was hoping that was an omen. When Fox heard that, he roundly and firmly rejected J.T.'s account that he went five for five. "It's not true," Fox argues. We'll administer the truth serum later on.

Anyway the governor assumed her position, everyone from my crew held their collective breath, and Fox declared, to everyone's chagrin, that there is a shadow under the governor's right cheek. No, not a deadly shadow! There goes her reelection bid. Now, to be honest here, this is serious stuff and I really did understand Fox's position. It was his job to make his candidate look as good as he could. She joked that she did not want to appear like the "Bearded Lady." Fat chance of that, hey?

But my crew was getting hotter by the minute. Fox would not relent. I moved him out of the studio for a time out. He walked the governor to her SUV. She split, and Fox came back into master control where we watched the Tigs on the tube, and he mentions to me, "Don't give up your Fox-TV connection." That was short hand for, he was hacked at the KAR folks and if I was going to do anymore debates with him, it would be with FOX and not public TV. It was not music to my ears. I asked him to stay put while I went back to the crew in Studio A. I was not in the best of moods. This whole debate thing from the get go had been a pain in the you know what, and I had frankly just about had it. I could not explain all this to the crew, but made it clear I was not happy and pretty much told them to do whatever Fox wanted. I am usually called Timmy by these guys, but there were no terms of endearment that afternoon. We ended the stalemate by agreeing to bring the governor back to the studio on the day of the debate for one more lighting check, and fortunately there was no shadow. The Bearded Lady would not be on stage that night.

On the day of the debate, I went to the crew and personally apologized for my conduct the day before. I did not want any hard feelings going into the studio that night since we had an important job to do. Everyone graciously accepted my apology and when I explained what I had been through for almost three months, they understood the genesis of my rant.

Debate day. Finally. Dick DeVos came through the studio that morning. He seemed cool, calm and collected. He stood in his spot, asked which camera was his for the closing statements and requested that the TV monitor be turned off even though the pro-tracted rules that his side negotiated said the monitors should be on. So much for that. We took him to the Green Room where he dined on chocolate cookies and diet Coke later that night. He went off to his workout about 1 p.m. and I went home to do my two miles on the treadmill, shower, and put the finishing touches on my questions. Then it was back to the studio for three live shots on FOX and TV-10.

I was nervous. In fact I had been on and off nervous for about two weeks leading up to this thing. The night before the de-bate, I awoke at 2 a.m. and could not get back to sleep. I was going over the questions trying to figure this angle and that. If one of the candidates said this, how would I counter. Silly stuff, I know, but just serious enough to keep me from getting two hours of badly needed sleep.

Before I left for the studio with Gayle, I called my 92-year-old mom. She wished me good luck. I asked her to say a prayer for me. I didn't have to ask. She already had. So off we went. At this point I told Gayle this whole thing was analogous to planning a wedding. After arduous months of planning every detail, you just want to get it over with. I was ready to get in the ring and get it over with.

We drove into the back parking lot at the Communications

Arts and Science complex on the Michigan State University campus. It looked like a high tech circus had come to town. There were "sat" trucks all over the joint. They came from as far away as Traverse City, Detroit, Grand Rapids, Saginaw, Flint, you name it. The media contingency reached 100. Apparently this first debate was a big deal. I did the live shots and then talked to some public TV donors who were watching from Studio B. I told them how Gayle and I had purchased a brand new tie for the debate and how, on the way home, I lost it by dropping the bag on the sidewalk. Fortunately the guy who sold it, found it. Remember TV is all about hair and ties. I then positioned myself at the east entrance where DeVos was set to come in.

At about 6:45, he walked through the sliding doors.

I pretended I could not remember his name, "You're DeVere, De-something or other?" He laughed as we shook hands. He was greeted by the MSU president who had problems of her own. East Lansing was coming unglued over the performance of a certain football coach and a certain football team. Dr. Lou Anna Simon told me that her husband was getting lots of calls from concerned Spartan loyalists and he, of course, was passing all that good stuff along to her. She shared none of this with DeVos who had his own worries to contend with as the clock ticked toward the live broadcast at 8 bells. I walked him to the Green Room, deposited him there with his coke and cookies that I bought, by the way, and said, "See you in the studio in a little bit."

Back to my post to await the arrival of Betsy DeVos. There had been some question as to whether she would be there. "It is Dick's call" an insider shared with me. "He'll have to decide if it is a plus or a distraction." As she walked in with the children, I figured he concluded it was a plus. Mrs. D and kids were ushered off to the Green Room where she would watch the debate along with key staffers. Next it was time for the governor. The original arrival time was about 7:15. At about 7:20 she rolls in and it's off to the studio for that final light check. Her two daughters Ce Ce and Kate are tagging along with hubby Dan. The governor seems relaxed as we walk along with flash bulbs popping as we go by the pressroom where it is standing room only. With the set check out of the way, she retires to her Green Room, and I decide it's time to suit up. Charlie is in his seat. I join him. We have about 20 minutes to airtime.

They check my earpiece to make sure I can hear the time cues. There is also a person inside the booth who will be timing each answer so that each candidate gets equal time. If there is an imbalance, someone will whisper it in my ear, and I will make adjustments along the way. I had made that commitment to McNeilly from the DeVos side when he raised the concern about equal time.

Then out of nowhere, the governor strolls confidently into the arena and walks right by me, "Do I make you nervous?" she inquired. What? Me nervous? She moves to her podium and starts making notes on the 4 by 6 cards and two pencils and two pens that are there per the infamous debate agreement. Moments later DeVos comes in. He says nothing. His game face is firmly in place. The two candidates do not shake hands. He's nervous, too. A close DeVos associate after the fact shared this: "Do you remember your first time on television? You were not debating a professional. Need I say more?"

DeVos starts writing on his note cards, too. From my ringside seat, I watch them both. Every once in awhile she sneaks a peak over at him and vice versa. The silence is finally broken as the floor director moves into position; everyone can hear his squeaky shoes.

"Stosh, you gotta take those things off," I half joked with him. It was a distraction yet comical as the candidates laughed, breaking the tension. The governor observed that the shoes were more of a problem for her opponent since the floor director was closer to DeVos than he was to the governor.

"Three minutes," Stosh shouts to drown out his noisy shoes. I say to myself, it looks like this is really going to happen. What started out with a phone call on the treadmill in July has come to pass. As I always do, I quietly closed my eyes and said a little prayer. I wanted to be fair above all else. As for the governor, she said her prayer in the waiting room before she came down. I assumed that somewhere along the line the very religious DeVos had done the same thing. But apparently only one set of prayers was answered that night—and it wasn't his.

23

The Lashing in East Lansing

The opening music for the debate was playing in my ear—30 seconds from airtime. There were nine people in the studio: the two candidates, two correspondents, three camera operators, one floor director, and one state trooper hidden in the corner for security reasons. Little did the nine folks know that we had company. Over a million viewers were out there in TV land waiting for the first debate. That is not a misprint—over one million interested citizens who wanted to see Jennifer Granholm and Dick DeVos up close and personal.

"Good evening and welcome to the first debate for governor." With those opening words, the butterflies disappeared. The game was finally underway and once it began, there was no time to worry about being worried. "We have with us tonight the major party candidates for governor and they are." She says, "Jennifer Granholm." He says, "Dick DeVos." They said their names right.

Good start. I explain that the minority party candidates are not here because they failed to meet the qualifying standards established by the Michigan Public TV folks. Next, I welcome Charlie, remind everyone there are no rules for the debate, and fire the first question at DeVos.

I was looking for a question that would stir the pot from the opening bell and since I knew DeVos was hacked off about some of her commercials, I thought this was a good place to start. "Did we need a law making it illegal to lie in commercials and if so, was his opponent in trouble with that law?" DeVos smiles, but instead of accusing her of bending the truth with the China ads, the Amway stuff, and a host of other attacks, all he could muster up was, "Certainly some of the campaign rhetoric has been disappointing." Dis-a-what?

I asked if the commercials had "crossed the truth line?" He says that he is "very comfortable" with his ads, but I remind him I want to know about her spots. He concedes "She has taken disparate facts and attempted to mislead the people of Michigan to an erroneous conclusion." Pretty tough stuff, hey? As for Granholm, the former prosecutor, she says, "He's guilty." She points to a current DeVos spot claiming she never met with Honda to bring jobs back to Michigan. "That is an absolute falsehood." And in case you missed it, she drives home her point concluding, "He would be guilty as charged. It's an outright lie." What she said was true. Her first time in Tokyo she had a sit down with Honda. What she deliberately left out of her answer, which she is good at doing, is the fact that during the second visit, when Honda was on the brink of making its decision, she was overscheduled and could not meet. She sent her team instead. I reminded her of that omission. In her Green Room, her guys were reportedly shouting, "Shut up Skubick" because I was ruining her pefectly good answer. She delects my inquiry and repeats that his ad is still not true. Then she tells the viewers, "It's important for people to know the facts." Or I might add, only the facts she wants them to know. Then she beautifully blends into China. Only took her about 7 minutes. "He didn't make jobs in Michigan," she asserts, but he did create them in China. DeVos finally gets into the game. He stands his ground on the Honda meeting issue saying,

"I think it is a fact" that she didn't meet with the company on the second trip. But she hits back, "That's not what your ad says, sir." Then he tries once more to rebut the China jobs issue, saying it is "absolutely untrue," and once more he confides he is disappointed with her repeated accusations.

But it went down hill from there for the challenger. As one GOP insider noted, "It was like watching a hockey game. She threw down her gloves in the first 30 seconds, and he headed for the bench." He came off the bench long enough to deliver his best line of the night which followed a monologue by Granholm on the early success of her economic recovery program. He retorted, "It's hard to say the plan is working when the people are not."

We actually discovered a few things we did not know. DeVos would have vetoed a tobacco tax increase which she signed, because it was hurting businesses along the state's border. He also opposed the blowing up the Detroit Board of Education that former Governor John Engler recommended, and Granholm agreed with DeVos. By far the question that produced the most outrage from the viewers was the one on Ricky Holland, the little 7-year-old who was murdered. I brought it up in a careful manner so as not to be misunderstood. It was misunderstood anyway. The question to DeVos was, did he hold the governor "indirectly responsible" for the Holland death and the death of three people who were murdered by Patrick Selepak. He was the convict who was given a parole when he should have been in the slammer.

DeVos felt that a governor must "stand up and take responsibility" for an error within her administration. "I think it's a question of leadership. The people of Michigan need to know they're safe in their own homes." It was an okay answer, but he could have been stronger. Why not, "Governor, I am not blaming you with the death of four persons, but let's be honest here. Those persons died on your watch. The question is could you have done more to protect their lives? Do you know how to do that? Well, I do and if the buck does not stop at your desk, it sure as heck will stop at mine."

The governor took the offensive on her handling of the Selepak case. She said once the "mistake" was uncovered, she fired a bunch of employees in her corrections department. As for the

Holland case, a state agency did an investigation into her human service department's conduct, but she correctly reported she could not comment. The Ingham County Prosecutor Stuart Dunnings III put a lid on it pending the outcome of the murder trial involving the foster parents. Dunnings is a democrat so I asked him afterwards if he had done it to protect the governor from any incriminating evidence. He denied it and pointed out he made the decision to sit on the report long before the Holland issue became a political issue.

Many viewers blasted me for raising the issue. "I was so appalled at the question you raised...about the death of Ricky Holland," wrote someone from Muskegon. Another chimed in, the question was "ridiculously unfair." And on it went. I beg to differ. Those deaths occurred on the governor's watch. It was her corrections folks who gave Selepak a "Get out of Jail" card. The Child Protective Service workers assigned to the Holland case worked in the Granholm administration. They were in the Holland home looking for abuse. Either they didn't find it, or if they did, they did nothing about it. The Holland question was a classic accountability question and fair game. Not everyone agreed.

But the bombshell in the broadcast was delivered by the governor. Her team tried to get me to light the fuse. The morning of the debate, I got a phone call hinting that if I asked a question about "disclosure" and Mr. DeVos, I might get a newsworthy answer. I tried to fill in some of the blanks but did not get much from this source. After I hung up, I thought about it for a second and concluded I did not want to carry the water for her. I figured if she had something she wanted to pop, she would have to do it herself. She did.

Just past the half way mark of the broadcast, the governor looked at DeVos and recounted that over the weekend she had been reviewing his financial disclosure statement. (A little light reading to keep her amused in her spare time no doubt.) And she discovered that DeVos did not say anything about his holdings in the Alterra nursing home chain. Come to find out, the chain had a record of abusing senior citizens. The well-trained barrister was very careful not to accuse DeVos of being responsible, but she clearly hoped the audience would reach that conclusion on its own. All she really said was he did not disclose the investment.

DeVos said he found the charges "disappointing." He denied any wrongdoing; said his family owned only one-percent of the company stock, and decried the "tragic situation and unfortunate set of circumstances." Then he told the audience it turned out to be a "bad investment." Not exactly the best thing to say. Besides when he decided to run for governor he didn't own the stock anymore so there was no reason to disclose it, he explains.

Ignoring that critical point, the governor told Charlie Cain that maybe DeVos did not want us to know about his investment because of the abuse problem. DeVos countered it was only recently that he discovered the problems with the bankrupt company. Some believe the governor had another agenda. She wanted the audience to know that DeVos was rich. At one point with a delightful smile on her face and looking him right in the eye she commented on the $200 million he plunked into the failed venture. "That's a big investment, even for you." The reporters in the other studio laughed.

The democrats the next day tried to attach legs to the story. They kept it alive for four days and kept DeVos on the defensive and off his economic message but the "legs" fell off and the story died. There was even the hint that some viewers felt the governor hit below the belt by bringing it up in the first place.

After the nursing home questions, I cross-examined the governor on her personal convictions and whether she had compromised them for her own political gain. She asked for examples. I rattled off four: reparations, the Ten Commandments in the capitol, Detroit charter schools, and dove hunting. She had clearly changed her tune on each one of them, but even though I pressed, she would not concede that she changed her mind in order to win votes.

DeVos had his own problems on the prickly issue of abortion. Everywhere he went he proudly called himself a pro-life believer. He also personally believed that a woman should not be permitted an abortion in cases of rape and incest. That's what he felt inside, but trying to get him to admit that for public consumption continued to be a challenge. Just as the governor was attuned to statements that might cost her votes, DeVos also knew any chance he had of attracting pro-choice voters would evaporate if they knew he did not support the rape and incest exception. The question was asked twice and DeVos would only say, "I'm on the pro-life side of that debate...different people have different views" and then he looked at the governor and told her that her "self-proclaimed mentor," former Attorney General Frank Kelley, was "compatible" with DeVos on all this. The only exception DeVos favored was to save the life of the mother. Granholm called that, "far out of the mainstream."

I glanced at the clock. We were running out of time. Next was another unpopular question with some viewers. Let me pause here to explain a bias. I'm not fond of questions that are longer than the answers. Sometimes reporters feel they have to justify their questions by prefacing them with a ton of background. I think it is better to get in and get out with a short question. However, having said that, omitting the context can get you in trouble and that happened on the next inquiry.

"On a scale of one to ten, ten being the best grade, how much influence does your spouse have on your decision-making process?" Lots of folks thought that was off the wall. Here's the context I did not give that night. Word on the street was that both Dan Mulhern and Betsy DeVos had plenty of sway over their mates. I'm not saying that is wrong, but there were many in our town who believed that and feared it was detrimental to the governor and DeVos.

Some complained that the First Hubby was too nice and had no killer instinct that you needed to survive in this game. His was a collegial style based on the assumption that if everyone tried to work together, things would be all right. That's great if you're running a day camp for little kids, but in the rough and tumble world of politics, it could be deadly. I ran all this past a person who had a birds-eye seat and who saw Mulhern in action. He denied that Mulhern was calling the shots. What about the notion that his management style is to sit around, sing two verse of Kumbaya and all be right with the world? "That would be an unfair analysis," my source argues. Well what about reports than when she leaves a cabinet meeting, he takes over? Not true on that, too. In the GOP there were murmurings about Betsy being the power behind the throne, and if her hubby was elected, she might be the next republican Hillary Clinton. No one in the media had really written about this, but I had heard the conjecture which formed the foundation for the question.

DeVos went first. "I have great respect for my wife's ability in that area and I love my wife, very, very much." Can't go wrong with that, but I would not be deterred. I wanted to know about her influence not his love. He did disclose that she was more interested in the "political" side of the equation and not the governing side. He did not pick a number nor did he confirm that she possessed more power than the voting public knew about. In other words he danced.

The governor borrowed his tap shoes for her response. "It's hard to put a number on it; he's my best friend." Talk about drilling a dry hole. Someone suggested we needed a debate between Dan and Betsy.

With only thirty seconds remaining, Charlie got in a good one. "Tell the viewers something about yourself that they do not know." DeVos said he was a runner and had participated in three tri-athlones to keep in shape. Granholm told the oft-repeated story that hubby Dan had wanted to be a priest, "Before he met me. Thank God," she smiled. With that they gave their well-rehearsed closing statements and it was over. Well not quite.

Next came the infamous spin session. The reporters who had been watching now jumped into action as they mobbed DeVos on the nursing home "revelations." There must have been fifty media types jockeying to stick their cameras and microphones in his face. The governor, meanwhile, scooted out the side door to meet with reporters outside after they were done accosting DeVos. I walked toward the studio door, exchanged a few pleasantries with players from both camps, and saw my wife standing against the wall. Her smile told me everything had gone well. We hugged knowing that life would now sort of return to normal with this debate in the history books.

The newspaper columnists on the day after had lots of material to munch on. DeVos took some surprising hits at the hands of the conservative commentators. Daniel Howes from the *News* wrote, "With apologies to Republican challenger Dick DeVos, what was most "disappointing" about Monday's debate with Gov. Granholm was his performance." Nolan Finley piled on. "As for DeVos, he's got to find his cojones." Jim Schaefer at the *Free Press* asked, "What was more painful: watching DeVos try to smile while fending off accusations about his investments or watching Granholm lower her voice to get sincere with the people of Michigan?" Brian Dickerson from the *Freep* centered on DeVos's "verbal tics," suggesting that a focus group told him not to be angry, mad, or disgusted but it was O.K. to be disappointed. And Rochelle Riley came in from left field with, "The only person who showed up to debate was "Off the Record" host Tim Skubick, who asked hard questions and didn't let either candidate engage in planned sound bites....If the candidates continue to fail on pocketbook issues, then I, quite frankly, plan to vote for Tim Skubick." Oh dear.

And as if that was not bad enough, if you opened to the *Detroit News* editorial page just after the debate you saw a cartoon. A male viewer and his wife are looking at a TV screen with the title "Governor Debate." The cut line from the man reads, "He was aggressive, challenged the governor, and didn't back down. I'm voting for Tim Skubick." Thank goodness only about 8% of the newspaper readers stop on the editorial page. But thanks to H. Payne for the plug. What do they say, "Don't care what you say about me, just spell the name right." He did.

Bill Ballenger made the biggest post-debate splash as he suggested, "It's the worst performance in a debate I've seen in four decades...." Columnist Jack Lessenberry echoed that as he called it the "the worst performance by a major candidate for governor that anyone can remember." David Vizard from the *Bay City Times* even suggested it was time for DeVos to "withdraw from the race immediately...DeVos is burying himself."

While I got some favorable viewer comments, a bunch of folks were livid and blunt. "His republican partisanship was both obvious and overwhelming." "I write in the wake of your shameful conduct...you are a DeVos partisan." "You were so deferential to her...you enabled her great staging and acting and catered to her throughout." And my personal favorite: "You, sir, acted liked a colossal ASS." A relative, no doubt.

Does that stuff hurt? Not really. But by the same token it's no fun to read either. Despite negative viewer remarks, both sides felt I was fair. DeVos confided to someone after the fact that I "didn't let her off the hook." And Fox said I treated both candidates the same and he predicted, "I feel this effects the outcome" of the race.

One person I also ran into after the debate was my timekeeper. I was concerned that both candidates got equal face time. I was disheartened to learn that in the heat of the moment with so much going on in the control room, he forgot to start the clock. If he had, it would have revealed that she got five and a half more minutes than he did. I was not happy with that. A two-minute differential or less would have been more to my liking.

I asked my research assistant Rachel Moblo to run the numbers on how long each one spoke and the results were quite revealing. Take a guess at the average length of the DeVos sound bites during the debate? It was 39 seconds. 39 seconds. His longest answer was 1:50. He had 18 responses that were under a minute and only 9 answers over a minute. I concluded that he had his chance to talk longer which would have cut into the 5-minute deficit. But for some reason, he chose not to or couldn't. She on the other hand talked forever and at one point did 3 solid minutes on her economic plan. No one in a debate had ever run the clock like that.

Granholm's handlers did their private post-debate commentary. One was "stunned" that he wasn't better and suggested he was "Quayled." That's a not so flattering reference to the former GOP Vice President Dan Quayle who was not very adroit on his feet. GOP Chair Saul Anuzis must have had his fingers crossed when he suggested, "Given the political realities, given the issues, and given the expectations...Dick DeVos came out the clear winner!!! (Saul, your nose is growing.)

Only 8% of the viewers agreed with Pinocchio, err, Anuzis. Thirty-one percent gave it to Granholm and the rest gave it to both or neither. But even though she won the debate, the polls suggest she lost ground in the head to head. Going into the debate, she was at 50% and he was at 42%. When the dust settled after the debate, she lost four points. He lost two. The fence sitters almost doubled. It was an amazing finding. Obviously not everyone liked what they saw with some voters moving away from both of them.

Greg McNeilly, who told reporters he was more nervous than the candidate at the start of the debate, suggested that if you removed the Alterra story from the debate, "It was a win for us." Nonetheless he conceded his guy had some work to do on his stage demeanor. First, DeVos needed to figure out where to look and when. Either look at the camera or moderator but don't switch back and forth. You would have thought that by this stage of the game they would have figured that out. DeVos also had a head tilt as if he was trying to get water out of his ear. It was unnatural and weird. McNeilly also concluded his guy needed to be more assertive. But could a gentleman do that? I wondered.

John Truscott told the *Free Press* that DeVos had too many people giving him advice adding, "Dick is a nice, respectful guy. He is who he is. We're not going to try to change that. He's not the kind to go attacking someone."

Before putting this chapter to bed, some personal observations. When I saw the program the next morning after finally getting a good night's sleep, I felt that DeVos was not as bad as I thought he was during the debate. But I thought he lacked passion. The governor on the other hand had it coming out her ears. I thought he had been over handled as Truscott suggested. I wondered if they were afraid to let Dick be Dick for fear that if the real DeVos came out, voters would not like him. The length of his answers also bothered me. If you have command of an issue you should be able to talk for longer than 39 seconds. Did this guy have any depth? Was he a mile long and a quarter inch deep? Was he the creation of the media handlers who obviously did not do a bang-up job in getting him ready for the big one?

I knew that the Dick DeVos I observed in the SUV that day last summer was not the guy who appeared in Studio A. On the road he was easy to talk with, he readily shared his feelings on issues, and seemed to be a man who knew where he was headed, plus he had a good sense of humor. While most observers blamed him for not answering the questions in the debate, it bothered me more that when he got that "deer-in-the-headlights" look, he automatically fell back on his standard and canned lines that he mouthed in his commercials. You know the stuff about being a businessman and knowing how to create jobs. In a nutshell, he did not appear confident. He did not appear in control and he sure as heck did not look gubernatorial, and in this game, image means a lot with the voters who are more inclined to vote from their gut than their brains.

The more I thought about his showing in debates one and two, the more it appeared to me that if this man was elected, I would be writing about this "depth-of-knowledge" issue again. Would he be the man in charge or would he be manipulated by those around him? He was fond of saying that if everyone in the room agreed with him, one of them was not needed. But was it just talk? Would he lead based on his convictions or would he be malleable? Would the buck stop at his desk, and if it did, would he have the gravitas to make the best decision for the state?

As for the impact the first debate would have on the outcome, one GOP insider confided to me in an email, "The dem partisans were happy, the Republican partisans disappointed. That leaves about 100,000 undecided." This source says those folks were confused by what they saw. The Granholm they witnessed was combative and not necessarily the likeable woman they thought they knew. By the same token, "DeVos didn't convince them he could step up and do that much better of a job...." And if there was any good news in a lousy debate performance, this source optimistically concluded, "He has nowhere to go but up..It can ONLY get better." And in the next debate it did.

24

The Real Dick DeVos?

A new and improved Dick DeVos showed up for the second tele-vised debate replacing the old and battered DeVos who tanked in the first one. He started his second performance by calling the governor a liar and closed by asking voters to fire her. In-between he got in some punches to boot. In other words within one week he did a 180 degree flip. Some debate commentators even gave him the "W" over the incumbent governor. Talk about your come-back kid.

Obviously on this October 14, 2006, date we don't know the outcome but if he turns out to be the winner, the governor shares part of the credit. It's ironic, but what she did to him inspired her op-ponent to revamp his act and regain some badly needed momentum going into the home stretch…momentum that democrats had sucked out of his campaign for the last month or so.

Here's what happened. When the governor hit him with the nursing home stuff in debate one, DeVos was not only surprised, he was upset. He personally decided to do something about it, and with the help of his handlers, his personal reformation was apparent just 30 seconds into the broadcast in Grand Rapids at WOOD-TV 8.

"I learned a few things in the first debate," DeVos began in his opening remarks. What he learned was that the "Governor looked straight into the camera and lied" about the infamous nursing home issue. I was watching from the media bull pen and thought this was not the same guy. He told the audience that earlier he had been "disappointed" with her behavior but now he was "furious." Only problem was, he did not act nor sound furious. Regardless, it was a good opening and set the tone for the rest of the night.

The governor opened by acknowledging that the Detroit Tigers were playing in the American League Championship series and she thanked the viewers for watching her instead of pitcher Justin Verlander. Her statement sounded great, but was a tad misleading in that her debate team had deliberately chosen that date just because there was the conflict with the ball game. My source believes the other side never bothered to check that little point. In other words, Granholm and company did not want a big audience. That not withstanding, she launched into her opening statement completely ignoring the liar stuff that DeVos put on the table. Nor did she seem concerned that the guy at the podium next to her was furious. She wanted to talk about her plans to turn the economy around. Hadn't we heard that before? Yep, and we were going to hear it again and again whether the press corps liked it or not. With opening comments out of the way, a panel of three reporters took over led by Rick Ablin and his partners Devin Scillian from WDIV-TV, Detroit, and Mike Wendland from the *Detroit Free Press*.

This debate was tightly structured which played into DeVos's hand. Reporters could ask one question. The candidate got two minutes to respond, followed by a one-minute response from the second candidate. If the first candidate wanted another thirty seconds, he or she got it. There were no follow-up questions although that rule was broken a few times.

DeVos took the first toss up. He was asked to list three things he would do to reinvigorate the economy that the governor had not done. He listed six and asked, "Is that sufficient?" He seemed to be saying, they accused me of not having command of the subject in the first debate, here's proof to the contrary. The competitive governor matched him with six ideas of her own. As the thing went on, you could see that DeVos had learned from his mistakes. Gone was the slanted head trying to get the water out of his ear. Gone was the confusion on where to look. Gone was the deer-in-the-headlight gaze. At one point he even gave it back to her when she got him on the single business tax replacement question. The governor was one response away from landing a nice punch, but the moderator blew the whistle and the opportunity was lost.

Granholm laid off the nursing home angle and hammered away at DeVos for cutting Michigan jobs while creating jobs in China. She concluded that that effort made him "someone who was part of the problem, not someone who is part of the solution." And for good measure she acknowledged that DeVos was a CEO, but with skills that "were not transferable to being governor."

Revamping the line, "There you go again" once used by former President Ronald Reagan, DeVos fired back, "Here you go again." Then he said her statement was a "lie." He added, "The governor is willing to do anything and say anything to keep her job in Michigan." Nobody hit one out of the park and while the governor seemed a little off balance at times, she gave a steady performance and appeared pleased that she could talk about her beloved job's agenda. DeVos finally figured out how to segue from a reporter's question into what he wanted to talk about. He even got in a plug for his website which he failed to do last time out.

He made some news with his plan to eliminate the personal property tax on business equipment. That meant very little to the typical viewer, but if you own a company and have machines on the factory floor, you pay a tax on that stuff. DeVos wanted to wipe out the $1.7 billion tax. The governor saw an opening and jumped in with both feet demanding to know how he would replace that revenue on top of the $1.9 billion from the SBT. DeVos did not offer a solution. Once again, the old DeVos reappeared. He was long on the ideas, but real short on the "how to." That was now a recurring theme in his campaign. It wasn't until after the program that his handlers tried to clean up the mess by filling in some details that DeVos left out.

And before you knew it, it was time for closing statements. DeVos went first as he rattled off all the things that were wrong in

Michigan from the lousy real estate market to the kids leaving the state. "It's not personal, but we know they're [meaning her] not getting the job done and it's time to make a change." He noted that if he had been running things they way she ran them, "I'd be gone by now." And then he moved in for the kill which was rare for him. He suggested it was time to "sever the relationship" and everyone sat up when he concluded, "Unfortunately, we have to fire the governor and head in a new direction." And then he slammed home his point by asking what all good republicans do when they run against an incumbent democrat, "Are you better off today than you were four years ago? If the answer is no, it's time for a change."

Granholm got the mike next and reworked his question. "We have a lot of differences my opponent and I. I guess the question for him would be, is he better off than he was four years ago? My guess is he is, because he is somebody who supported unfair trade agreements that got Michigan into this mess in the first place." It was a good retort. Then she hit him again for all his foreign investments. "That is not leadership for Michigan." She concluded by explaining the "seeds had been planted" for an economic turnaround and she asked for "your vote" to continue the job of growing them.

With the program out of the way, everyone in the press pit wanted to know the score in the game. The Tigers were beating the Oakland A's 3 to 0 and went on to win. The media pack moved into the TV-8 spin room where DeVos was holding court. Walking up the back stairs to the studio, it dawned on me that the DeVos we saw this night was not the same one we had seen a week ago and I was wondering, "Who is the real Dick DeVos?" I also wondered if the handlers remolded his image, his message, his everything that resulted in a stronger looking contender? It wasn't long before I asked exactly that. "Did your handlers get to you?" DeVos did not flinch as he glared at me with, "The only one who got to me was me." Great line and it was delivered with the passion that was woefully missing from his earlier "furious" line. He goes on to explain that the guy you saw in the first debate was trying to be a gentleman, but the person "you saw tonight is the Dick DeVos who is ready to lead."

State Democratic Party Chair Mark Brewer would have none

of that. He said the handlers did get to DeVos, and it was no surprise he was on the attack given his lousy showing a week earlier. He again accused DeVos of having no substance. Granholm spokesperson Chris DeWitt earned his pay telling reporters, "This was Dick DeVos's second job interview and there is no reason he should be hired by the people of the State of Michigan." All of this was quite predictable and frankly, I am not sure why the media devotes so much time and energy to these spin sessions. Everyone in the room knows that neither side is going to concede defeat, but you have to cover it anyway. Who knows somebody might say something that was actually newsworthy.

Next it was out to the parking lot where Granholm supporters were gathered with their signs as they shouted "Four more years. Four more years." Wonder if they knew they swiped that from a republican named Nixon...as in Richard M.? Somebody from the state GOP got a picture of all this with a parking lot sign in the middle of the demonstrators. It read: "Wrong Way" and stood out like the proverbial sore thumb. GOP Chair Saul Anuzis made sure the "wrong way" sign, his metaphor for Granholm, was on his web site the next day.

Granholm emerged and handled the first soft ball of the night on her economic recovery plan. She loved that. But I was trying to think of something a tad more challenging. It struck me that each time DeVos asked the "better off than four years ago" question during the broadcast, she never directly answered it, so I tried. "With all due respect governor you never answered the better off question." "Tim, [When she starts out that way, I know I have her attention.] the U.S. auto industry is not better off than four years ago." "But what about individuals?" I wanted to know. She would not bite. She stayed on the auto industry theme and then segued into blaming DeVos for creating the policies that, yes we know, "got us into this mess in the first place."

Just a side bar note on hearing the same lines over and over again from candidates. I do not mean to be disrespectful. I understand they have to repeat and repeat the same thing because each time it's a new audience. But the danger is, the press corps begins to tune out. And in fact the governor has joked on the stump, "You've heard all this before." But she still has to say it again. We just don't have to report it.

By now it is about 9:45 p.m., and it's time to head back for a live shot at 11 on "News Ten." I wrote the story in the van and began with the "Fire the governor" line. I suggested that he had won the debate just because he had done so much better.

By the time I got home around 11:30, there was an email waiting for me from Mr. McNeilly. He had been standing next to DeVos during the spin session and heard my question about who is the real DDV. McNeilly shared with me two documents that demonstrated to him that it was the candidate and not the handlers who had reconstructed his image at least for his opening and closing assaults.

Go back to the night before the debate. McNeilly sends the boss a draft for opening and closing comments. The memo reads: "Dick—Attached is a draft for the 1 minute opening, 2 minute close in the debate. Re-write, delete, etc as you see fit. It's your delivery, so it has to be your way." The remarks contain a litany of what's wrong in Michigan and it reads, "If you're tired of broken promises and no results, then vote for change....Let's take Michigan forward, in a new direction." The closing is along the same lines although the script is direct, "Michigan wants real leadership...the buck stops at the top with our governor...and I'll be a governor who has the guts to make the tough decisions that are needed to turn our state around...Everyone makes mistakes. That's life. But one difference between the governor and I [sic]. I will always take responsibility" etc., etc. DeVos comes in on the day of the debate and announces, "I didn't like the copy." McNeilly goes, "O.K., thoughts on what direction you'd like to go?" On the spot McNeilly says DDV "proceeds to give out loud, from no notes, the opening and close he used tonight. Totally him, totally from his heart on this." As DeVos himself said, "The only one who got to me was me."

The next morning DeVos declares himself the debate winner on the Frank Beckmann show on WJR Radio, but he did not get the pop out of the Grand Rapids event he hoped for. The TV audience in Detroit was about 700,000 less than it was for the first debate. Nobody reported what the outstate viewership was, but with the

Tigers on the air, it's safe to assume a million plus folks did not see the revised edition of Dick DeVos. That means all the folks who saw him on October 2 were stuck with that lack-luster image he projected.

And to make matters worse, the new poll that came out three days after the debate showed he slipped and she gained. Go figure. After the first debate that the governor won, she lost four points. After the second debate that he won, he gained only two points to her five. The EPIC-MRA folks had her breaking the magical 50% plateau but just by a smidgen. It was Granholm 51%. DeVos with 42%. The voters on the fence dropped from 12% to 5%. In other words her performance moved her into a 9-point lead. As the *Detroit News* reported, "The last time Granholm was over the 50-percent mark was in February, [2006] when she led DeVos 53%-46%." It took her eight months of slogging along to finally get a lead that looked like a lead.

There was more good news for her. She increased her margin with pro-choice voters by 9 points. Union folks came home with 75% backing her and 22% backing him. And in the vital female and independent category, Granholm won both. She was sitting pretty for the first time in a long time. But it was not time to declare victory and go home. Not by any means. DeVos could read the numbers and when a challenger is down, you can only do one thing, get up and strike back. He did so by delivering perhaps the best speech of his short-lived political career, and I missed it.

Photog Steve Coon and I were set to head to Detroit to cover a joint appearance on Friday, October 13, how fitting. We just got onto I-96 when it felt as though we were transported to some desolate and backwater two-lane highway in the Upper Peninsula. It was a total white out. The first winter storm of the season. We decided to chuck it. I had a book to finish, and I did not want to do it from a hospital bed.

Consequently, I had to read the DeVos speech and soak up the reportage of my colleagues. The popular wisdom was he was very good. Two good performances in a row. Something new for him and it came in front of an audience of 1200 influential business types at the Detroit Economic Club. Each candidate got 15 minutes.

DeVos showed some guts by allowing Oakland County Executive L. Brooks Patterson do the intro. Patterson is the lovable "Clown Prince" of state GOP politics, and he did not disappoint.

"I'm supposed to introduce Dick DeVos. Or as Beth Chapel [of the Economic Club] calls him...Mr. Dick. [laughter] Actually, I don't know what I can say about Dick DeVos that hasn't already been said about Kenneth Ley." More laughter. Ley was the convicted and dead CEO who ran Enron into the ground. "Sheky" Patterson finally got off stage and DeVos opens with, "I'm not someone who is afraid of taking risks...just look at who I asked to introduce me." But that was the last time he made a funny. The rest of his speech, with the governor sitting 10 feet from him, was dead serious.

"I know what your thinking. You're thinking about the job that Jennifer Granholm has done and you're not happy....You like the governor, but you just don't know whether to trust her to run state government for another fours years. At the same time, you're not sure about me." No truer statement could have been made. Voters around the state knew DeVos from the commercials but lots of them saw a different DeVos in the first debate and yet another one in the second debate. He was largely an unknown quantity, but he promised in his speech that he would resolve their concerns about "where I will lead Michigan as governor."

Then he bangs out a top-ten list that was not written by David Letterman. He outlines in crisp fashion the "first ten action steps I will take on New Year's Day, after taking the oath of office." He pledges to take personal control of the Michigan Economic Development Corporation. Never mind that it is a quasi-private and quasi-government agency that the governor can't control. Then he calls for more spending for higher ed, the cutting of red tape, he'll open ten trade offices in Japan, and on and on including number ten, "I will meet with Detroit Mayor Kwame Kilpatrick, and I will tell him that Detroit's success is critical to Michigan's success." The only thing missing from that line was a "Take that Governor Granholm." What DeVos did not reveal in his speech was that he had already held several private meetings with the mayor, and Kilpatrick had assigned a personal liaison from his office to confer with DeVos during the campaign.

DeVos also zings the current governor. "This governor will finally get the job done when it comes to creating a regional transit system." Oh man. He better be careful. Every single governor I have covered since Bill Milliken made the same promise that turned out to be empty. I figure the only way DeVos can meet that promise is to use his own wealth to buy the subways and hire the workers to build it. Then in his speech he goes back to an issue that was raised in the first debate and second time out, he is more forceful. "I've been asked if I believe the governor is responsible for these tragic events and my answer is yes." He refers to the Holland and Selepak cases. Two events that refuse to go away in this race. In case the governor missed the point, he adds, "You cannot solve a problem if you will not take responsibility for it."

All in all, it is a hard-hitting message. He pulls no punches and lands a few of his own right on her chinny-chin-chin. Afterward she is not amused as she tells reporters DeVos is "desperate" because he is behind in the polls. In her speech she told the audience she was interviewing for the job and took a jab at DeVos, "At a job interview you're supposed to tell what you're all about and [not] run down the other guy." She lays out her economic accomplishments and notes, "I even received a letter from one of Mr. DeVos's companies praising us for this....I've signed 84 targeted tax cuts. I'm a fiscal hawk—I ask for your vote," she concluded her talk.

DeVos got some kudos from the media for the Econ Club event, but he got none from the voters. There was no TV coverage. So for most citizens it was a non-event. And to make matters worse for him, it got minimal newspaper coverage because that night the Tigers whooped the Oakland A's for the third time, and that was all over the papers the next morning. Sure DeVos was now hitting some home runs. Only problem was, with the Tigers on their way to the World Series, the only home runs covered by the media were in Comerica Park. DeVos was now the victim of Tiger-mania in the media.

25
Slugfest in Southfield

It's days like these that political reporters think, maybe I should have gone into sports. The race for the World Series has supplanted the race for governor. The fact that the Tigers beat the Oakland A's with a dramatic home run in the bottom of the ninth with two outs no less, somehow makes the ball game between Ms. Granholm and Mr. DeVos less compelling, at least that would be the impression from reading the morning papers.

But the *Detroit Free Press* did have a story on the inside front page. It hinted ever so faintly that DeVos was set to do his best imitation of the Oakland Athletics. Pollster J. Ann Selzer, noting the 49% to 41% advantage for Granholm suggested, "It would take a huge effort for DeVos to pull it out." I could hear the dull thud over on the other side of town at DeVos headquarters.

The most telling part of the column by Chris Christoff was not the words but the graphic just below the headline that read, "Granholm Surges." It was one of those typical line charts with one line for her and one for him. In July, the graph shows DeVos at 47% and the governor down at 42% and then his line gradually and steadily moves down as her's moves up. The two lines eventually cross making a prophetic "X" in August as he hits 44% and she takes a slim lead of 46%. Her line ends on October 11 with her firmly ahead. This "X" graph may tell the whole story when the votes are counted on election night. He won the race when it didn't count, and he lost it when it did? He peaked too soon would be the ancillary conclusion. Republicans rushed to counter that John Mathias Engler was behind at this point, and he won. Yes, but is DDV another JME?

You did not hear any champagne corks popping over on Oxford Road in the executive residence. The two adult occupants know full well this is not over. A long time Granholm confidant and I finally hooked up for a long delayed interview and I inquired as to the significance of this Granholm lead. "Nobody is sitting on their heels. We take nothing for granted," was the wise comment. This source had been through many a war to know that winning a battle meant nothing. But Granholm's current lead did mean one thing. "Where she sits today is validation of her decision not to go up against DeVos when he started running all his ads." Remember the governor took a ton of hits for sitting on her cash, while he was spending his. But given where she was at this moment, the decision to sit tight, despite all the heat, "was one of the most important decisions of the campaign," this Granholm friend reveals.

Yet there was a related factor to consider. In the beginning there was speculation that DeVos might shell out close to $60 million to get elected. Whether that was true or not, this source says, "We assumed it was right. In essence it became the truth. It drove the thinking that we were going to be outspent." Thus in that context, the tactical move not to match him dollar for dollar was an even gutsier move. In theory with all his spending, by the time she got in the game, it could have been over. But lucky for her it did not work out that way. In fact here she sits today in the middle of October with a lead over him despite being outspent.

While we were on the subject of important decisions, this source confided that a campaign comes down to a "finite number of critical decisions." If that was the case, I wanted to know what else was in that category with about 25 days to go.

Up near the top was the China decision by the Granholm campaign to start early and run long and hard on the fact that he created jobs in China. "It resonates with voters and became a tuning fork issue." Meaning what? I asked. It boils down to, "Whose side are you on?" From the movement of union members back to Granholm, many blue collars folks concluded DeVos was on the wrong side. In other words, the China ads, gong and all, worked for Granholm according to her friend.

What else was on the list of critical strategy moves? The first debate was. As was laid out earlier, the Granholm inner circle thought this was a "very important decision" to get him into an unstructured format that lots of folks would see. "It was the worst format for him. It gave her the potential to control the dialogue and it would be the one with the largest audience." With a little chuckle this person observes, "She took charge of the hour" and it showed that DeVos was not the guy all the viewers had seen in the commercials. Thus going into the program they knew what they wanted and coming out they had it.

For the last two weeks, it's been life in the bubble with a flurry of debates. Now on the eve of the last one, it's time to pick apart some of the outside-the-bubble-issues that are impacting this contest. By the time you read this, the name Mark Foley will be but a bad memory. While the former Florida congressman is not on the ballot in Michigan, his sending of suggestive e-mails to underage pages in Congress is a sub-rosa element nonetheless. Not everyone agrees, but one gets the feeling the whole GOP is in a funk. The president gets most of the blame for Michigan's ugly economy. The president gets no points for the daily bombings in Iraq, and the religious right within the party is appalled at the email scandal even though Letterman and Leno are having a field day with it. If the national polls are correct this could be a watershed year for the democrats who are poised to exploit the hand ringing in the GOP ranks.

I called it the "Republican Malaise" on OTR this week which means many republicans may find something else to do other than vote on Election Day because they are so discouraged. That helps Granholm. During the broadcast I asked the snowstorm question to test my hypothesis. If there is a blizzard on Election Day, who will show up at the polls? That's another way of saying, which party has the passion to vote? Bill Ballenger thought republicans would be there. The AP's Kathy Barks Hoffman did not agree. Ballenger did make a good point that during his lectures around the state, he found very few democrats who were eager to vote for Granholm.

In fact he felt the only reason they would support her is that they disliked DeVos even more. That coincided with the sentiment I was picking up that this thing was coming down to a choice of the "lesser of two evils" in some voter's minds. I was also sensing, with no data to back it up, that some moderate GOP types were saying they backed DeVos in public, but in the privacy of the voting booth where DeVos could not see, they'd either vote for Granholm or not vote at all. In the latter case, it was a defacto vote for her. I knew of one state lawmaker who had a DeVos sign on his front lawn but was going to vote for Granholm.

Before moving to the final debate, several thoughts emerge from the Christoff column on the new survey. Here are factors that may or may not determine the outcome: She wins on the charisma scale, trustworthiness, charm, hard worker, brainy and tuned in to average Michiganders. He beats her on the vision thing as the first President Bush used to say. On having a strong faith in God, they are virtually tied, although 40% didn't know the two were very religious. There's a reason for that; neither has played that up.

Four years ago, then governor candidate Granholm and former seminarian and candidate David Bonior exchanged so many Bible verses in a debate that it felt like a Billy Graham crusade. So far in this race, the Good Book has not been quoted as much. By the way while on the subject of religion, remember that I theorized that she was lighting candles to land the new Toyota engine plant in Michigan before the election. Well forget it. I have two good sources who contend she should save her matches. It's not going to happen, as the Japanese carmaker does not want to get in the middle of this dogfight. To underscore that attitude, there were unconfirmed reports that Toyota was less than overjoyed when some video appeared in a Granholm commercial showing a groundbreaking at the company's research and development facility near Ann Arbor.

Toyota and Honda did not come up in the final televised debate but lots of other stuff did as the candidates rolled in for the slugfest in Southfield on the evening of October 16, 2006.

On WWJ Radio the morning of the debate, anchors Joe Donovan and Roberta Jasina wanted to know how high the stakes were for this final meeting. They were much higher for Mr. DeVos than for the governor. She was the one with a nine-point lead. He had to slice into that. She was the one with some momentum, although he was doing better. She was the master debater while he was the one with the checkered debate history. That did not instill much confidence in the DeVos debate team which had been through a lot and not all of it good.

I had a DeVos source who shared with me the overall analysis of the first two debates going into this most critical final meeting. Even though they started two weeks before the first session to "practice in front of a podium, Dick was a little stiff but getting much better. A week out we met every day and practiced." That's when Brooks Patterson and John Truscott played the part of Granholm. (More on that shortly.) In fact this source says Truscott was so good that after he "basically took the head off of DeVos," the candidate said, "I don't like you very much any more." Everyone laughed. Everyone was still in a good mood immediately after the first debate, but it was short-lived. Then the "public responses rolled in…we were devastated for him—it wasn't fair and it was our fault" for over prepping him.

For the second session, "We completely changed tactics." DeVos himself was showing some new life when he appeared at a *Grand Rapids Press* editorial board meeting that day. When he got a question about democratic U.S. Senator Carl Levin being critical about China jobs, DeVos lashed out with, "Carl Levin doesn't have a clue what he's talking about." This source says DeVos showed some fire and when he showed up at WOOD-TV that night, "He was a different person—quiet but confident. When he walked into the studio, an aide told him, "Let's see that Carl Levin fire." DeVos smiled.

With all those ups and downs over the first two debates, it was time to meet the governor for the last time. Given his on again-off again performances, who knew what would happen next? This source says DeVos was "probably more nervous at this one because there was so much riding on it." The strategy was to let "Dick be Dick." It had taken them a long time to arrive at the obvious.

I arrived at WXYZ Broadcast House around 7 p.m., about an hour before airtime. It is always rather melancholy going back there since I worked at "Wixie" radio in my first real news job after college.

The weather this night was damp and chilly, but that did not deter the demonstrators from both camps who established a beach-head in front of the station. Like a roving circus that moved from town to town, the debate groupies who were in East Lansing and then Grand Rapids were back with their signs that they feverously waved as everyone entered the station grounds. One sign caught the governor's attention, but we would not hear about that until after the debate.

Providing a little comic relief while we waited for the opening bell was L. Brooks Patterson. Fresh off his laugh-filled performance at the Detroit Economic Club just three days earlier, I got Mr. P. on camera and discovered something very interesting. He was pretending to be Jennifer Granholm.

You are taught in journalism school never to ask a question without knowing the answer, and I knew the answer to my first inquiry. "Did you play the role of the governor in debate preparations for Mr. DeVos?" Brooks laughs and confirms it, and I ask him how he got ready to do that? "I walked around the house in high heels for a week," he delivers his first punch line. I asked him if he wore a wig? He apparently did not. Getting serious for a moment, he added, "I tried to study up on the issues and then when the questions came, I tried to anticipate how she would answer them. I just tried to give him some low shots below the belt [chuckle] to get him ready for the debate." I wondered if he was aggressive? "I was all over him like an old suit, but even as hard as I attacked, I had no idea that the Alterra shot was coming. [the nursing home/abuse thing she popped on Mr. D. in debate one] I hope I played a constructive role," Brooksy concluded although he conceded the first debate left lots to be desired.

"Have you ever played the governor before?" I ended the interview. "No, but Mulhern [First Gentleman] made a pass at me." How can you top that? Nor would you even want to try.

Also hanging out in the lobby were the two party chairs. Brewer predicted a round of nasty ads going into the home stretch from the other side and he pitched me on the "malaise" stuff in the national GOP claiming the party was "imploding." His GOP amigo Saul Anuzis offered, "What malaise?" He was spinning me because privately he was saying there were concerns about the scandals within his own party. He also shared one tidbit as we came down the home stretch. He had 40,000 volunteers standing at the ready to make over 3 million phone calls to get the GOP faithful to the polls on Election Day. 3 million!

We were now about 10 minutes from airtime. In the media bullpen, the same crew that had covered the other two debates had assembled. Times must be tough at WXYZ. In years past there was free pizza for everyone. Now there was pop, water, and some potato chips. There was no collection plate next to the meager goodies.

Meanwhile inside the studio, Mark Fox and Chris DeWitt dropped off the governor at the stage door. Just before she went in, she turns to Fox and comments that DeVos has spent a ton of money on his commercials. He says, "That's the second worse investment he has made," with the first one being the investment in Alterra which DeVos himself conceded was not a good one. The governor laughed. Fox warns her not to use the line in the debate. At about the same time, the challenger shows up. Fox tells me the governor moved to say hello, but DeVos moved right past her to his podium. This was not a happy camper as I would amazingly discover in a rare and startling moment right after the debate in the back hallway.

The rules for this debate were restrictive just like the second meeting. There were time limits on the answers and responses and no opportunity for the two to go back and forth. As an added twist, a group of undecided voters was in the studio to offer up their questions as well. The governor liked this format and it was assumed that DeVos, who had worked many an Amway convention, would do well, too.

Moderator Chuck Stokes from TV-7 outlined the rules, and

they were off with anchorwoman Dianna Lewis's first toss up. It was right down the governor's alley as Ms. Lewis wanted to know what was the one thing the governor would do to change the state's economy. The governor picks up her Louisville Slugger bat, and whacks the softball out of the park. She says something about her 21st Century Jobs Program, but then catches everyone off guard as she segues into a hardball of her own.

Following the DeVos speech at the Econ Club in which he listed the names of foster care children who had been murdered on the governor's watch, the Granholm camp had done damage control to mute the criticism. Now the governor was taking matters into her own hands as she looked right in the camera and basically told DeVos to knock it off.

"Mr. DeVos, if you have a beef with me bring it on. I can take it. But leave the deceased children's name[s] out of it. If you're determined to pick a fight, I would ask you to pick one with someone your own size. Use my name. But let's leave the names of deceased children out of it."

It was a masterful preemptive strike. By ordering him to keep the "deceased" out of the debate, she was neutralizing one of the issues he wanted to use against her, namely that she had mismanaged her departments which led to those tragic deaths. If DeVos did go there during the debate, she would just make her point over and over again that he was using the kids for his own political gain. DeVos did not bring it up. The strategy worked. But the governor was not done. After taking questions on banning smoking in restaurants, she was for it, he was not, and the single business tax, the governor moved in with another "Alterra-like" surprise. She discloses that when DeVos was CEO of Amway, the company took advantage of a tax loophole as he incorporated subsidiaries in Bermuda to avoid paying his "fair share of American taxes."

DeVos, acting like he did in the first debate, did not come out swinging. "You're doing it again. You know that's not true and you're doing it again." And for old-time sake he trots out this one again, "That's disappointing." Aw, shucks. But before DeVos can refute the claim in detail, the moderator jumps in and explains he will get his turn later on. Once again, the governor scores a point.

DeVos is left standing at the gate. This was a theme in all three debates and one that did not serve him well.

Just before the Bermuda surprise, out of nowhere, the debate is stopped and they go to a Channel 7 "Action News" promo. Everyone in the bullpen was going, "What the hell was that?" I wrote down, "Tacky." Come to find out there were major problems with DeVos's microphone. You could hear it crackling on the air. The station went to the filler to give the technicians time to fix the problem. There must have been a debate-bug on the loose in the state because in the U.S. Senate debate that ran the day before, due to technical problems, the entire broadcast was delayed by ten whole minutes.

We are now 25 minutes into this debate, and it's time for the studio audience to get into the act. Christine, a small business owner, announces that she and husband Brian are thinking about leaving the state because their plumbing business is going down the toilet. (Sorry, couldn't resist.) She tells both candidates she is "terrified about what the future holds." DeVos gets to go first and he must be thinking, at last a softball for me.

"The governor does not have the experience to know what it takes" to run a small business. He shares with Christine that he grew up with parents in a small business, too. He does not say he feels her pain, however. And then he pulls off an ad-lib that had his handlers cheering in the backroom. They had never heard it before but he says, the governor has "never signed the front of a paycheck."

Granholm takes a different tact and gets personal. "It's Christine?" the governor asks in her best consoling voice. Then she asks about the woman's children, their ages and the governor notes she has young children, too. My. My. She does not ask for the woman's favorite meatloaf recipe, however. The governor says she wants jobs for her children as well, and reports, "We are going through some restructuring." Next she warns her newly found friend Christine that if DeVos gets his way by ending the SBT, there will be even greater problems in Michigan. She admonishes him to explain again how he will replace the revenue if the business tax is cut. "This is not Washington. Two plus two in Lansing still equals four," she lectures her opponent. And then the governor ends her response which reveals her essence. She contends that Michigan is a "magical state" and "We're going to be O.K." DeVos did not have the opportunity but he should have said, "Tell that to the 7% of the people without a job tonight." More on missed opportunities in the next chapter.

The debate rolls on. On those rare occasions when the candidates wanted to get into it with each other, they could not, which caused moderator Stokes to lament, "You all negotiated these rules." Amen, brother Chuck. There were questions on funding for higher education, Canadian trash, revenue sharing, property taxes, and public transit. None of this makes any news. We move to closing statements as the clock winds down to 9 p.m.

DeVos was very good this night on his repeated theme that the governor has had four years and there are no results, so he comes back to that in his closing remarks. He notes that she "continues to mis-state the facts" while at the same time "letting the state down." He notes she has "failed on every count and failed to protect Michigan while she tries to protect her job."

Granholm repeats her economic stuff and manages to play the class warfare card one more time. She notes that her opponent is an "expert yachtsman," which is code for rich guy, and she asserts that his philosophy is "each man for himself." She says, "I'm captain of the ship" with the attitude of "We are all in this boat together." And that's that.

The debate season is now officially over, but one more spin session to endure. The Granholm folks are woefully weak on propping up the Bermuda tax break charge. We are told the details are coming...and so is Christmas. She also expands on her remarks about him using the "deceased children" and notes that when her SUV drove in that night, she saw pictures of Ricky Holland on some placards...placards held by DeVos supporters.

For his part DeVos claims his company never used the tax loophole and he refers everyone to the company for more details. The story does not get legs. But the accusation must have touched off something in DeVos. I was the lone reporter to witness that "something" as I followed him out of the studio where he marched toward his vehicle as they put the third debate in the history books.

26

Anger, Cheaters, Daughters, and Abortion

The Tigers open the World Series tonight, October 21, 2006, in Motown. The state is awash in Tiger-fever. In yesterday's paper there were dozens of sports stories, but not one, single, column inch on the race for governor. However, there are new efforts by Granholm and DeVos to weasel their way into the sports coverage. Hey, if you can't beat 'em, join 'em.

On the Dick DeVos web sight his last name is spelled with the Olde English "D" just like the one on the Tiger's home uniforms. And outside the ballpark on game night, DeVos and his entire family handed out t-shirts with the same lettering on the "D" for DeVos.

In the polls, Michigan is feeling better about itself. Prior to the baseball playoffs, only 27% of the voters thought the economy would improve, and now with the best of seven series on the line, the number is 34%. Still not great, but the incumbent governor will take it. Up is better than down anytime. Wonder if she is angling to toss out the first pitch in one of the games—even though she admittedly concedes, "I throw like a girl."

Both sides are aware that getting a political story out these days is a challenge. "It's impossible to break through with any message," suggests John Truscott. That is echoed by Chris DeWitt, "The focus is going to be on the games." But that doesn't mean they aren't trying. DeVos beat the governor to the punch on lining up a bet with the Governor of Missouri, home of the St. Louis Cards who are in the series, too. DeVos will send a case of Faygo pop, a case of Vernors ginger ale to Governor Matt Blunt if the Tigers lose, and Blunt promises to send along some beer if he loses. Hope he keeps those messy Clydesdale horses right where they are.

As for Governor Granholm, she put Little Caesar's pizzas and Vernors on the line, and she'll don a Cardinals uniform. She extracted from her Missouri counterpart a commitment to be photographed wearing a Tiger's jersey. Plus, regarding the Tiger manager, Blunt has to hold a sign saying "Jim Leyand is My Tiger." He also has to sing "Take Me Out to the Ball Game" on a Detroit radio station. All of this made it into the newspapers. But that may be it. In fact for the next two weeks, DeVos will focus on the west side of the state with a bus tour that basically ignores Southeast Michigan. Granholm who missed the first game, will surely get a seat for at least one of the remaining games. And some bad news for both candidates: a sign was seen in the stands, "Leyland for Governor."

Back to the action in the race for governor. The Debate World Series was over and the third meeting was another rating success. 252,000 households, or just over half a million viewers tuned in. They not only tuned in, they stayed glued to their sets. During the first quarter hour the rating was 12.2% and it steadily grew at the conclusion to 13.7%. Compare that to a rained-out baseball game on FOX which netted a 4.9% rating.

And glory be, "Deal or No Deal" lost again. It could only muster an 11.8% showing. If you roll in the 190,000 households that viewed the second debate with the record breaking one million for the first meeting, you had over 1.8 million viewers for all three debates. Who says citizens are not interested in politics? But despite the good numbers, it was not good news for DeVos. He had a viewer deficit problem. About 200,000 who saw him in the first debate, did not see him improve in the other two. So they got only one impression of the challenger, and it was not very good.

What you are about to read next is the recounting of one of the most unusual moments on the campaign trail for me. It happened after the last debate. I was one of two eyewitnesses. Let's set the stage. DeVos does his post-debate spin where he is asked about "using the deceased children." At first he pretends like he doesn't know anything about it. "I have no idea what the governor is talking about." Rick Albin of TV-8 will have none of that and reminds the candidate that he himself mentioned those children at the Econ Club and in an earlier debate. Now his memory apparently comes back. "I did reference their names because these are young people who lost their lives." Then he implies that the Granholm administration had the "responsibility" to protect them. "And they lost their lives. They deserve the dignity to have their names mentioned. But that's all I have done...." So what he was saying is that in order to dignify the deaths, he mentioned them in the debates, and by implication he was not exploiting them. I thought it was an unusual justification.

Then he takes a Bermuda tax break question. He denies his company took the tax break, and shortly thereafter he's done for the night and heads out the studio door...with yours truly following about 30 steps behind. I had not had a chance to get in any questions for my TV story that night, and I thought I might catch up with him at his car. Just as I make a right turn outside the studio, I see the candidate walking toward the door, and as the door opens, he slams his fist against it as it closes. Bam. This was no love tap. It was a right-hand punch that I thought might have injured his hand. For a second, I wasn't sure what I had just seen, but I continued to follow him out. He did not bang on the walls, he did not kick anyone, he did not push anyone around. He just marched steadily down the hallway, and out into the driveway. I shouted out just as he moved toward the back seat.

"Mr. DeVos. What did I just see?"

"You saw what you saw," he confirmed the incident without saying it. Now his aides moved in to close the door on him...and me. I needed more, however, and did not back away as I stuck my head inside the back door and I asked for an explanation. He gave it to me. "The continued misrepresentations does get frustrating." And with that, the door closed. I dashed for the steps outside the station to jot down the quote. I had a feeling I might be using it again. None of this was captured on camera.

I needed to get back inside, but the station door was locked. Standing on the inside near the door was Lt. Governor John Cherry. He had two choices, let me in or keep me out. He laughed from the other side of the door as he paused for a moment knowing that he had me at his mercy. But then he gently opened it for me. I joked with him, "You missed your chance."

I attended the Granholm spin session, wondering if I should ask her about what I had just seen in the hallway. I decided there was no need to share that in front of the entire press corps. I waited until she was ready to leave and I followed her out, too.

"Oh no," she blurted out when she saw me come up from behind as she was ready to step into her car with her two daughters and husband getting in first. I gave a verbal description of the fist pounding. I wanted her response. She offered that perhaps he was "frustrated that he created the problem." Then she was off into the night, too. I was left to ponder what I would do with this story.

My camera guy and I got into the van to head back to Lansing for my live shot at 11 p.m. I called Gayle to see if there were any calls. There were two. One from Chris DeWitt and one from Greg McNeilly. There's a surprise. DeWitt wasted little time. He wanted to know if "DeVos had slammed the car door in my face and whether he had slammed the door outside the studio?" I answered no to both inquiries. Apparently a stagehand had seen the same thing I had seen, but got the story twisted. Notice, DeWitt did not ask if DeVos had slammed his fist on the door.

McNeilly was next. He wanted to spin me on the winner and loser angle on the story I was about to do. Prior to talking with him, I reviewed my notes from the debate. I thought both candidates did well, but I felt DeVos needed more than a tie. And the more I thought about it, I concluded I would give it to her because the challenger was woefully unprepared on four issues. Four issues he could have used to "muscle her into a corner, but instead left her merrily dancing in the center of the ring," as I wrote in my weekly column that week. McNeilly did not like the sound of that when I shared it with him to get his take. He went on about how DeVos had "controlled the agenda." I conceded that he did do well by repeating that she had four years in office and had little to show for it. He said his guy had interacted well with the audience. I agreed, but by the third debate I felt DeVos needed to be scoring more points against her instead of playing so much defense.

Then out of fairness, I changed the conversation. I shared with him what I had just seen backstage. He was not aware of it. I could almost hear the wheels grinding in his head, "What does this mean? How will Skubick play this thing?" He had a right to be worried. Candidates who want to project the image of being in charge and in control, don't going around banging on doors after a debate performance...or do they? Then I could hear the concern in his voice as he went grasping for straws. He wondered if there was something that I needed for this book? I was not offended. "Deals" or trade-offs are not unusual. In fact, the governor's office had done that when it found out I was writing something that the boss might not like. The objective was to get me off one issue and onto something different. It was an accepted part of the game, but the reporter was under no obligation to play, and on this one, I was making no deals. I asked McNeilly if he had discussed this with the candidate. He had not. Again out of fairness, since I knew this was a highly sensitive issue, I agreed not to include the incident in my story at 11, but I told him I would have to report it at some point even though he continued to argue that what I saw was a "private moment." Maybe so, but it was done in public.

I did the live shot at 11 and came home to kiss Gayle goodnight as I headed down to the P.C. to write this week's column. It was due in the morning before I left town on a speaking tour around the state. I decided to write about the knock out punches that DeVos missed in the debate and not the one he landed on the door that night. I first suggested that DeVos was a victim of his own success. Having done so much better in the second debate, the expectation bar had been raised for the last one. I concluded that while he gave an acceptable performance, he didn't reach the bar. He could have surpassed it and won the thing going away had he been more up to speed on the issues.

Item: She boasted about spending more on higher education and her Merit Scholarship Program. DeVos should have countered, "But governor in your first year in office, you actually cut the higher ed budget."

Item: The governor in the debate went on and on about doing more for the inner cities including Detroit. DeVos should have countered, "But governor when House republicans tried to increase state aid to the cities by 2%, you killed the deal."

Item: The governor continued to get on DeVos's case for not explaining how he would replace the $1.9 billion in lost revenue from the SBT. Even by the third debate DeVos had not yet figured out that she didn't have a plan either. He never called her on it by saying, "Excuse me governor, but your plan does not address the problem. Your plan only lowers the rate of the SBT. But, we don't have an SBT anymore. Your rate-lowering plan is bogus. Instead of griping about me, what's your idea for filling in the budget hole?"

Item: The question of school funding and the property tax for schools came up. And the governor glowed about her historic increases in state aid but DeVos missed this final opportunity. "With all due respect, when you were a candidate for governor four years ago, you said you would tweak Proposal A, the property tax-school funding plan. Four years later, where is your tweaker? You've done nothing."

Four chances to win the debate. Four chances blown. How come?

DeVos is obviously no student of state government. It appears he has a limited knowledge of state political history, too. If he did know about those four issues, he forgot to use that knowledge in the debate. If he didn't know, then his handlers are to blame for not filling him in. She was vulnerable on countless occasions during all of the debates, but he couldn't deliver a counter-punch to save his soul. It's easy to say, "Fire the governor." It is more difficult to justify it with real life examples. Predicated on that, I scored it two debate wins for her, one win for him.

Glasses. In his final appearance, DeVos showed up with his cheaters on and viewers noticed. At a speech in Grand Blanc four days after the show, folks wanted to know the why and wherefore behind that. Here's the inside skinny from one of my DeVos sources. "He's actually more comfortable wearing them and wears them around the office or at small functions all the time," it was explained to me. Then at the Econ Club event he had to wear them in order to read his speech. This source says the response he got was "very re-affirming." Plus, I was told the glasses "frame better his eye expressions and context a rather long face that he has." However, the glasses were never focus grouped nor were they "scientifically analyzed."

Pollster Eddie Sarpolus was more direct when I asked him about the glasses for a TV story. "People just don't trust Dick DeVos. The eyes seem beady...that seems to be turning off voters, especially female voters." So his eyes are too close together? I followed up. "Yes, they are," and Sarpolus labeled that a political liability since "80% of the vote is based on how people look at you. They don't like beady eyes." I ran that notion past the group in Grand Blanc and they agreed. I thought it was stunning how the governor's race might come down to glasses or no glasses. On that front, I noted, both candidates were tied. She wore glasses, too.

There was one other cosmetic factor regarding Mr. DeVos. His smile. Oh, I was getting plenty of comments about that on the stump and come to find out the DeVos folks were aware of it as well. This source tells me, "Dick does have a rather large smile and like most people, when he smiles his eyes get very small." (Notice the word beady is not used but there it is.)

I noted in my emails to this source that former GOP candidate for governor, Dick Posthumus from the DeVos side of the state had the same exaggerated toothy grin. I wondered if it was a West Michigan thing. Look, there is nothing wrong with smiling. I just observed that with both men, they sometimes smiled at the wrong time which seemed out of place, and I knew lots of voters saw that. As a result DeVos was sent to smile school. He was "encouraged to have a more neutral expression during non-speaking." In other words, don't smile so much. I told this source that I thought DeVos was getting better at controlling his facial expressions. I was sure that made this source smile.

Reconfiguring a candidate's image was certainly not unique to the DeVos campaign. And in a TV-driven era, it is foolhardy not to address it. When John Engler first ran for governor, he was put on a crash apple diet that resulted in him almost looking thin by the time he unseated Jim Blanchard. Who can forget that they tried to re-invent the alpha male image of former presidential candidate Al Gore. Stock in the earth-tone sweater industry shot up after he showed up in that new garb. Bill Clinton died his hair and who knows how many other "things" were done to other candidates over the years. There was even a piece in the *Free Press* the other day about the governor's mole on the right side of her face. Should she slice it or not? Trust me, the mole stays, even if Ms. Granholm goes.

With just about two weeks to go, the campaign now shifts to the air wars. In the air, a new commercial appeared featuring DeVos sitting at the table reading the newspaper. Are we done with him dashing through a factory? Apparently so, as we see this young woman who tells us, "Are you still trying to decide who to vote for governor? Hear me out." Then we see family pictures of DeVos, his wife and four kids romping through the clover, or whatever they romp through at their home. We see this young lady give DeVos a hug and then we hear, "And he's got an independent streak. Nobody pulls his chain." Then she sheepishly grins, as she adds, "Almost nobody." And finally we discover this unsolicited testimonial is from, "Elissa DeVos, and I hope you vote for my dad."

When the family members show up in commercials, what gives? Sarpolus has his take. At this read, the DeVos negatives with voters are higher than President Bush which is to say they are pretty awful. The "Elissa" ad is designed to make DeVos appear "softer" and more "trustworthy." Heck, if the kid likes him, he must be okay. Right?

That spot began at the same time an ad with several other women appeared on behalf of the candidate. Only they weren't family members. They were former Granholm supporters who have seen the light. "Jennifer Granholm hasn't done the job she said she was going to do when she was elected four years ago," the first defector begins. Woman 2 joins in, "I cannot take the chance on having her not come through again….Good try and thank you, but it's time to move on."

The DeVos folks believe the governor is shaky when it comes to segments of the female vote, although she is not as shaky as in the past. Most recent data shows her winning the overall female vote 50% to 40%. But she loses females under 40 by 5 points and she ties him for the older women with no college education. Nonetheless "she is vulnerable and has been for two years with women," Sarpolus explains. A few short days after the commercials went up, I got word from inside the DeVos camp that the overnight tracking data showed the race closing to within five points. This may explain why the governor countered with a new ad of her own which sent shock waves through the republican leadership ranks. "Did you see the abortion commercial?" an obviously excited Saul Anuzis asked when he got me on the phone. I had not. He was elated and thought the spot might be the thing that turned it around for his guy. What? The governor runs a commercial that helps the enemy? I wanted to hear more about that.

The commercial itself features a woman's face and the voice over begins, "Jennifer Granholm personally opposes abortion." She believes this is a "deeply personal and private decision" between the woman and her doctor and politicians should stay out. Then the ad calls DeVos "extreme" because he does not favor the rape and incest exclusions. It concludes by saying its time to take a stand.

Anuzis is overjoyed. He thinks he has caught the governor in a mistruth. He has quotes from her years ago saying she was pro-choice and always had been. The ad says she opposes abortion. However, there are many pro-choice women who oppose abortion. The "lie" he thinks he has does not exist. It may look to some that the governor is trying to have it both ways, but she would disagree. Regardless, he immediately puts the spot on his web sight and notifies the two thousand or so folks who follow his daily musings.

He figures this is the break he has needed to awaken the sleeping giant in his party, that is, the right wing—true believers. They've been on a starvation diet during this whole campaign, having gotten no red meat from DeVos because he's been instructed to lay off the wedge issues. The GOP chair thinks this will motivate those voters to get in the game, to show up on Election Day, to forget about the malaise stuff and vote for DeVos. Man oh man, if he is right, would it not be the irony of ironies that a Granholm spot, designed to hold onto her female vote, turned out to be a deciding factor which cost her the election?

"That's just wrong," argues a very good source embedded in the Pro-Choice movement. "Abortion will not be a mobilizing factor for the GOP. They don't wake up in the morning thinking about abortion. They are worried about what the president is doing, Iraq, and the ethical problems." This source says, "I was glad to see the abortion ad. It is aimed at women who make their decisions late and it is one way to point out the differences between Granholm and DeVos."

Having said that, this source concedes that noncollege educated women under forty continue to be a challenge. "They are hard to get to. They are busy and not paying attention. They are by-standers" in the election process. Nonetheless, a source I have at Emily's List says a targeted mailing of 150,000 has gone out on the abortion issue and it tags DeVos as "extreme" especially on the rape and incest exceptions. Other mailings to other clusters of voters hit the education issue and his support of vouchers.

Note the word "cluster" in that previous sentence. Years ago when political parties did GOTV or get out the vote efforts, they were not very sophisticated. They knew where the Rs and Ds lived. They could identify union and non-union households, etc. But now, they can identify over a dozen subgroups of voters. Republicans used this "cluster" approach very effectively in the second election of George W. Bush. Democrats were late coming to the party but the inside data shared with me for this book reveals the Ds are in the game now. Get a load of this.

The Garin-Hart-Yang Research Group published their "Michigan Project...Overview of Clusters" report in July. Researchers interviewed 8,000 women voters and came up with not one, not two, but 36 unique clusters. Here are just some of those: They found 9% of the democratic base vote to be "Educated Liberal Elites." Their traits were: 86% follow the news about politics and government; 92% are pro-choice; 87% back gay marriage; 84% are white; 9% are African Americans. Another cluster is the so-called

"Young on-Line Liberals." To them, religion and faith have no role. Almost half rely on the internet for news. They are disproportionately found in Oakland and Macomb counties. And the list of clusters goes on with "Financially Stressed Union Members and Minorities," "Bread and Butter Graying Democrats," "Secular Seniors" and "Younger Main-Street Democrats."

Knowing where the voters are and what messages they respond to allows the Granholm folks to mold a message that will bring them into her camp. They can also tell which groups don't much like her. I had no idea this kind of refined research was going on. And I was even more surprised to find out that two training sessions were quietly held in the state with 85 special interest groups who were instructed on how to use this massive research. Out of that grew the Voter Activation Network or VAN which will swing into full tilt as the election goes closer.

A month ago my source was concerned, but now there is more confidence that Granholm will win. The reason, "Since February DeVos hammered her on jobs and the economy and it has not worked. Now where else do they go?" Having said that, however, this same contact continues to fret about voter turnout in Detroit. "The governor has not closed the deal in Detroit." And there is history to suggest this is a huge concern. For example in the 2004 race for president, 51% of the Detroit voters showed up for John Kerry. In marked contrast in 2002 when she first ran for governor only 36% of Detroiters bothered to vote for her. That's why Jessie Jackson, Al Sharpton, Bill Clinton, and the aforementioned John Kerry have all been in the state for her.

The governor's Detroit problem was spotlighted in the paper the other day. A piece in the *Free Press* noted that DeVos released his Urban Agenda during an appearance in Detroit. He told the paper, "You're seeing a more concerted effort from me. We're participating on urban radio.... You'll see our advertisements asking people to consider voting Republican for the first time." Speaking in Highland Park, right next door to Detroit, DeVos made a little news by announcing his first State of the State address would be done in Detroit. He called it "symbolic," but told his urban audience that it was time to start talking about bringing Michigan back and "that recovery has got to include the city of Detroit."

On the same day, the governor was 45 minutes late for a meeting of the Michigan Welfare Rights Organization composed of black democratic women. It is rare for Granholm to be late and to make matters worse, after twenty minutes she stood up to leave only to hear voices raised and hands clenched as leader Maureen Taylor lectured the governor, "We're in crisis. We have 45,000 people without water....We've got to win this election but on Nov. 8th [the day after] we're really going to have a meeting." All of this reminded me of the Adolph Mongo flap where he complained about Granholm taking the black vote for granted. I did not attend the session, but if writer Rochelle Riley had it right, that was the same attitude expressed by the black women. If the governor was mending fences in Motown, it was apparent from the tenor of that meeting that she was not done yet. The outcome on November 7 was riding on whether she got the job done.

27
Heading for Home

Two weeks to go as they come around third and head for home. Monday, October 23, on the campaign trail, began with a great opening line from one of the candidates, but a not-so-great closing line from one of his aides. I was summarily informed I had just done my last interview with Dick DeVos.

It was another gloomy day sans sun in Michigan but there was still joy in the realm. The Tigers had tied up the World Series with a stunning performance by Kenny Rogers, the 41 year-old pitching sensation who has tossed 24 scoreless innings. GOP challenger Dick DeVos, who turned 51 over the weekend, was hoping to shut-out the governor in two weeks as he jumped out of his blue SUV and extended his hand to me. "Dick DeVos. Rush chairman. Damn glad to meet ya," he quoted the famous line from the Animal House movie with his ever present smile. And I retorted, "Now go over there and stand in the corner...." I had seen the movie, too. DeVos was at an elementary school in Williamston, a tiny community outside of Lansing. He was there to read to the kids, and I was there to tend to some unfinished business.

I was still sitting on the story concerning the fist-pounding incident after the last debate, and I wanted to chat on camera about that. I walked with him into the principal's office where he signed in. Soon, other reporters showed up. That complicated the situation. I did not want to reveal my story in front of them so the two of us conferred in the hallway away from everyone else.

"I want to talk with you about your post-debate impressions and I also need to talk about the incident after the last debate." He showed no signs of not wanting to discuss it. I informed him there were other reporters in the room. To avoid sharing the story with them, I explained I would not include all the details when I asked him about the back stage occurrence. He nodded that he understood, and we moved toward the interview chairs in our converted TV studio in the school office.

On the way I had a different thought. I asked John Truscott if he could clear out the reporters before I talked with the candidate. He said he would and did. I took my seat while DeVos reviewed his "blue book" which had been handed to him. Each candidate gets a briefing book on what the event is about, who are the important folks to know, and what they are supposed to do. It was the same type of book that Jessica McCall hauled around for the governor. After DeVos glanced at his agenda, he came over and took his seat right across from me.

I wanted a sit-down interview so that he would feel more comfortable. Plus, when you are standing up, it usually signals a shorter exchange, and I knew I needed more time to get this story right. We started with his reflections on the debate season. Someone had told me that DeVos felt that was the most challenging thing he had ever done. I asked if that was true? He says, "Debates are very challenging for someone who's not been brought up to argue in public, and in fact...the idea of arguing in public was not encouraged at all." I jumped in, "Especially with a woman." DeVos bursts into instant laugher as he caught the significance of the statement referring to his female opponent. When he stopped laughing he noted, "There were multiple challenges different than anything I had experienced."

So the obvious follow-up was, "If you had to do it over again, what would you change?" He did not retreat, "I would have been a little more careful on the selection of the moderators on the first debate." Now he has me laughing and he joins in. After I stop, I inform him he had no choice on that. Then in a more serious vein, he reflects that the "unstructured format" of the public TV debate was "the most challenging" and "I might have done that a bit differently." I inferred that if this guy gets elected, he would never consent to that format again. But all and all he concludes that he did get better as the debates went on. I thought he had that right.

Now to the "incident." I wanted to know what was going on? "I had been just very frustrated with some of the debates. It's the sort of thing that makes people—that drives people, frankly, out of politics or keeps them away from getting involved in political leadership." He says during the course of the three meetings with her, "the governor [was] continuing to say things that I believe that she knew were not true, and her lobbing those in, and continuing to distract from the real issues. And that's very very frustrating when you are in a time-limited environment...."

His reaction was exactly what the governor and her handlers wanted to provoke. They wanted to keep him off his message, keep him on the defensive and back him into a corner where it is tough to think clearly. In a word they wanted to frustrate him, and DeVos was confirming just that.

He wanted to "stay focused" on the issues that he thought the citizens of Michigan wanted to learn about, but "yet the personal attacks, the negativism that the governor brought to the table was very disappointing [there's that word again] and very frustrating at times." As a captain of industry, no wonder this stuff was foreign to him. Can you imagine a CEO in a boardroom engaged in an argument with an opponent who wants to talk about everything but the subject at hand? DeVos would have none of that, I was sure, but in the political board room, he didn't know quite how to navigate those waters. It showed, and in the end, he drowned.

The fact that he slammed his fist on the door was one thing, but I felt the public needed to know if this was a pattern in his behavior. I had already asked about that with his staff and got reassurances that it was not, but I wanted to hear that from him. So I next asked, "As a result of that frustration, you were acting out? That was not a temper tantrum, was it?" He does not pause and gets right into it. "It was just frustration. We all get, we all get frustrated sometimes where things happen that we're not pleased about. But we work through those things, and we get back on track, get back on focus. But the debates are a very intense environment, very competitive."

Then he thinks back to his high school days while playing football. He remembers the intensity before, during and after the game. My next question reflects my desire not to blow this thing out of proportion, but just as I say that, I hear Truscott, who is standing off to the side say, "We gotta go." I noticed that he got that word from Greg McNeilly who was late coming to the picnic. I could also see that "look" in McNeilly's eyes, but I marched on basically ignoring Truscott's "gotta go" admonition.

"There's nothing else that we should read into this. That you know, you have a bad temper or anything like that?" Again he did not back off. "I mean, no. People who have been with me know that one of the characteristics about me is that I'm very competitive. But that's happened mostly in a quiet environment, and it's expressed, it's expressed, expressed by me in a way that conveys, if you know me, it does convey my intensity. But most of the time folks don't see it, but it's very much there."

DeVos was not unlike the governor who has had her own private moments, very few of which get into the public domain. A former GOP leader once told me she was so upset during one negotiating session that she stormed out of her own office, leaving the republican to joke, "I just inherited a new office." The governor has also cursed from time to time but a close aide says this behavior does not last long. "Does she have a bad day?" this source told me, "No, she has a bad 15 minutes or half hour and then she is back to normal."

DeVos smartly ended the interview in the principal's office with, "It's that kind of competitiveness that I would definitely intend to bring to the people of Michigan...to get Michigan back on track. That kind of competitiveness to go to work on behalf of the citizens of Michigan." And with that we ended the interview—and commenced a pointed discussion with the disgruntled campaign chair.

DeVos strolled off to the library to read to the kids leaving

me to deal with McNeilly. He let me know he was upset. I told him
that I had talked with DeVos. This was no ambush interview, and I
needed his side on camera for the story I was going to do. McNeilly
still wanted me to sit on this incident as he continued to invoke the
"private-moment" defense. I was still not in a sitting mood.

"With two weeks to go, you probably don't care that this
was your last interview," he tells me. "Yes, I do care," I quickly responded. Please note that all of this is very civil, with no shouting,
certainly no fist pounding against the door, yet I wonder what the
office attendants must have been thinking as McNeilly and I tried to
problem solve in public. I reaffirm that I will check with him before
I run any story. In my mind it was the only fair thing to do, and I
have extended the same courtesy to the other side. That seemed to
lower his temperature a bit. I moved to hear the candidate read out
loud.

Unfortunately, as I walked quietly into the room with the
kids seated on the floor and DeVos on a tiny chair in front of them
with a book, it was all too reminiscent of a similar library scene
from September 11, 2001. Only instead of the president reading, it
was a candidate for governor as the kids sat attentively listening to
"One Nation" which was a combined civic and math lesson. The
kids learned there were nine players on a baseball team and nine
members on the U.S. Supreme Court.

One student asked the candidate why he was running? Wish
I had thought of that. DeVos talks about working hard and trying to
give back to the state. Everyone then poses for pictures. With the
TV cameras capturing every move, the kids ask which channel is
this going to be on, and then it was the media's turn. It didn't take
long for the subject to shift from jobs to the Tigers. DeVos wisely
says that his biggest challenge these days is, "We'd all rather be
watching the World Series. That's the truth of it." He basically says
that trumps the race for governor. Nonetheless he gets on that bus
and moves around the state keeping one eye on the Tigs and another
on the polls. One of those polls has him down by 11 points, while
another has the race tightening.

It's about noon and I have to decide what story to do that
night. I am concerned enough about the "fist" story that I do not

want to rush into it. I want to move methodically to avoid any mis-cues. So I decide to wait one more day and instead do a story on the impact of the Tigers on the race for governor. Democratic Party Chair Mark Brewer rejects the thesis that all this feel-good baseball news helps the governor. "I don't think so," Mr. Wet Blanket Brewer begins. "I think people are reading way too much into this. We've got pundits with way too much time on their hands." He concludes, "It doesn't help or hurt one person or the other." Brewer does con-cede that it is a "challenge" to get a political message through all the din surrounding the series. I write the story, go home, and begin work on the other story.

First I transcribe the entire interview with DeVos concerning the frustrations, the competitiveness, etc. Then I make a first stab at a TV story not knowing if "News 10" will even air it. I reflect that if I was first starting out in this business, I might be tempted to write this lead: "Candidate for governor loses it during post-debate, fist-pounding incident back stage." Kind of catchy, hey? And ex-actly what's wrong with news coverage these days. All sizzle and no context. Sure the sensational part of the story needed to be in there, but the context was needed, too. To understand the story, the viewers needed to know that in the debates DeVos got increasingly frustrated which is how I set up the anchor lead in. I completed the draft, and then kept my word by calling McNeilly. He was on the campaign bus about to dive into a pizza. It was about 10 p.m., and they were headed to Detroit.

We talked about the script. He was still sensitive but profes-sional enough to know that I was going to do the piece. And we fi-nally agreed that what I had written was okay. We also discussed the article that would run in the MIRS newsletter. At one point I used the question about, "Was this a temper tantrum?" McNeilly did not like the sound of that. That was the last impression he wanted to leave on the reader's mind. I explained that I had to leave it in. It was part of why I was doing the story in the first place. Was this candidate often out of control or was this an isolated incident? I argued that to preserve the integrity of my reporting, the question needed to stay in. Otherwise the other side might correctly ask, "How come you never asked if his behavior was part of a pattern?" I did not want to be accused of pulling my punches. I thought the pointed question I asked DeVos was proof that I was not cutting him any slack.

We ended the phone conversation, but before we did, I told him if he had any other thoughts, he could call in the morning before I produced the story. He did not. But I had to get back in touch with him after I talked with my news director at "News 10." He signed off on doing the story but felt I needed to get a response from the other side on the DeVos charge that the governor had been lying in all these debates. That is what created all his frustrations. It was a good suggestion. Again to be fair, I emailed McNeilly and shared this with him. He was again worried that the other side would exploit the story. I told him I had been directed to ask about the "lies" angle. I figured after the story ran, if the other side wanted to pick up on the "pounding" incident that would be up to them. I was on my way to a speech in Ludington when the story aired. I never saw it, but there were no gripes from either side. A few days later, however, DeWitt was on the phone. He had read the account and asked me why I didn't confirm for him on the night of the last debate that DeVos hit his fist on the car door? "Because he didn't hit his fist on the car door," I explained. "It was on the door outside the studio." DeWitt laughed and conceded he did not ask the right question. "Next time I will ask, "Did he hit his fist anywhere?" Who says you can't teach an ole P.R. guy new tricks?

Speaking of phones, thirty years ago a book on a race for governor would not have included the new-fangled term "Robo calls." Who hasn't received one and been perturbed by these incessant computer generated calls? Political parties were paying about 3 cents per call and during one night thousands of "pitches" could be made urging the unsuspecting "victim" to vote for this person or that. The state AFL-CIO was up in arms over some anonymous calls criticizing the governor and ending with the phrase, "Brought to you by Michigan working families." That was a line that appeared in union literature. Union president Mark Gaffney smelled a rat or in this case an elephant.

Surrounded by two speakers, a laptop computer, and a giant screen, Gaffney called in the capitol scribes and promptly tagged the state GOP with making these "fraudulent" calls. He argued republicans wanted to create the appearance that the union was not backing Granholm. "We had absolutely nothing to do with it," responded GOP Chair Saul Anuzis who wondered if it was the union making "a clever move" to "scare" union members into voting for Granholm. The two sides agreed to disagree.

Everyone in both camps was spending a lot of worry time over last minute desperation moves by the other side that might flip this race on its ear. I figure if the governor had her wish, she'd like to do a commercial with her "friend" in Traverse City former Governor Bill Milliken. It might be the closer she needs to shut out DeVos, but alas it is not going to happen. That conclusion is based on comments from a key source familiar with the thinking in the Milliken household. It is true that the current governor did ask for the former governor's blessing but a "reluctant" Mr. Milliken turned her down.

He still believes in the two party system and concludes, according to this source, that if he repeats another "John Kerry," he would "effectively rule out any possibility to influence the GOP in the responsible directions" he wants to move his party. In the last presidential sweepstakes Milliken broke ranks with President Bush and embraced democrat Kerry. Therefore he concluded, "at least up to now, I could not do as she has requested."

Granholm then wanted to know if that meant he would pop for DeVos. This source quotes Milliken, "that under no circumstances would I do that." Both the former governor and former first lady, as we heard in that interview in June, felt DeVos "has backed too many extreme right-wing causes over the years and will continue to do so." Word was the Millikens felt with DeVos spending his own fortune on the contest, now pegged at an unbelievable $35 million, that was "tantamount to buying it." This source also reports the moderate former governor believed that the "simplistic approach" DeVos brought to the state's problems was "mind-boggling." But for DeVos, keeping Milliken on the fence was a partial win which he would take. It was one more example of DeVos successfully neutralizing a factor that could help Granholm in a close contest.

While Granholm was working the former governor, both she and her opponent were lobbying someone a bit more obscure—Kia

Hagens, a mother of twins from Detroit. The *Detroit Free Press* in recent days did a story on undecided voters and found Ms. Hagens. She told the paper that her main issue was not jobs but getting a cup of coffee somewhere other than a gas station. There are no Starbucks in the inner city nor are there any Target stores, she observed. Days after the piece ran, the phone rang in the Hagens's household. Husband John told his wife, "The governor's on the phone." "Mom," Granholm began, "don't the twins have you up yet?" Then Hagens's says the governor gave her the floor, and she took it. "Can we talk about something other than Amway?"

The governor explains she is pushing for more housing to draw businesses to the city. Hagens listens but remains undecided. She tells the *Freep*'s writer Tina Lam that an email went out to her friends, "Guess who called me this morning? The governor." But Hagens is not done. Four hours later she was driving along I-75 when her cell phone rings. This time the voice on the other end is not female. "This is Dick DeVos," he begins. Hagens says, "I was doing a Snoopy dance in my car" as she listens to her second pitch for her vote. She notes that there is no chitchat with DeVos, as he cuts to the chase asking for her support. He talks about his turnaround plan and wants to send her a copy. Two hours later, a DeVos operative shows up on her front steps with the documents. In her eighth-grade American history class, she takes advantage of this learning moment telling her captivated students, "It shows how much my vote counts." Despite those unusual personal contacts, she remains on the fence. What a hoot if the election came down to one vote and it was hers.

It's always precarious to draw firm conclusions based on a few events, but this DeVos exchange with Ms. Hagens is a carbon copy of the one with the plumber's wife during the last debate. He is all business. There is no touchy-feely expression of concern. Contrast that with Granholm. "What's your name, again? I have kids, too. And how are the twins doing?" All of that is a prelude to the connection, and don't kid yourself, voters want to feel that. They want to be touched. The two-handed handshake is one physical way to get there for a candidate, but the need goes into the metaphysical, as well.

Voters want to feel they have something in common with the candidate. Candidates need to show they can listen, respect, and then do something about a person's problems. There's no question that DeVos is devoted to doing just that, but he doesn't show it all the time. Maybe it's a familial, cultural or personality thing or all three for him? But you either have it or you don't, and in this image-driven and media-dominated biz, if you don't, it will cost you votes. Unfair? Certainly. Reality? You bet. And you can't teach any of this in candidate school. Sure you might fake it for a while, but over the long haul, voters figure it out. DeVos made the connection when his daughter appeared in an ad but disconnected with the two female voters he met. Elections come down to the intangible of trying to empathize with voters which is why Granholm shared some motherly advice in her next commercial.

28

Microtargeting and Other Goodies

The Cinderella Detroit Tiger story is resolved. Turns out Cinderella did not have trouble AT the ball. Tiger pitchers had trouble WITH the ball as they tossed it in all the wrong places. Couple that with a lousy .198 team batting average, and the beloved Bengals handed the St. Louis Cards the World Series on a silver platter. The rainy, windy, and ugly weather outside the window is a fitting postscript to the end of a disappointing season finale. There's always next year for Detroit, but the players in the gubernatorial ball game have only ten days to play.

The governor is up with her "Mom" ad. "I was taught by one of the toughest economists the world has ever know—my mom," Granholm begins in another commercial where she looks into the camera against the now familiar black drape background. Granholm notes that her Irish mom "never wasted a nickel and never gave us money." Learning that nickel-pinching lesson as a kid allows the grown-up governor to report that she is one tough cookie on cutting the state budget, but she also tells viewers she will not slice health care, schools, or raise your taxes. "My mom taught me to make tough choices, and to tell people exactly where I stand." It's a good spot, but perhaps not as good as the ones DeVos was running with his daughter and those former and now anti-Granholm women. They were moving the numbers for him.

In the most recent EPIC-MRA survey, the governor's once comfortable lead of nine points was now sliced to five and Ed Sarpolus says the DeVos female ads account for the movement. But in every polling cloud there are silver and dark linings. The dark ones for the challenger were pretty obvious—on the trust scale DeVos was losing. Of the two contenders, a majority of voters felt they knew more about her than him and that she knew more about them than he did. Despite all his commercials, the debates and everything else, DeVos has moved from 39% to 41% on the trust scale. She is at 46%. Sarpolus tells the media that DeVos does not have enough time to convince voters to trust him. His only two remaining options are to promote a strong get-out-the-vote effort and convince voters that Granholm is not the person for the job. If you apply the theory that voters will decide based on their gut and not their brains, the lack of trust was critical. In fact I was telling audiences this race was Granholm's to lose. But DeVos had a secret weapon to win.

You've heard of microwaving, micromanaging and microeconomics. Add this "micro" to your ever expanding vocabulary—microtargeting. During my visit with GOP chair Saul Anuzis on the Robo call story we talked about earlier, I was leaving when he pulls this blue book off his mahogany cadenza behind his desk. "Michigan Micro Tactics" is the title and as he flips it open, you see 33 subgroups of voters. In my head I'm thinking this is the GOP equivalent to the cluster model used by Emily's List and democrats to cull out voting segments. The republican document is equally as fascinating. Michigan-bred researcher Alex Gage gets credit for inventing this beast four years earlier. It has every imaginable category of voter. About the only thing missing is what these folks eat for breakfast, and I figure, if they tried hard enough, they could uncover that, too.

Anuzis commands a computer file on 7.3 million voters and phone numbers for an astonishing 5.3 million of those—including mine. "Let's see what we can find out when we pull you up," Anuzis warms to the task with a smile. He punches in my name and within seconds, up pops my home address, my home phone number, and a big fat "I." I knew the "I" would be there, because I am an independent voter with a track record of voting the person not the party. Anuzis has nothing else on me on the screen, but there is one icon that he does not push. If he does, it would reveal my income, the type of car I drive, the magazines I buy, the value of our house, all my census data, whether I own a boat (do not; can't swim), and other personal goodies such as a person's willingness to display a yard sign for a candidate. Are you kidding me? Oh yeah, he could also determine if I own a snowmobile. If I did I would have lots of company.

Turns out Michigan leads the nation with 400,000 snowmobilers, all of whom are squeezed into some tiny bar in the Upper Peninsula at this very moment listening to a Travis Twitt CD. Anuzis loves these guys and gals because they could determine the outcome of the election. Over a year ago, the governor vetoed a bill that the snowmobile lobby wanted. Anuzis used his handy-dandy microtargeting list to notify each and everyone about the veto. Then he launched a seven-city tour into towns that depend on snowmobilers to stay alive. He reminded the local newspaper editorial boards that Granholm was hurting their economy. And he's fixin' at this moment to recontact those 400,000 and remind them about the veto and urge them to vote for DeVos. Pretty nifty, hey?

But the GOP microstuff is not limited to the wilds of up north. There are forty-four thousand voters in Detroit that Anuzis and company have their eyes and computers on. These are voters who could be persuaded to vote for DeVos or at least, not vote for her. That number doesn't sound like a lot but it's a critical subgroup that could reduce the Granholm margin of victory in that city. "If we could get her vote down under 85% [of the Detroit vote], we'd be solid," the likeable Lithuanian says.

The GOP created this list by going door-to-door and even staging a June-teenth celebration in Detroit and other inner cities around the state. June 19 each year is the day African-Americans believe is their true Emancipation Day. The chair reveals he does not announce that this is a GOP event so lots of blacks show up. He tells the audience that republicans are concerned about their needs and while some are very skeptical, at least he gets them thinking about the party platform. At one event he reports he even got a standing ovation.

The most amazing thing I learn in this candid exchange, and Anuzis swears it is true, 50% of the citizens the party contacted in Detroit think DeVos is a democrat. They obviously got that impression from watching his ads. Now you understand why they leave the "R" for republican out of those commercials. Turns out the crafty media wizards can fool some of the voters all of the time. Not to belabor the point, but in a close contest, that could also be a deciding factor.

Let's pause here for a second. I just got a phone call from Kia Hagens, the undecided female voter in Detroit who was the subject of that newspaper article mentioned in the last chapter. She has still not made a decision, but confesses if she had to vote today, she would vote for the "current governor" but with "reservations." As we talk, I can tell she is not overjoyed with either candidate. "I love the governor," she blurts out, but "I will not vote based on personality. Wonderful people can't do everything." Ditto for her feelings about DeVos. "He's a wonderful businessman but that doesn't mean he can run the state well." This is obviously a "thinking" voter, and she reassures me she will vote "my head and not my heart." A woman with a sincere sense of duty and a great sense of humor, I offer her a third alternative, voting for neither. She laughs and so do I. She rejects that notion adding, "I will vote for governor even if I have to write myself in." Then she graciously asks when she can buy the book and laughs at the title. Ms. Hagens, I will make sure you get a copy.

Now back to our story. Anuzis, with his blue book packed full of intimate knowledge on 7 million voters has reduced this thing to its simplest terms. He has 1.87 million self-identified republicans in his files, 1.09 million democrats, and 623,000 independents, plus one—me. He needs to cobble together 50.1% of the total vote to win, and he's confident that his microtargeting will get him there, but others within the GOP are not so sure. In fact some of them, on the eve of this election, appear to be plotting to oust the chairman.

This is incredible. Just when the entire state GOP apparatus needs to be yanking in the same direction to unseat her, some plotters are hankering to unseat Anuzis. This could not come at a worse time for republicans, but several key sources all but confirmed they had heard the rumor, too. I got wind of this story from an Anuzis supporter who received calls from other party officials who were aware of the alleged plot. The name Chuck Yob and Secretary of State Terri Lynn Land were mentioned as possible co-conspirators.

Yob is the guy who years ago suggested that the GOP needed to find a woman to run for secretary of state because, "Women like that sort of work." Then Governor John Engler and his cronies wanted Yob's neck and everything else he possessed, but Yob somehow weathered the storm and remains a key player. He would not confirm his role in the move to get Anuzis and neither would Secretary of State Land. Her office dished out this evasive statement saying Land "found the rumor to be rather odd since she was the first one to support Saul Anuzis for party chair." Notice, the statement did not address the question I asked, "Was she part of this move to get rid of Anuzis?" It was a clever dodge but fairly transparent.

So assume for the moment that this is happening. The question is how come? The answer is 2008 presidential politics and 2010 gubernatorial politics. Stop laughing and read on. First of all two camps are lining up in Michigan for the 2008 race with some folks in the John McCain camp and others in the Mitt Romney stronghold. Romney is the son of former Michigan Governor George. McCain won the Michigan presidential primary by beating George W. Bush the first time he ran. Stay with me now. Yob is pushing for McCain and there are some who feel Anuzis is pushing too hard for Romney. Thus the effort to get rid of Anuzis.

On the 2010 race for governor, which is ions away, Land is interested in seeking that post. She would never confirm this, but there are some who believe she will not be crying on election night if DeVos loses. That would clear the way for her to run four years from now, and wouldn't it be nice if she had her guy as party chair.

She has a guy in mind, David Dishaw. I have a source who says he's eager to do it and is one of those who is unhappy with Anuzis.

But the chairman is correctly asking, why is all this going on when the focus should be on Election Day? He argues, "Anyone focusing on the chairman's race at this point in time should re-evaluate their priorities." And there was also a private email that went out from West Michigan republican Peter Secchia to party big wigs. It was titled: "Holy Moly." Secchia in bold red letters writes, "How stupid is this? What the devil is going on? Let's get off this and get off it now! We have an election to win." Candidate DeVos writes back to Secchia, "I couldn't agree more." I report this to underscore what an 11th -hour gift this is for Granholm. It's all she could hope for—an intra party feud that could hamper Anuzis in his get-out-the-vote strategy to beat her while others scheme to fire him.

The democratic GOTV effort was very much on the governor's mind when she rallied with about 100 Lansing supporters prior to launching the first leg of her 2,200-mile and 20-city "Putting Michigan First Express" bus tour. It was a glorious morning as the thermometer began its steady climb to a balmy 65 degrees under sunny skies. I was convinced it would be the last time everyone felt that warm until next April. The governor arrived and did her 15-minute rah-rah-stump speech and then played weather reporter. She noted that on the way to the rally she had checked the long-range forecast: rainy and cold for November 7. On this Halloween eve, that forecast brought back scary memories.

She told reporters after the rally that four years ago she went into the election with a 14-point lead. But the rain and cold on Election Day, she says, depressed the democratic turnout and she slipped into office by a slim 4 percentage points. She was worried history would repeat itself, and this time she did not have a 14-point cushion. She could lose and that was the same concern she shared with the First Gentleman.

Dan Mulhern was coming off one of his marathon runs two days earlier and was in his usual low-keyed mood as he started this conversation with the same opening line he used the last time we talked. "How's the book coming?" He confesses he wanted to slip me some inside stuff but fought back the temptation. He also wanted to know who all my inside sources were? Nice try Daniel.

So when you wake up at night, what do you worry about?" I shifted the topic to harvest something I could use for the book. "I don't wake up at night," he confidently reported. So when you are awake what scares you? He hits the GOTV thing, too. He observes that the democrats are "very noisy about everything we do," but he confesses the other side is "very quiet and under the radar screen" when it comes to getting their troops to the polls. I sense his apprehension as he concedes a cold and rainy day is not what he wants next week. I'm figuring the gov and the first hub are hoping the weatherman is a democrat.

Mulhern rips off a pretty good line when I ask if the voters know the real Dick DeVos? "I don't know," he begins. "Sixty-million dollars of advertising is okay if you're selling Coke or if you're selling McDonald's—the people will buy that. But a fast food candidate? I don't think that works." He then hits the trust issue and says voters know that "Jennifer" did not create the auto industry mess, but they trust her to get the state back on track.

Back at the bus, I ask the governor the same question. "When you wake up at night, what do you worry about?" "Tim Skubick" she laughs as she asks me to repeat the question. This time she talks about turnout but boasts that, "We're going to have a slam dunk GOTV...including in Detroit." And to nail that down, Jessie Jackson and Al Sharpton will reprise their visit to Motown as the clock ticks toward "E" day.

She was in a very upbeat frame of mind although her voice was a little raspy. She reveals that's because she was screaming for all the entrants in the *Free Press* Marathon last Saturday. Think about it. She is moving into the critical final week of her own marathon when she will need her voice the most, and she's outside screaming at runners. Classic Granholm, i.e., all competitive, all the time.

Finally she and the gang are ready to hop on the bus. I follow her on as she introduces me to John. "He was our bus driver four years ago," she informs me as I sense she thinks John is some sort of a good luck charm. That triggered my memory to that cold and rainy Election Day when I got word that Granholm was on a bus "flying to Detroit at about 85 miles an hour." She wanted to get to the hotel to count votes. So I ask her, "Is this the guy who went 85 miles an hour?" I can tell she remembers the incident, however she deflects the question but old John does not. "The bus does not go that fast," he tells me. To which I jokingly retort, "Is that because there is a governor on it?" (For you nonbus mechanics out there, a "governor" is a devise they install to keep drivers from speeding.) John's a gamer and I can see why Granholm likes him. He adds, "Now there are two governors on it." Game, set, match to driver John.

And with that, she is off to Battle Creek. I slowly walk back to the news truck to soak up the rays. I'm thinking she is poised to win which was the prevailing attitude I sensed in the crowd. Later that morning a DeVos source reports she still has a four point lead based on their internal tracking polls, but "others are showing it wider and even some more narrow. It's a strange wind out there." How true. A strange wind indeed; one that could still blow either way.

I finally connected with one of the key players in the Granholm campaign who had a pretty good seat to all the critical decisions, and this person was confident the wind was blowing in Granholm's direction. In fact this person confessed that the governor had run a flawless effort. But what about the governor's infamous line about being "blown away in five years" that was appearing over and over again in GOP anti-Granholm ads? This source actually thought it turned out to be a plus because the other side wasted a lot of time on it with no results. "It hasn't moved any votes," this person contends.

The Granholm confidant was "stunned" that DeVos didn't offer the voters any solutions to the economic problems he was talking about. And when he did respond to the China charge by calling it "bull," this source says he never explained it away. The feeling was that DeVos "wasn't deep."

Other insights I picked up from the conversation: While it looked like the entire Democratic Party was clamoring for the governor to respond to the first batch of DeVos ads in February, the inner circle spent only one day debating the pros and cons and decided to hold back. "It wasn't a big debate," my source reports.

And on the first televised debate this observer says, "I was blown away that he did not come back at her when she attacked....It was a defining moment." And if there is one final notion this source wants to leave with readers it is this: "We did not package her. Who she is and what she believes" is what you see. "We did not attempt to make her into something she was not." And by inference this source concludes that was a mistake the other side made with their candidate. And the latest polling data seemed to underscore that as the voters were still not sure who Dick DeVos really was—with 7 days to go.

29

The Numbers Don't Lie...or Do They?

Nobody has ever become Michigan governor with 42% of the vote. And unless Dick DeVos can magically get out of the rut he's been in since September, that statement will hold. That's a polite way of saying, looks like he's a goner as we begin this chapter with four days to go.

The *Detroit News* and WXYZ-TV 7 reported a Granholm margin of 52% to 42% this week of October 30, 2006. The ten-point spread was obviously the lead in the story, but there was also a chart showing the numbers since last fall and that had more wallop than the polling figures. Starting in September, DeVos recorded 42% of the vote, then it was 40% in early October, back to 42% in mid-October, with an up-tick to 43% after that, and now back to 42% one week before the vote. To repeat, nobody has ever become governor with 42% of the vote.

"He's been stuck in the low forties," pollster Ed Sarpolus

bluntly suggests. But Granholm has not shown much movement either. She continues to hover around the 50% mark going from 50% in early September, dipping to 46% in early October, and now back to 52%. Of the two candidates who are stuck, however, she is the one poised for victory. Sarpolus says if you toss in the 6% of the undecided voters, most of who will go for DeVos, the race is much closer.

You are always sifting this data looking for any new story angles, and this one produced one. Retirees have pretty much been ignored in this race as both contenders focused on creating jobs. These folks could care less. They were anxiety-ridden, and with good reason, over the loss of health care and retirement benefits. "Nobody has talked to these voters," Sarpolus observes. Apparently Granholm has, as she enjoyed 59% of that vote to his 35%. His 35% is linked to the democratic ads telling voters that the DeVos health care plan is, "get a job." That two-second sound bite was resonating with retirees and the general population as well. It also fit perfectly into the democratic mosaic of the challenger as a heartless business guy more concerned with the bottom-line than with the average Joe. The characterizations were working as the polls revealed that 44% of the voters had a negative feeling about DeVos compared to her 37%. However, pollster Steve Mitchell recounts that "60% of the voters said they had a "favorable impression" of Jim Blanchard— just before they booted him out of office. Just one final note on health care blueprints. The democrats neglected to tell everyone that the governor's health care plan was only a piece of paper. And even under the best circumstances, it would not become a reality for half a year or more.

A source just shared the nightly tracking data. These are smaller surveys of about 200 people every night for three nights running. On Monday, October 30, Granholm had a hefty 51%-39% lead. It did not change the next night but then last night, an unbelievable flip. She was at 44% and he was at 46%. Was that a blip, a trend, or a what? I had no idea, but I asked around. If it was a trend, we had ourselves a horse race. If it was an anomaly, it provided only a momentary adrenaline rush for Team DeVos. Days later it was looking more and more like a flash in the pan.

In these dying days no one was saying it publicly, but in secret you were starting to hear disparaging remarks about the DeVos effort. In an attempt to pump themselves up, his backers trotted out examples of previous races where the polls were wrong. Pollster Mitchell reminded me that four years ago, challenger Dick Posthumus was down 51%-38% to Granholm. As the election inched closer, so did D.P. One week out it was down to seven points, and she crossed the finish line with a relatively unimpressive 3.8% victory. And when DeVos-ites really needed a kick in the pants, they resurrected again and again the John Engler come-from-behind win over Jim Blanchard in 1990.

Speaking of Posthumus, he re-emerged with an 11th hour "I believe" letter to party leaders. In it, he lamented how he came close to unseating Granholm, whom he labeled "the media darling from day one." He complained about the "know-it-alls in Washington" who could have helped with more money, but had "already written the obituary on my campaign." That was then and now was now as Alto, Michigan's favorite son, turned up the "I BELIEVE" volume. He said the race was a virtual dead heat. It was not. He said Granholm was no longer the darling and the Washington folks were sending workers "in droves." One key factor he left out, DeVos was spending something like a million dollars a day in last minute advertising. Posthumus urged everyone to get involved. You just have to "BELIEVE," he concluded his pitch.

But with yet another poll showing her with a 49%-42% advantage, it was getting increasingly tough for everyone to believe. Rather than have faith, some sources seemed to be grasping at straws. I fielded a call from a staunch GOPer who confessed it was all but over, yet he did assert that a CBS network TV crew had been in town. The network boys were doing a story on the Ricky Holland case or some other aspect of the foster childcare story, or so he hoped. "And word is the Granholm people are trying to get the network to sit on the story until after the election." Hey, I love a good conspiracy story as much as the next guy, so it was worth a call to the governor's press office. Media secretary Liz Boyd confirmed the network news guys had interviewed Marianne Udow who runs the Human Services Department, but Boyd said it was not about the

Holland case or anything else that might toss a monkey wrench in the Granholm re-election machine.

Boyd was also busy the next day peddling a *Washington Post* article she did want me to review. "The governor wanted to be sure you saw this story," she advised me. It was a political blog from the world-renowned newspaper as it revisited the "Ten Best Incumbent Campaigns" in the nation. I was pretty sure if I read far enough, I would run across the name of Boyd's boss. Sure enough. "Granholm started the cycle as one of the most targeted governors in the country," the piece began. It noted that GOP hopes "rose even higher" when Dick DeVos decided to open his wallet. However in the end, "What once looked like a toss-up now tilts slightly but significantly in her favor."

There were still more "Hail Mary's" in play from the GOP side of the scrimmage line. Thursday afternoon before the election, some fast food storeowners were shot in Oakland County. I got an email from one DeVos source claiming the story was "huge" because the perpetrators were reportedly out of some adult foster care home which may or may not have been under the jurisdiction of the Granholm administration. Could it be another Selepak story in the making? Was this an answer to a prayer and another opportunity to blame Granholm for more deaths? Turns out the "huge" story was huge all right—a huge dud. The story never got into the paper.

Newspapers that had been sitting on the sidelines swung into action as a batch of editorial endorsements got into print about seven days out. Of the 14 biggies, Granholm bagged ten while DeVos got the rest. Most notable was the Traverse City *Record Eagle*. "Granholm deserves another term" the editors told their decidedly GOP readers. DeVos did pick up the *Oakland Press* which glowed over the fact that he had run a "major corporation," and "if anyone should know how to turn around Michigan's economy, he should." DeVos also scored in vote-rich Macomb County where The *Macomb Daily* concluded, "When something isn't working, it's time to try something different."

The *Grand Rapids Press* on the editorial page embraced its native son, but in the news hole there was a not-so-flattering "he said, he said" story dating back to DeVos's high school football days. The candidate often repeated this tender recollection about a walk he took with his coach. "It was a warm day, and I remember he told me, 'Dick, I am going to start you because you have leadership skills and the team responds to your leadership.'" Man, right out of *Profiles in Courage*. Only problem was the coach says it never happened. Oops. Frank Rosengren told writer Ed Golder, "He used my name and it isn't true." There were also conflicting memories on whether DeVos even started a game at Q.B. The DeVos campaign got into the game and denounced Rosengren for folding in to pressure from the Michigan Education Association which "told him to say this." The coach fired back, "I don't even know who the MEA bosses are." He did recall that DeVos was a "good kid" but "the scene he describes never took place." Clearly the coach was shopping the story as he called 8 reporters offering his version of the alleged non-pep talk. Ah, but a few days later he suggested that maybe DeVos did start a game or two. And several days after that, the coach was back peddling like Lance Armstrong—in reverse. Rosengren told the Press he had regrets about challenging DeVos since other players reported DeVos did play quarterback. Rosengren conceded that while he still could not recall the pep talk, it would make sense that he gave DeVos one before the game. On a similar note, on the stump I also ran into one of the candidate's high school teachers. She remembered DeVos as someone who did his work on time and was not that well-liked because of his wealth.

A national Catholic advocacy group also got into the act complaining about a Granholm ad that appeared in three church newspapers. "She has the audacity to portray herself as a friend of Catholics," argued Fidelis of Michigan President Joseph Cella. The ad was unique. The governor rarely appears with her family except on her Christmas cards but apparently when votes are in-play, the rule is revised. There she was with the three kids and her hubby with the headline, "Governor Jennifer Granholm Promoting the Common Good."

She tells the readers that because she has dealt with the down trodden, it creates a "much deeper appreciation for the leaders in the Bible—from Abraham and the prophets to Jesus" who did not "focus on individual piety alone, but sought to shape a good people and a just society." Cella was livid as he reminded everyone of her pro-abortion stance. Nonetheless, in the latest polling material she had 46% of the Catholic vote and 25% of the Pro-Life vote to boot. That must have made the Right to Life crew stew.

The stars were rolling into the state on the last weekend. Presidential hopefuls were all over the landscape. John McCain did a commercial and rode the bus with DeVos. Mitt Romney got a bus seat but probably not next to McCain since they were fighting each other for Michigan '08 support. And everyone had to move over for Rudy Giuliani, the popular former New York 9-11 hero who had his eyes on the White House, too.

The governor was no slouch as she hooked up for the second time with former President Bill Clinton who was still wildly popular among African American voters. They rallied at 10 a.m. on Saturday morning at Wayne State University in Detroit. The mayor of Detroit also fired off a radio commercial that aired in his city reminding everyone about the Blanchard loss in 1990 to John Engler.

Then a voice from the past showed up on my answering machine—Adolph Mongo. Remember him? Last July he was a household word as the firestorm over his Hitler ad dominated the news coverage. Since then, nobody had heard a peep from him. So I called and left a message. Within half a day he was on the other end of my line, complaining about the Granholm folks "beating up on me still." Regardless, he was predicting a win for the incumbent in Detroit with over 85% of the vote. He also criticized DeVos for spending all his money on commercials but never aimed one at Detroit. He did credit DeVos for opening an office there and doing more than any other republican since Bill Milliken, but Mongo concluded, "I'd be surprised if he got more than 10%-15% of the Detroit vote." Mongo did offer to DeVos that list of 25,000 angry Detroit voters who were fed up with being taken for granted by the democrats. DeVos didn't want it. "They got scared of me," Mongo suggests while correctly adding, "in a close race the list would have helped him."

Elsewhere the *Detroit Free Press* ran some interesting copy on the two contenders. Voters learned, probably for the first time, that DeVos dropped out of Calvin College to work in the family business. He later got a degree from the Northwood Institute in Midland. He also gave up smoking because his future wife could not stand tobacco breath. Press Corps colleague Dawson Bell also reported that DeVos could "mangle a phrase" from time to time including the one on WJR Radio when he told an interviewer, "If it walks like a duck, it's a duck." DeVos seemed to play off that in a radio ad where he confessed, "I'm not perfect. Not near as smooth at politics as Governor Granholm is. But I'll make changes happen from Day 1 in office."

He also made a revealing confession during a Q and A on WWJ Newsradio 950 when someone asked, "What don't the voters know about you?" DeVos immediately said, "My passion." And to flesh that out he brought up his cultural upbringing again. Just as he was unprepared to argue in the debates because it was verboten in his family, an outward expression of passion was frowned on as well. "But don't mistake the lack of passion on the outside for the passion on the inside," he tried to assuage the radio audience.

In the *Freep* column on Granholm, readers learned that she was a self-taught sketch artist, her favorite rock star was Bruce Springsteen, she likes to fish, knows how to drive a stick shift, and went to the Soviet Union in 1981 to deliver clothes, eyeglasses, and medicine to Soviet Jews. I was surprised the GOP did not try to exploit that. How about something such as, "Dick DeVos went to China to create jobs in Michigan, but Jennifer Granholm went to Communist Russia. Who knows what she did there?"

In the same column First Hub Mr. Mulhern offered his personal take on her attitude during hard times. "Jennifer has always been a person who doesn't cry over spilled milk. She's never been a person of self-pity. She is all about accept, adjust, and advance." Writer Chris Christoff noted that during this campaign Granholm "flickered from political nurturer to puncher," revealing a more aggressive side that some had never seen. That was especially evident in the debates, and there was one school of thought in town that suggested she went too far. A close advisor, however, strongly disagrees suggesting that voters needed to see that this female governor was not afraid to fight for her beliefs.

Meanwhile, I continue to field communications from DeVos

backers who apparently have not read the Posthumus "I Believe" correspondence. "If you spend $40 million dollars and lose, you have to point to yourself," this well-connected GOP source confides. "Either you're not capable of connecting with people or the people you've paid [to connect you to people] weren't capable." This source concluded it was getting late and if DeVos did not show some movement, "It's not going to happen for DeVos....He's toast." Another contact was praying for lousy weather so democrats would stay home. If "it rained or snowed...[then] he might win." The forecast was for 58° with partly cloudy skies and some light rain on November 7 with no blizzard in sight. Apparently the weather guy was a democrat.

While the candidates and their surrogates ride around in a bus, in the real world typical citizens this Saturday before the balloting are lamenting the fact that neither the Michigan State University vs. Purdue or University of Michigan vs. Ball State games will be on TV. That means husbands will be relegated to raking leaves or checking off all those items on the honey-do list. There is also great angst among all good Spartans as yet another hunt is underway for a new football coach. John L. Smith got the ax this week as that story took over where the Tigers losing the World Series left off. But fear not. The political parties will do everything they can to interrupt what serenity there is in the state with an unending series of knocks on the door and rings on the phone—not to mention a ton of political junk mail that the post office will be dumping in mail boxes all over the land.

The GOP will make 3.2 million phone calls to microtargeted voters. It will knock on 360,000 doors while passing out 400,000 signs on behalf of republican candidates. And to cap it off, one million mailings will go out including 600,00 churches around the state. Not to be outdone, the democrats will wear out their fists knocking on 2 million doors and wear out their fingers making three million phone calls of their own. Some lucky folks will avoid all this. They voted absentee. In Grand Rapids two years ago, 2,000 voted that way. The number this year is 8,000. Similar reports out of Oakland County, including Livonia, show a 20% increase of 11,500 absentee votes waiting to be counted.

Embattled state GOP chair Saul Anuzis was taking credit for that increase. He learned that 435,000 absentee ballots were sent back to local clerks, and he boasts "our target Republicans account for 269,000 or 62% of all ballots returned so far." That's an impressive number. If you assume all of those republicans vote for DeVos, that's a great "get" for him. But Granholm was getting about 12% of the GOP vote in a last minute survey, and Anuzis did tell his troops his data was not a "precise measurement of what our actual vote among the absentee voters will be." Maybe it was another attempt to keep the race alive, even though the polls suggested something else.

Lots of tongues were wagging on the Sunday before the election. The *Detroit Free Press* had a caricature of Granholm and DeVos on the front page. Over her head is the number 52%. Over his, 39% and then the headline reads: "Granholm Surges in Poll With Boost from Women." To the unaware citizen, that headline said one thing. The race was over. In the Granholm camp there must have been fears that her backers would think just that and stay home since she had it in the bag.

The GOP challenger was riding with former New York Mayor Rudy Giuliani on the Saturday before the election when he got the 52%-39% results more than sixteen hours before the story hit the street. "We expected it," reports a key campaign advisor. "We knew all week they were gonna release their poll then—it didn't phase anyone, so it was a yawner." Translation: it was old and out-of-date news. Pollster Steve Mitchell, whom democrats reject as a front for the GOP, had the race narrowing. In fact, on the day before the vote, he had it Granholm 46% and DeVos 44% with 7% on the fence and 3% who refused to answer. Mitchell had her winning the all-important female vote by a 50%-38% margin and the independents by 41% to 35%.

"It can't be two points," protested Ed Sarpolus who accused Mitchell of faulty methodology. Sarpolus had Granholm with a comfortable lead as she continued to hover around 50% and DeVos remained right where he had been since the fall. Former Governor Jim Blanchard also checked in on his cell as he sat in a plane headed for D.C. He had been on the tour with Granholm and his old pal Bill

Clinton. He was feeling confident although he, along with count-less other democrats, was mindful of the well-oiled GOP GOTV machine. Nonetheless, Blanchard concluded DeVos did not parlay his stature as a successful captain of industry into votes. "Being a businessman can cook your goose in public life," he observed. That's because some of the tough decisions in the boardroom "look insensitive to voters." If you're slashing budgets "to please share-holders," Blanchard argues, the voters may not understand. He had a point and the effective use of the China issue by the democrats was a prime example.

After chatting with Blanchard, I recalled how John Engler found a simple symbol to unseat Blanchard. And it struck me that DeVos did not have his symbol to defeat Granholm. To explain: in 1990 everywhere challenger John Engler went, he brandished a nickel and handed them out to voters. It was a symbol of the weekly tax relief voters would get if they supported Blanchard. It worked. Granholm's symbol was China, gong and all. It worked, and when the *Free Press* asked voters which comment from Granholm was most damaging to DeVos, 31%, or one out of every three voters re-sponded, "created jobs in China." Conversely, despite the expertise on his bench, his cash in the bank, and a state economy in the tank, DeVos never crafted a simple symbol to encapsulate his message for the electorate, which is why almost one out of four voters said DeVos said nothing that damaged the governor. Twenty-five percent did parrot his line that she was a failed leader.

Hindsight being what it is, he could have printed thousands of unemployment cards and everywhere he went, he could have handed them out and said, "If you vote for her, it's only a matter of time before you get one of these. Vote for me and you won't." Simple, direct, and carrying the impact of a ten-pound sledge ham-mer that could have shattered her China to smithereens.

It's a wonderful Michigan Monday morn as the candidates head out for the last day on the trail which is where I'm going after putting the finishing touches on this chapter. At 6:30 a.m., WWJ news radio 950 anchor Roberta Jasina wanted to know, "what has disappointed you more about this campaign than any other?" I thought for a second. "I wish it had lasted longer." She laughed. I laughed. It was the only lie I had ever reported on the radio—"to my knowledge," as the politicians like to add just in case the grand jury is listening.

30

Blown Away

The call came at 12:40 p.m. on the day before the candidates for governor handed the issue to the voters — at last. Campaign manager Greg McNeilly and his counterpart in the Granholm shop, Howard Eldelson, exchanged phone numbers so they could reach each other on election night. Either Jennifer Granholm or Dick DeVos would be using that number to concede defeat to the winner. At this hour, who would be dialing was still in doubt although the Granholm folks were "cautiously optimistic," but if DeVos was concerned, he sure didn't show it as I caught up with him in Jackson around lunchtime, November 6, 2006.

The tie-less and jacket-less candidate bounding out of his giant "Time for Change" bus was not the same guy who jumped out of a black SUV almost 15 months earlier on a dead-end road in Oakland County. That's where my journey with him began with my first question on school vouchers. It was ending here with a question about going to Disney World. After today, I would not see DeVos until after the election. He would watch the votes from Lansing, while I was headed to Detroit to cover the Granholm victory party or wake. I continued to feel it was the former, but I had my doubts.

Before meeting DeVos at Gilbert's Restaurant, I huddled with pollster Ed Sarpolus. He now had the race at 49% for her and 42% for him with the rest undecided. But he warned, again, if DeVos netted the independent voters who were waiting for the last minute to decide, he could narrow the race to 51% to 49% or even win it. The gap was closing because young voters were moving toward DeVos. He had enjoyed a lead with that group from the opening bell, but many of them don't vote. Sarpolus reminded me that when Kwame Kilpatrick ran for mayor, he made a huge comeback on the backs of that voting segment. If it happened once in Detroit, it might happen again.

DeVos was still not conceding Motown to Granholm. He spent all day Sunday in local churches and authorized a unique mailing to over 200,000 Detroiters. On one side the brochure read, "Vote No on Proposal 2 to ban affirmative action." When you turned the page it said, "Vote for DeVos."

Back to the survey. Sarpolus shared other interesting results. He learned that 52% of the voters saw the debates in October, with one third of those watching all three. There was a kicker. For those who saw the debates, Granholm had a lead of 53%-39%. Among voters who didn't see any of them, the candidates were tied at 45% to 45%. In other words, DeVos took a hit in the debates, but half of the electorate never saw it. That was good news for him.

There was bad news, too. Voters continue to believe Granholm was more honest. They feel she understands their problems, and here was a biggie for DeVos. On the issues of abortion, gay marriage, stem cells, and intelligent design, voters did not think DeVos shared their views on those questions. Forty-six percent felt Granholm did. Because DeVos avoided the wedge issues, he may have lost voter support. Ed also tested the Amway issue for the last time. He found that 39% said DeVos's association with Amway hurt him, 27% said it helped, and another 27% had no opinion. Sarpolus felt the results showed the democrats had successfully exploited the DeVos-Amway link.

Back at the restaurant, DeVos finished his pep talk to get out the vote and shook every one of the 30 pair of hands in the place. He then took a question on those undecided voters. Was he frustrated at this late hour that some were still not sure? "Folks in Michigan are pretty independent. I think a lot of them have an inkling, but they're not quite ready to put the marker down yet." He was sure when the "common-sense" voters made a decision, they would see it was "time for a change."

Once more he revisited two old issues, his passion and President Bush. "Inside this rather quiet West Michigan exterior is a passion—to make this state great. We cannot have a repeat of the last four years. I'm excited about getting to work." When he was told that 39% of Michigan voters still blamed President Bush for the ugly economy and only 27% faulted Granholm, he concluded, "sooner or later you can't keep blaming everybody else. True leaders do not apportion blame."

It was time for him to go, so I lobbed in one more. "If you lose, will you go to Disney World?" It was the hardest and longest I had heard him laugh, after which he offered, "I haven't even thought about that possibility, Tim." He had thought about going to work as the governor-elect in two days.

He shook a few more hands, and then I walked out back with him to the bus. "Any regrets?" I asked. He had none. "So you are sleeping at night?" Yes, he was. He and Dan Mulhern had something in common. He confessed that sometimes "the brain does kick in" but when it did, he was always thinking about things in the future and not the problems of the past. That gave me an opening to take care of a problem I had with him.

He was not fond of the title of this book, or as he told me, it did not move the needle. I had asked the governor and him for their comments. The governor called the title "cute" but did not register any protest, but I could tell some of her underlings were not overjoyed, and the feeling was mutual in the DeVos camp.

Long story short, I shared all this with the publishers who were sensitive to my concerns about not wanting to offend either candidate. But the bookstores said they loved the title, and since it was not my call, the decision was made to go with "See Dick and Jen Run." I informed Mr. DeVos. I had heard in one of his commercials that he was a businessman so I asked him to put on that hat to understand the decision. I apologized for not being able to substitute something else. Outside the bus, I asked if he accepted that apology. He said he did, although I could tell he was still not elated. And neither was McNeilly who had a wonderful rejoinder. Readapting a line that Granholm used on DeVos, he said with a smile, "Skubick. Putting profits over people." Good one.

The contrast between the DeVos bus and the Granholm contingency that rolled into Lansing later that afternoon was striking. There was no hootin' and shoutin' when DeVos arrived. Rather businesslike, he went about shaking hands and while his audience applauded, the joint was not rockin'. Granholm's self-described "slap-happy crew" was a whole 'nother thang.

Reporters were hanging around outside the Beaner's coffee shop which was a favorite haunt for lawmakers and capitol staffers given it's close proximity to the state capitol building. When I arrived, I saw a director's chair sitting on the sidewalk with a camera crew preparing to do something. I asked one of the Granholm folks, "What gives?" The governor was going to do two live shots with the TV anchors in South Bend, Indiana, and in Traverse City since her bus would not trek there.

I nudged public radio buddy Rick Pluta. "Look at the background behind her chair." A huge moving van was parked across the street as workers were moving somebody out. Pluta caught the significance of that as did I. DeVos had run commercials complaining that under Granholm, more folks were moving out than moving in. She was about to appear on the tube with that going on behind her. Yes, but when the Granholm express rolled in, it rolled right in front of the moving van. So much for a last minute boost for DeVos.

A smiling Granholm moved briskly off the bus into the horde of reporters as her shouting supporters provided a live audience back drop. "Welcome to the dog pile," she woofed. That was the term, she reported, that one of her media advisors used to describe the gaggle of reporters poised to bark out some questions. "What about that high number of undecided voters at this late hour?" She didn't think it was that high and suggested that "many of them are busy and have two jobs which is a good reason for them to vote democratic."

She then warned everyone to "disregard" all the final commercials blanketing the airwaves, saying they "are false." She did not say she was disappointed as somebody else continually said.

Next she floated a little conspiracy theory. She accused White House operative Karl Rove, sometimes known as the "Brain for George Bush," with concocting Robo calls using the voices of candidates Rove wanted to defeat. She said the calls were being placed at 1 or 2 a.m. "to get people angry." She called it a dirty trick. Then she laid into Rove's boss.

In my TV story that night I was focusing on how Bush was still getting the wrap for Michigan's retarded economy, and since the governor was benefiting from that, I asked if she was sending a thank you note to Bush for helping her out. All of a sudden the Granholm grin turned serious. "He owes Michigan an apology. He owes the auto industry an apology. He needs to come to Michigan and meet with the auto makers." Then she gets a steely glare in her eyes as she says this election "is going to be a referendum on George Bush." The country needs to do something "before he hurts the nation any further." Guess that meant there would be no note of appreciation from her to him.

After the rest of the press corps dabbled in this and that, I had to get in my Disney question to her. "If you lose, will you go to Disney World?" She turned back to the camera, "No, but my heart will be there" and off she went to shake some hands, pose for pictures, and do her rock star thing with the tiny crowd crammed into the coffee shop.

Just as Lt. Governor John Cherry gets up a head of steam to introduce her, she motions me to come over. She whispers in my ear, "I didn't understand your Disney question. Now I get it" about going there if she lost. I told her I thought she was quicker on her feet than that. She blamed it on "cognitive dissonance" and laughed. Cognitive what?

Cherry is really into it now as he semi-pleads with the audience to give "just a few more hours," warning that to pack it in now could mean defeat. With that, campaigner Granholm morphs into a cheerleader shouting, "No sleep. No sleep." The crowd joins in and segues into "Four more years." All this is vintage Granholm.

She loves the smell of the grease paint and the roar of the crowd, only this is not a Broadway play; it's a bid for her political life.

Cherry finally gives her the mike as she introduces her mom and dad, her uncle and his wife, her husband and her department directors. She goes into the standard stuff about getting out the vote, but ends with a nice line, "If we do that, the other side is just going to be blown away." The crowd loves the little dig at the DeVos ad with the same line.

As the rally ends, the governor morphs again, this time from campaigner to football lineswoman. She wants to make sure I don't get a chance to chat with her parents, so as they go walking by, she grins and blocks me out while giving me an elbow in the side until they are safely back on the bus. All I was going to do was ask them if they knew what a sinking fund was?

Election morning. I'm on the computer at a little past 2 a.m. and there is the last survey from GOP pollster Mitchell. You remember? He's the guy none of the democrats like. Well, I was guessing they would like what he was reporting this time: a respectable 51%-44% lead for her with 5% undecided. I immediately e-mailed my FOX 2 morning producer to give him the data for my 6:35 a.m. phoner in four hours. After I sent the info, I had second thoughts. If I used the numbers in my report, it might influence the outcome in some way. I recalled the tidal wave of criticism the network TV boys got when they "called" the election at 8 p.m. on election night before the West Coast had a chance to vote. That resulted in some folks not voting. I rewrote the producer and told him to yank the numbers. He did.

I got back to bed about 3:30. The phone woke me up at 6 a.m. Ugh. WWJ wanted a live report on the ballot proposals that Michigan voters were deciding today. I did that, then the FOX 2 bit at 6:30, more radio reports at 7, 7:30, 8, 8:30, and 9. In-between, there was another report for a Lansing station and a twenty-minute give-and-take for a Detroit FM station. All that was interspersed with e-mails from the DeVos camp. They were not tossing in the towel, but I figured they were praying for a miracle. Chris DeWitt also called offering an unnamed guest for OTR this week. I wanted the governor. He laughed. The First Family was skipping a vacation in Disney World and saying "Hola" to Mexico for the next week. Man, I had a full day in, and it wasn't even noon; yet, it was great fun. Gayle and I finally voted around 10:30.

There was only one more assignment to cover. Election night. I'm in the car at 3 p.m., but before I leave, a quick call to Sarpolus. He has a poll showing Granholm with a comfortable lead of 50%-43%. What in the heck are those 7% undecided folks doing?

The weatherman turned out to be a republican after all. It rained all over the place and it was not a slight drizzle either. Even though the temps were mild, it was an ugly day and not an answer to the governor's prayers. As I drove along I-96 headed to the Ren Cen hotel in Detroit, I contemplated the possibility of a new DeVos administration vs. moving into year nine of covering Granholm. Let's be honest. It is always easier to continue with folks you know than to start from scratch. Besides I had seen enough from the DeVos side to have concerns over his accessibility if he won. I might go months without seeing the guy. After all, he staged one formal news conference during the entire campaign, and he didn't hang around very long for that. Plus you heard things about how aggressive the DeVos folks were on the stump. Three young democratic workers could attest to that. John Groen, Jordan Acker, and Patrick Schefsky were assigned the grunt work of dogging DeVos and video taping everything he said. They called themselves MI-3 for Michigan 3, borrowing the phrase from the James Bond movies.

Because the DeVos campaign did not post his public appearances, this trio spent countless hours surfing the Internet, trying to find groups that had DDV on their meeting schedule. In all they found 200 such meetings, and they quickly got to be a pain in the butt for DeVos and company. DeVos handlers tried to kick them out of a public library and hassled them at other locations as the candidate was clearly irritated. Nonetheless their recognizance collected over 200 videotapes of DeVos remarks which the dems used to sift his every word for a slip-up that they could use against him. What will they do with all the tapes? "Sell 'em on EBay," one of the three musketeers laughed.

While DeVos was getting flak from the folks in Grand Rapids for staging his "victory party" in Lansing and not in G.R., the governor was returning to the scene where it all began four years ago. The Marriott Hotel in the middle of the new GM building in downtown Detroit was not exactly a beehive of activity when I rolled in just after 4 p.m. "When does the governor arrive?" I asked the three valet parking guys at the front door. They didn't know. Turns out "Elvis" was already in the building fixin' to get some last minute face time on the tube.

I asked Liz Boyd if I could sit in on the "live shots" the governor was doing via satellite. "If I do that for you, I'd have to do it for everyone else," she suggested nodding her head toward the 25 TV reporters on the riser next to us. "Come on Liz. Who would know? She did send a message on her blackberry to somebody higher up the food chain and the answer was no. But magically ten minutes later she walked up to me, "Come on. Follow me."

I dashed off with her as we moved down one of those circular runways that confuses everyone who goes there. I had no idea where we were headed, but I figured it out when I saw three of the governor's security guards standing in front of two closed doors. "Security breach," I jokingly announced to them as they graciously opened the door into a makeshift TV studio. Sitting far off in the corner in a red blazer in a director's chair, without a moving van behind her, was Ms. Granholm. I was instructed to keep my mouth shut as she was on the air live with some anchorperson out there in TV land.

As I quietly watch the scene unfold, it struck me how far this political game has advanced since my first campaign with Bill Milliken in 1970. If Milliken wanted to do some last-minute Election Day campaigning, he jumped in a car and went there. Now Granholm jumped in a chair and the satellite did the rest. She was reaching thousands of voters and urging voters to get to the polls. She finished her pitch, and the all clear was sounded. She acknowledged me with a head nod. I asked her how she was doing? Politically she was winning. Voice-wise she was losing.

Heidi Hanson, one of Granholm's media go-betweens, told me afterwards that the governor lost her voice at a stopover the night before at Yesterdogs, a hot dog joint in Grand Rapids. And it only got worse when the Granholm bus rolled into Ann Arbor at the U of M for a 1 a.m. rally with over 500 cheering students who were obviously on a study break. And to compound the problem, the governor had a lousy three hours sleep.

Remaining in her chair, she motioned me over. "Having trouble with my voice," she semi-squeaked to me. It was painful to hear her talk. "Are you done with the book?" she wanted to know. Weeks ago, she had advised me to write the final chapter with her as the winner. I told her I would finish the project the day after the election. Then, as she waited for the next live shot with TV-7 in Detroit, she shared with me her personal analysis of what was unfolding across the state at that very moment. She was winning but did not share her internal polling data to prove it. "He didn't have a plan," she continued. "He thought people would just buy the 'change' message. He needed to do more than that." Next we discussed his "Turnaround Plan" that he touted when voters asked him what he would do if elected. She dismissed it as a lot of "pictures and charts and generalities." She seems amazed that he fought her on the 21st Century Jobs package and the merit scholarship program for college kids, which was something concrete the state could do to flip the economy around. She also discloses that the "fighting" language she used in her stump speech "really resonated" the most with voters, especially when she talked about health care.

Our free-flowing backroom exchange comes to a grinding halt with word that TV-7 is ready to go. I back away from her chair and sit down on a nearby riser to see what anchor Steve Clark is going to extract from the gov. I can't hear his questions, but I hear an answer that sounds familiar. "There is a huge contrast in this race," she says. And then a little later, "I will fight for you." Heard that, too. Then Clark apparently wants to know about how tough it is to get that message out when you only have thirty seconds or less to do it. She acknowledges the challenge and then reminds the Detroit viewers if they want more information, they could "go to WKAR.org and watch the first debate." Hey, a plug is a plug and a freebie to boot.

The all-clear is sounded and Chris DeWitt, who's been keeping an eye on me along with Ms. Boyd, cannot restrain himself as he looks at me and ribs me about the .org bit. "This is going to cost me," as I look at her. The governor laughs as I wonder out loud why that particular debate, as if I didn't know? "Because I remembered WKAR.org." Wasn't that the one where somebody looked awful?

Anyway, she had one more live shot to do, and I needed to get back to the hall for my own live shot on FOX 2 at 5:30. I thanked her for the private audience and suggested we could talk later on...if she had a voice left. I did my thing, explaining to the Detroit TV audience that the outcome in the city was critical to a Granholm victory and I recounted what both candidates had done to impress those voters. Nobody in the studio asked me who was going to win. I had a sense Granholm would, but then I found out for sure. And what a shocker!

Remember during speeches around the state, I was telling everyone we would be up late on election night as this race was going to be very close. Where was Tim Kiska when I needed him? Kiska is the former *Detroit Free Press* writer who has reinvented himself into a one-man guru of Michigan exit polls. He was on the other end of the line as he unofficially brought the race to an end. "She wins in a landslide." "What?" He had her at a whopping 56% and DeVos at 44%. So much for our being up late. I was stunned. No, I was more than stunned, I was shocked. DeVos had imploded. $40 mil down the crapper, and nothing to show for it. He didn't do much better than other gubernatorial losers who spent fewer dollars. I asked my namesake if he was comfortable with the numbers. Based on a 3000-person sample, he was taking it to the bank.

Within minutes, one Chris DeWitt showed up. He had earlier asked what I knew. At the time I knew nothing. Now I did. He wanted to know. I am always uncomfortable sharing info with campaigns, so I let him do a guessing game. "You give me a number and I'll respond," I suggested. He started at 58%. I motioned lower. He landed on 56%-42%. I smiled, "You're in the ballpark." He got the message. He also later confirmed to me that before he asked, he had already gotten the same info from another reporter who had gotten the same stuff I had. Small world.

Of course, I could not use any of this earth-shaking information until after the polls closed. Even though the battle was over, I still felt a responsibility to be fair. So I quietly moved to the room next door where Northwest Airlines had staged a seminar. I grabbed a chair and dialed John Truscott. He sounded tired as he reflected he had been at this thing for 18 months. "Have you heard?" I began to break the bad news to him. He had not. "Do you have any polling numbers?" He did not. I explained that I did. We commenced the same guessing game I had just gone through with DeWitt. "Is it bigger than six points?" he asked. I said, "yes," adding, "let me put it this way, it is not recountable," meaning it was not close enough to recount the votes. He shared a sincere thank you for the information and we ended the call.

Even though the race was history, I still had stuff to do. I caught up with Mark Brewer back in the Ren Cen ballroom. The Democratic Party chair agreed that China, Amway, and the first debate were critical factors in the outcome, but he added, "Don't forget about the governor." He credited her with running a wonderful campaign. Sound bites out of the way, he was kind enough to give me even more with the camera off. Turns out the "China" issue surfaced in the spring of 2005, and it didn't take a ton of skullduggery to uncover the fact that DeVos laid off workers in Michigan and created jobs in China. Brewer says Amway announced all of it. Once he discovered it, he says, "It was the biggest ah-ha moment in my political career." But there was an internal discussion on whether to use it. Another source remembers, "There was about an hour of heated discussion about it." But once the decision was finalized, this insider says, "We pretty much never looked back at it formally as a group."

Brewer reports, "There was no guarantee it would work." If it did, he speculated they might milk it for two or three months and that would be it. DeVos kept it alive, the chair says. "He kept changing his story." Another contact suggests, "They weren't ready to respond effectively to the attack…it was unbelievable to me."

By now, word was beginning to filter out that Granholm had slammed dunked the rich guy. Later that night one Granholm staffer suggested a title for this chapter, "How to Bury a Billionaire." Thanks to Chuck Wilbur for that, but as you read, I decided to go with "Blown Away," which was the banner headline on the front of the *Detroit News* today. There was one out-of-character remark from another Granholm staffer as this person breezed by me. "People gave us a lot of flak for four years. They're going to be sorry." That sounded like something John Engler would say since he was never averse to settling a score. I filed it for future reference.

There was not much more to do except wait for DeVos to toss in the towel and for her to declare victory, and then go home. Just before 11 p.m., and just in time for all the local newscasts around the state, they cranked up the entrance music. She is a huge fan of the Motown sound so somebody selected the Temptations singing, "Get Ready, Here I Come" to get the winner on stage. And then there she was—walking out with her husband whom she kissed at the podium, but not like Tipper and Al Gore. Mr. Mulhern went back stage, leaving her alone to soak in the cheers, the adulation, and that unique feel of success that only a handful of governor's have experienced.

"I spoke a few minutes ago to Dick DeVos," but before she can continue the audience erupts into wild applause, "He offered his congratulations and best wishes." Later she said he was very sincere and very gracious. She talks in this speech, as she did in this same room four years earlier when she was first elected, about this being One Michigan and she pledges to work for everyone, including "the person with a Cadillac and the person who assembles Cadillacs." She proclaims this victory is for the "people of Michigan." She, of course, thanks her family, the mayor of Detroit, who was not on the stage, and all the voters and ends with "I love you all."

Struggling with camera in toe, I managed to plow through the throng in front of her and squeeze in one more question. "What's first on your agenda?" The answer should have been sleep and some hot tea for her throat, but she says she wants that merit scholarship program passed by the Michigan House. Just before she ducks back stage to meet and greet more supporters, my last question of the night. "Did you ever think you would lose?" She laughs, "Oh, you bet." "When?" "Probably during the summer when he was up ten points."

Without a camera, I duck backstage to witness more smiles, more handshakes, and more pictures. I catch her once more as her bodyguards move her to the exit. "We took the house and senate," she gloats. I didn't believe her. I'd been in the bubble all night and missed all the other election news. Turns out democrats did sweep control from the GOP in the house, and the senate was, at that time, still in doubt although the GOP was claiming victory. This was huge for her. Instead of coping with two houses run by the GOP, she had one house that would make passage of her agenda easier. She was on the eve of a new day.

Meanwhile almost 90 miles away in a Lansing hotel, Dick DeVos was calling it a day. He had also taken to the stage moments after the governor began her victory speech. TV stations had to choose which one to cover. Since I could not be in two places at once, I listened to the audiotape and then watched the videotape. I came to one startling conclusion. If DeVos had performed during the early stages of the campaign in the same tone and texture that he demonstrated the night he lost, the outcome might not have been different, but it most certainly would have been closer.

In the early stages of the campaign, as he introduced himself to the state via his commercials, we saw a man who moved at a brisk pace through factories. He was all business. He appeared driven. He was a man on a mission to create jobs. In strong contrast, DeVos moves slowly to the podium this night with his wife at his side and three of his four children close at hand. Son Rick is not there. DeVos jokes, "We can't find him at the moment. Maybe he's still out campaigning," DeVos tells his supporters who laugh.

The reassuring image in the hotel ballroom is that of a common man, a family man, and someone who has something to share with the audience, other than the overwhelming desire to create more jobs. Think about it. This multimillion-dollar campaign never ran a single biography or bio ad telling us about his family, his roots, and what he shared with typical folks. His strategy guys were so anxious to introduce DeVos as the successful businessman that they forgot to let him say hello to Michigan residents as a man—without the business suit. Sure jobs are important, but voters want to know the guy on the inside, and without that, it's hard to build any sense of trust. That's exactly what he reveals the night he lost.

He is low-keyed but not maudlin. He even tries a little

humor, explaining that he was wearing his glasses, "So that I can see my notes." You could tell he is losing his voice, too. "This is the full extent of the voice I have left," as he explains why he is speaking so softly. Even though he speaks from those notes, they are not from some hotshot scriptwriter who focus-grouped every phrase to make the message work. The words are from inside. He begins by thanking his wife. He turns to her; she moves toward him and instinctively puts her head on his shoulder for a moment. He thanks her again for standing by him, and then they kiss. She fights back the tears while holding fast to his arm as they hug. He adds, "I love her very much." He does not need a fancy consultant to tell him how to say that. You can tell it's true, and the audience can feel it. He self-discloses that the race has been a "strain on the family," but they tackled it together once they all decided to get in. He then walks over to the children. The girls are wiping back the tears. They embrace. Creating jobs is the furthest thing from his mind. This is DeVos at his personal best. How ironic. Best speech. Last speech.

He's ready to move from the "thanks" to the "here's what we are all about" portion of his message. Next, he makes one of the most natural, yet revealing moves of the entire campaign. He simply removes his glasses while he is talking and gently places them in his breast pocket. If you want symbols, there it is. Without uttering a word he is telling the audience that what comes next is right from the heart, and it was.

"I did my best to deliver a message of hope and opportunity," DeVos continues, as there is dead silence in the ballroom. "I have no apology for the campaign we ran." Now the silence is broken with applause. He notes that "the future of our family has changed....We came to this campaign with an attitude of service....If this is not the way, I look forward to the way that we will be able to serve." On the last word, his voice falls off. A political consultant would have gone "Yes." But this was not consultant-driven.

More irony. The man who has trouble showing his feelings is weaving an emotional moment that touches everyone. This was Dick being Dick. And he closes with, "We're grateful for the privilege of having been a candidate for governor of this great State of Michigan. Thank you all very much." With that, there are family tears behind him, including wife Betsy, as the crowd joins in with its tears and applause as the family walks off stage together.

Most assuredly you don't want to launch a race for governor with everyone crying, but you do want to launch it with sincerity and a human touch that the common man and woman can feel. He hit a home run that night. It was real. It was him. He had passion. It was also, too late.

You would have thought after being through all this, he would have taken a time-out. But when I got home just moments ago on this day after the night before, there was an e-mail from him. Two weeks ago I had asked for his personal observations on the first debate. Now the ex-candidate begins, "Sorry for the delay Tim." And he matter of factly suggests that his agenda going into the first confrontation was not to "blow myself up...and avoid any "Dan Quayle" moments...which we did avoid." He reports that "I felt you and Charlie were actually fair and balanced in your questions." Then he hits a nerve for me. He relates his only criticism was that I allowed her to "run the clock." At all cost, I had wanted to avoid that imbalance to avoid the very justified criticism I had just read. Unfairness hurts me. I accept full blame and apologize to him in my e-mail, but also explain how the clock-watcher forgot to start the clock. A lousy excuse. He finishes with, "Hope this helps. Dick."

Politics is such a brutal sport. By design, at the end of the day, there is one winner and one loser. One family hugs out of joy; another hugs out of pain. But reflecting on everything that has happened that you and I have shared in this book, hopefully, you come away thankful that good persons are still willing to get in the ring, do the best they can, try to make a difference, and then let somebody else — the voters — decide the outcome. Participating in our beloved democracy is an honorable calling, and Dick and Jen and their troops have answered that call with class, passion, and personal sacrifice beyond compare. Next time you see them, share a word of thanks. They richly deserve it.